PHAIDON
Review copy

PIERRE KOENIG

JAMES STEELE
DAVID JENKINS

CONTENTS

5 Foreword
6 Introduction

8 'TOWARDS A STEEL ARCHITECTURE'
ENTERING ARCHITECTURAL PRACTICE & THE PURSUIT OF AN IDEAL

20 Koenig House #1
24 Lamel House
28 Squire House
29 Scott House
30 Burwash House
34 Radio Station KYOR
36 Metcalf House

38 'THE STYLE THAT NEARLY'
THE GENESIS OF THE CASE STUDY HOUSE PROGRAM

48 Bailey House (Case Study House #21)
60 Stahl House (Case Study House #22)
72 Beidelman House
74 Seidel House/Rollé Additions
84 Seidel Beach House
88 Johnson House/Riebe Addition
94 Iwata House
100 Mosque
102 Oberman House
110 Beagles House
114 Bethlehem Steel Exhibit Pavilion
116 EEI Factory & Sales
118 West House
119 Franklyn Dinner Club
120 Burton Pole House
122 Gantert House
128 Stuermer House
130 Koenig House #2
138 Schwartz House
146 Laguna House

148 'BLUEPRINT FOR MODERN LIVING'
THE MOCA SHOW & THE MODERNIST REVIVAL

152 Biographical Details
153 Chronological List of Projects
    Professional Affiliations
154 Awards
    Exhibitions
156 Select Bibliography
    Journals, Magazines, Newspapers
158 Other Media
    Tours & Lectures
159 Notes
160 Acknowledgements

FOREWORD

In 1962, having graduated from Manchester University, and thanks to a Henry Fellowship, I went to the United States to continue my studies at Yale.

America was a revelation, liberating and exhilarating in so many ways. The pace, for a student used to English habits, was vigorous and intense. The design studios were open twenty-four hours a day from the first day of term to the last. At the end of a programme we often worked through the last couple of nights, thanks to Paul Rudolph's habit of appearing just in time to savage every scheme in sight so that it all had to be done again.

Afterwards we would be exhausted, and that was our cue to take off. I travelled extensively, driving for days at a time, sometimes in the company of friends, sometimes alone.

America impressed me by the sheer scale of its infrastructure – its roads and bridges for example. I admired the vast clip-on trailers behind trucks, and the streamline aesthetic of the Greyhound buses and Airstream caravans. I was fascinated by lightweight agricultural structures, although they were not really 'designed' in the conventional sense, let alone regarded as architecture; they had, nonetheless, an extraordinary natural elegance and economy of means.

Arriving in Southern California I found a similar inspiration in the new architecture of the Case Study House Program, and the work of Charles and Ray Eames, Craig Ellwood and Pierre Koenig. Koenig's architecture especially left an indelible impression.

If I bring to mind what, for me, are some of the iconic images of twentieth-century architecture – light shining through the glass-block wall of the Maison de Verre; the volumetric clarity of the great workroom of Frank Lloyd Wright's Johnson Wax building, or the olympian roofscape of Le Corbusier's Unité in Marseilles – there is one image which burns more brightly and stays on the retina just that bit longer.

I am thinking, of course, of the heroic night-time view of Pierre Koenig's Case Study House #22 which seems so memorably to capture the whole spirit of late twentieth-century architecture. There, hovering almost weightlessly above the bright lights of Los Angeles, spread out like a carpet below, is an elegant, light, economical and transparent enclosure whose apparent simplicity belies the rigorous process of investigation that made it possible. If I had to choose one snapshot, one architectural moment, of which I would like to have been the author, this is surely it.

As both image and artefact, Case Study House #22 has long been a touchstone for contemporary architects, and Pierre Koenig's career – to which his wider body of work bears witness – is one of constancy, and truth to principles.

Pierre Koenig himself, like his architecture, is inspirational: still enquiring, exploring and inventing, never ready to rest on his laurels. I am very pleased to be able to celebrate with him the publication of this book and to share in his enthusiasm and curiosity for buildings yet to come.

Norman Foster, 1998

INTRODUCTION

An architectural revolution took place in Los Angeles soon after the end of the Second World War which had critical implications for the building industry. Pierre Koenig was in the thick of the fray. As one of a small group of architects in Southern California involved in the Case Study House Program, sponsored by *Arts and Architecture* magazine, Koenig challenged existing preconceptions about house construction, unchanged in America for decades, proposing, as an alternative, industrial production in line with the more sophisticated technologies developed as a result of the war. Of this pioneering Case Study House group, Koenig alone continues to advocate change from outdated, costly and inefficient building methods in favour of steel construction – as he has for the last half century. His impressive body of work, completed since the house he built for himself in Glendale in 1950 while still a student (as a reproof to academic critics who discouraged his inquiries into prefabrication techniques), stands as testimony to his consistent commitment to an ideal.

Designed at the age of twenty-five, when Koenig was in his third year at the School of Architecture at the University of Southern California (USC), his first house proved several things, not least that a steel house could be constructed at the same price – or less – than one of wood. It also revealed a fine grasp of the material; it even won him an AIA – *House and Home* Award of Merit, a fine achievement for a first building. Koenig is undoubtedly best known, however, for his Case Study Houses #21 and #22, the Bailey and Stahl houses, built in 1959 and 1960 respectively. The evocative night-time photograph of the Stahl House by Julius Shulman continues to be widely circulated in the media and has had a lasting effect on the public consciousness. The house encapsulates and has come to symbolize the singular character of the decade it brackets, epitomizing the optimism and innocence of the 1950s, before the

1

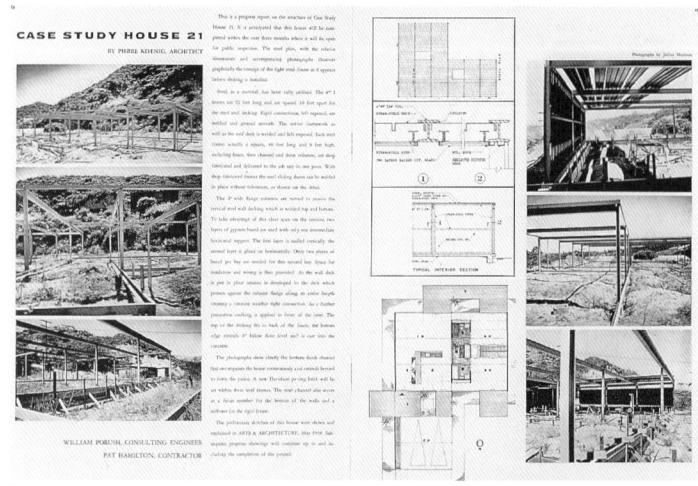

2

morality of progress was challenged, and when the United States was at the height of its political and economic power.

Called 'the style that nearly' by Reyner Banham in his classic study *Los Angeles: The Architecture of Four Ecologies*, the Case Study House Program was one of the most ambitious attempts to promote Modernist principles in the history of the movement. John Entenza, the Editor of *Arts and Architecture*, who conceived the idea for a combined media and construction blitz on domestic building conventions, sensed that veterans returning home from the War would welcome, and even demand, a more comfortable and less formal lifestyle. Entenza believed that the openness provided by long-span steel structures – facilitated by the industrial processes that Modernism promoted – made the International Style the logical choice for the more casual generation to come. The abandonment of boundaries between indoors and outdoors that he saw as the future living pattern in California was best achieved in houses that were not compartmentalized into function-related rooms, but conformed instead to the concept of a 'free flow of space' pioneered earlier in the century by architects such as Ludwig Mies van der Rohe. Not content simply to editorialize his convictions in his magazine, Entenza began to commission houses that attempted to embody these principles, making it possible, through product promotion and by trading advertising exposure for material costs, for clients who were willing to try his approach to have a new home. In return, the clients agreed to have their houses published, and to allow public access for tours for a short time after completion to promote the style.

Pierre Koenig was a relative late-comer to the tight-knit group of architects that Entenza enlisted in his campaign, a group which also included Charles and Ray Eames, Ralph Rapson, Richard Neutra, Raphael Soriano and Craig Ellwood, but his impact on the Program was nonetheless profound: for a short time it appeared that it might succeed in re-directing public opinion. The ingrained prejudices of the construction industry, however, were more difficult to dislodge, having been established through complex economic patterns and labour relations that resisted change. Even companies that manufactured the new materials that the architects specified for the Case Study Houses were, on the whole, remarkably unsupportive, thereby demonstrating the strength of the existing interconnected web of building industry convention.

By the time the Vietnam War had escalated into full mobilization in the early 1960s, the initiative had weakened and 'the style that nearly' had run out of steam. It was displaced in the media by daily reports of the conflict and deepening social upheaval. After three decades, however, it resurfaced in a landmark exhibition held in 1989–90 at the Los Angeles Museum of Contemporary Art (MOCA). 'Blueprints for Modern Living: History and Legacy of the Case Study Houses', which turned the spotlight back on Koenig's work, cast a quasi-objective, if admittedly nostalgic eye back to the brief period when it appeared that a breakthrough in contemporary house design might have been made. The popular response to the exhibition was phenomenal, however, and Koenig found himself firmly re-established within the canon as a major figure in the American Modern Movement.

Koenig's personal development as an architect and teacher (he has been a member of the architecture faculty at USC since 1964), his formative role in the Case Study House Program, and his most recent career following the impact of the MOCA exhibition are discussed respectively in the three succeeding chapters.

1 Pierre Koenig, Koenig House #1, 1950.
2 Bailey House (Case Study House #21) under construction, *Arts and Architecture* magazine, August 1958.
3 Case Study House #22 reconstructed for the MOCA exhibition, 1989.

'TOWARDS A STEEL ARCHITECTURE'
ENTERING ARCHITECTURAL PRACTICE
& THE PURSUIT OF AN IDEAL

It was my notion, when I started, to make anonymous architecture for ordinary people: to create houses that were better than ones done by anyone before – built more quickly and cheaply using steel and all the new materials that industry had to offer.
Pierre Koenig, Los Angeles, 1997

Pierre Koenig was born in San Francisco in 1925. In architecture it was the year of the landmark Paris Exposition des Arts Decoratifs – at which Konstantin Melnikov's USSR Pavilion and Le Corbusier's Pavillon de L'Esprit Nouveau made such a revolutionary impact – and European Modernism was beginning to stretch its legs. The same year in the United States saw the foundation of the Chrysler Motor Company in Detroit, as American industry set itself on a last accelerated dash before encountering head-on the economic crash and ensuing Depression in which Koenig was to grow up.

His mother and father were respectively of French and German descent. His father was a sales representative for an English woollens firm, and his mother looked after the family. It was the city in which he grew up, rather than any inherited sensibility, which was to spark the young Pierre's interest in architecture.

San Francisco in the 1930s was a busy Navy base, as well as being heavily industrialized in certain areas, and Koenig absorbed all of this. The Golden Gate Bridge, ships coming in and out of the Bay, and the foghorns that usually guided them left an indelible impression. His parents' house was less than a block from the water and Koenig remembers long solitary walks along the shore in what he describes as an 'enriched environment'. He would take a sketchbook and draw whatever caught his eye – construction sites, ships, the bridge, even automobiles.

At high school he remembers he could draw anything and always got straight A's in art, but in other subjects he was a weak student; he didn't study and got very poor grades. His teachers never thought of him as college material, and his parents struggled to think of a trade for him, convinced that he would have to find himself a job straight out of school. Koenig recalls being lumped with the 'dummies' in the class – buddies who, like him, never did well within the educational system. Others, however, including friends of his parents, were convinced that his skills were simply not being recognized by the system and that he would go far if only he could find his own direction.

Architecture for him at that time was only a source of practical pleasure. Among the sites he explored along the shore front, Bernard Maybeck's domed Rotunda – the surviving element of his Palace of Fine Arts – built for the 1906 Pan Pacific Exposition, and the surrounding park, was a favourite playground. Exploring the building one day Koenig discovered a construction ladder concealed within one of the building's enormous hollow wood and stucco columns leading up into the dome itself, which became a secret hide-away.

During the summer months, rural Sonoma replaced San Francisco, as Koenig went to stay with his paternal grandfather, and extended periods of solitude continued there. Koenig credits these long periods of being alone for the development of his creative imagination, since he was 'forced to make things up' in order to keep his mind occupied. Koenig's grandfather was an important mentor. An early supporter of Pierre's precocious minimalist tendencies, his grandfather urged his young grandson on when he crossed out a picture of a Neo-classical building in a brochure for the Pan Pacific Exhibition. Koenig has kept the brochure, complete with its heavily pencilled 'X' as a reminder of his grandfather's approval, and wryly exhibits it as proof that his Modernist instincts were there long before he ever imagined embarking on a course of formal architectural education.

In 1939 two things happened that were to prove significant in propelling Koenig along the road to architecture. The first – although it would be a while before its personal impact would be felt – was the outbreak of World War II; the second was his father's decision to uproot the family to escape

1

2

the Depression, which had gained a final stranglehold on San Francisco, and head south to the boom town of Los Angeles.

After San Francisco, which Koenig now looks back on as being 'old, foggy and damp, where everything was Victorian and smelt musty', Los Angeles was a breath of fresh air: 'It was warm, sunny and colourful; everything was new and bright and clean, especially the architecture.' He took to it straight away. The Koenig family moved into a small house in San Gabriel – between Downtown and Pasadena – and Pierre found a new group of friends who were set on studying architecture.

At seventeen, Koenig enlisted in the United States Army Advanced Special Training Program, which promised an accelerated college education, compressing four years into two. In 1943, however, after one semester at the University of Utah, the Program was cancelled abruptly and he was sent to Infantry School at Fort Benning, Georgia. The sixteen weeks of basic training that Koenig underwent there prepared him to join the 86th Infantry Division. Soon after, he was transferred to the 292nd Field Artillery Observation Battalion stationed at Brownwood, Texas, where he was trained as a flash ranging observer to optically locate enemy gunfire and mathematically transfer the information to map coordinates on a plotting table. Sent to the front lines first in France, and later in Germany, Koenig used these techniques to great effect, using logarithms and azimuths to triangulate positions communicated by telephone to corps divisions that could respond within forty seconds of an enemy Howitzer blast being spotted. Because of this skill, Koenig found himself one of the last GIs to be discharged, and it was not until 1946 that he returned home to the United States aboard the giant liner *Queen Mary*, which had been pressed into wartime service as a troop ship.

Soon after coming back to Los Angeles, Koenig applied to the University of Southern California School of Architecture under the GI bill which gave veterans preference and financial aid in completing their education; but he was to find that admission was still difficult. Faced with a two-year waiting list, he enrolled instead at Pasadena City College where he studied from 1946 to 1948. It was while he was enrolled at Pasadena City College, that Koenig first saw *Arts and Architecture* magazine, at the San Gabriel Library, and still remembers the impact it had on him. The first images he recalls seeing were the pen and ink renderings of a house in Florida by Paul Rudolf, and Ralph Rapson's sketches for the Greenbelt House, the latter an important landmark in the Case Study House Program, even though it was never built. It is worth noting that more than forty years later, the curators and designers of an exhibition about the Program in 1989 would identify the Rapson house and Koenig's Case Study House #22 as the defining brackets of the series.

At the end of his two years at Pasadena, having taken all the courses in architecture that were available, Koenig and his classmate, George Foy, determined to try again to enter the architecture programme at USC. Places were still hard to come by, however, and Koenig was again rebuffed; but refusing to take no for an answer, he and Foy sat themselves down in the Dean's outer office and stayed there every day for a week, from 8.00 am to 5.00 pm, until the Dean finally admitted them into the school.

When Koenig entered USC, the University had already established its reputation as the pre-eminent California institution in architectural education, after only three decades in operation. A Department of Architecture was first established there within the School of Fine Arts in 1919 – the first in Southern California – and grew rapidly with the help of the Los Angeles architectural community. A separate School of Architecture was organized in September 1925. Arthur Clason Weatherhead, the first Dean, was initially joined by five practicing architects as faculty, who also served as an advisory committee to the University. This established a pattern of professional involvement and pragmatism complementing academic inquiry, as well as a connection to the community that still exists in the school today. By the time Koenig applied for admission, the emphasis of the School had changed dramatically. Dean Arthur Gallion, who took over leadership in 1945, shook off the last vestiges of the old Beaux-Arts curriculum. He also added a Department of Industrial Design, advised by Norwood Teague and Raymond F. Loewy, whose innovations in process streamlining and the use of new materials have come to symbolize the optimism of the post-war period. The end of the war heralded an era of economic prosperity in America which corresponded with a period of tremendous population growth in Los Angeles, and the School intended to be in the vanguard of exploring ways in which the built environment could respond to radical change.

1 Pierre Koenig, 1943.
2 Pierre Koenig, 1945.
3 Ralph Rapson, Greenbelt House, 1945. Perspective drawing of living room and greenbelt.

The faculty in the School in the late 1940s and throughout the 1950s reflected these critical changes, with Gregory Ain, Robert Alexander, Harwell Hamilton Harris, Richard Neutra, Calvin Straub, Garrett Eckbo, William Pereira, and Alvin Lustig prominent in a concerted shift towards Modernism, tempered by the strong tradition of sensitivity to an ideal climate. This was the crucible into which Koenig entered.

Looking back, Koenig believes that he learned more from his peers than he did from the formal aspects of his architectural education at USC. Together he and George Foy were constantly experimenting with new ideas and forging new directions outside of their school assignments. Koenig and Foy would go hiking and camping together in the Sierras, and made short films based on their experiences. They made two 'ecology films' together, one on 8 mm film, the other on 16 mm. The first was entitled 'Water'; it traced a stream from the top of the Sierras – approximately 14,000 feet above sea level – to its base at Owens River. The film was roughly ten minutes long and was cut to music – Prokofiev's Scythian Suite. The second film, another 'short', was more generally about the Sierras. Both were environmental pieces and – whether consciously or not – shared ideas that Charles and Ray Eames were beginning to explore in short films such as their 'Blacktop', 1952, which offered an abstract cinematic exploration of the movement of water washing over an asphalt schoolyard – the 'blacktop' of the title – set to music by Johann Sebastian Bach.

Koenig and Foy also made films using a technique that involved scratching previously developed film – which could be obtained free from the studios – with a compass point or a needle, to reveal in various degrees the three layers of colour – red, green and blue – that made up the 'black' film. In this way, they were able to make simple animations, using mostly geometric forms, which again were set to music. Music, in fact, became important to Koenig at that time and has remained so throughout his life.

Although the University's curriculum was too rigidly formal for Koenig when he was a student, he recalls a number of teachers who were influential. Chief amongst them was Byron Davis who taught the first year design studio. Davis taught in the Bauhaus tradition, conducting many perceptual exercises (paint a cube so that its 'cube-ness' disappears and so on) and other tactile, visual, aural and light experiments which increased Koenig's awareness of the importance of all the senses in the design process. It was Davis's influence which also led Koenig into film-making and other extra-mural activities. Calvin Straub introduced Koenig to notions such as social relationships and social space in architecture, and set studio exercises that involved designing low-cost housing or housing for migratory populations, which were to have a profound impact on Koenig's later thinking. One of Koenig's last teachers at USC was Kenneth Lind. Lind was instrumental in teaching Koenig how the interrelationship of the spatial, structural and functional aspects of a design solution could be coordinated to optimize each of them. Lind explained how design could be explored as a 'process'. Koenig in his own design work emphasized the importance of structure in determining all the other elements of a plan and he also showed how this methodology could be applied to any design problem. For Koenig this became a basic set of tools, not limited to one system, one aesthetic or one structure, and it has influenced not just the way he has continued to approach design, but has formed the basis of his own teaching method. Much later, when they were both teaching together at USC in the early 1960s, Ralph Knowles based in science ideas that Koenig was already beginning to explore intuitively; he introduced him to sun-path studies and other aspects of passive climate control: ideas which Koenig has carried with him ever since.

As a student, Koenig demonstrated an independence of spirit no doubt rooted in his wartime experiences. His time in combat had changed his outlook on life; the notion of risk-taking, for example, was not something that scared him in the relative safety of Los Angeles. It followed, therefore, that when in his third year at USC, a studio instructor rejected his proposal for a steel building, he decided to build a house for himself out of the material, just to prove his point. Having grown up in the Depression, and experienced first-hand what it was like not to have money, he was not daunted by a lack of funds. He gathered together as much money as he could from personal savings and loans to build a house for himself in Glendale in 1950, acting as his own general contractor and using William Porush, who would join him on many later projects, as structural engineer.

Koenig wanted to explore an alternative to the wood frame – which was regarded as the *avant-garde* style of the moment in the USC studios –

4   Koenig House #1, *Arts and Architecture* magazine, October 1953.

4

because: 'it occurred to me that houses that were very slender were meant to be in steel, not wood'. But this idea was rejected by his professors with the argument that steel was intended for industrial, rather than residential, use and that it was too psychologically 'cold' to evoke a comfortable domestic feeling. Koenig believed, however, that steel would allow him to simplify the structural diagram that other students were attempting to construct in wood, that it had more clarity and integrity, and would allow him to clearly define an ideal way of building. Byron Davis, his first year instructor, had impressed Koenig with the social dimension of Modernism and planted the theoretical seed that prefabrication would lower costs and thus allow new housing to be affordable to all. This dimension, added to the diagrammatic clarity provided by steel construction, convinced Koenig that it was the best material with which to build. He still remembers Davis saying that in nature for everything created, something has to be destroyed, and Koenig used this Nietzschean idea as a rationale for rejecting existing methods and creating a new kind of architecture in steel.

After completing his studies at USC – and while most of his classmates were flocking to Richard Neutra – Koenig sought out, and worked briefly for Raphael Soriano to accrue professional experience credits before taking his licensing examination. Since he was also completing his first house at the time, he showed Soriano the drawings. He found that he and Soriano were working toward a common goal of optimizing a structural steel system for residential use by following through the logic of the most suitable span while taking advantage of standard component sizing. This is a critical aspect of steel construction because the higher structural strength of steel allows for longer spans and thinner floor decks than wood construction. The fact that he and Soriano had independently reached the same conclusions and the same new set of dimensions for steel construction was for Koenig an important confirmation of his new direction. By the time he came to design Case Study House #21, eight years later, all the elements of his steel vocabulary were firmly in place.

Koenig worked in Soriano's office on and off during the summer of 1950 – while his house took shape on site – completing the presentation renderings for Soriano's Case Study House which were published in the August 1950 issue of *Arts and Architecture* magazine. Then aged twenty-five, he found Soriano a sympathetic mentor: 'We were interested in the same things; and it turned out that I had something to offer him, and he to me. So it was an educational experience for both of us, and a lot of fun. I'm very grateful to him for taking me on.'

The design and construction of Koenig's first house in 1950 in Glendale is contemporaneous with the publication of the Eames and Entenza Houses (respectively Case Study Houses #8 and #9), the installation of Gregory Ain's model wooden house in the garden of the Museum of Modern Art in New York, and the completion of Soriano's house for Julius Shulman in Laurel Canyon. The built houses were in steel; all were experimental in some sense, pushing forward the boundaries of what could be done with the 'new' domestic material.

While building his first house Koenig demonstrated early on a genius for 'getting more from less'. He entered into detailed discussion with the contractor and suppliers for the house, and by consistent reiteration of the 'process' he had learned from Kenneth Lind – and working with the logic of the materials and systems available to him, he was able to reduce the cost of the house. Koenig has said about the process:

With a promised $5,000 loan from the bank, I designed my little experiment and sent it out to bid to various sub-contractors (I was the General Contractor). The prices added up to $12,000! Undaunted, I set out to find out what was wrong with my plans. I was convinced that I could build my steel house for $5.00 per square foot. I went to the steel contractor and spent a few days learning about fabrication and erection. I realized that I had designed a wood house. I learned how to turn the beams on the long direction of the plan – instead of transverse like a wood house. I learned how to minimize the number of parts by increasing spans. I learned how to cut down on waste. Then I went to a sliding glass door company and learned much the same thing – bigger and fewer doors were more economical. Armed with my new knowledge, I redesigned my house and sure enough the new bids added up to $5,000, including retaining walls for the hillside. These simple lessons have served me for my entire career and have given me the basis for expanding my knowledge to apply to bigger and more elaborate solutions.[1]

Construction was well under way in June 1950 when news broke of the North Korean invasion of South Korea, and the United States was once again at war. The effect on the building industry was immediate. Companies began hoarding materials as insurance against future shortages and as a result Koenig found himself without the steel decking necessary for the roof. After a three month delay Koenig persuaded the telephone company to sell him 1,000 square feet of decking from their stockpile.

The experience of his first house stood him in good stead. Thirty-five years and a number of houses later, when he came to build the second Koenig house, in Brentwood, he specified exactly the construction sequence for the triple-height steel frame, producing a twelve-stage erection drawing which showed the contractor how to erect the frame efficiently and, therefore, cheaply. By doing so he was able to knock $10,000 off the steel contractor's original price, and the frame was erected in under a week. As Koenig knew all too well, time on site is money. He also knew that while cost is largely dependent on market conditions, in the right hands steel construction is increasingly economical and time-efficient. An early illustration of this was the construction of Soriano's Shulman House in Laurel Canyon. At a time when building costs were soaring out of control – again because of the Korean War – Soriano tendered the project in both wood and steel. The contract bid for steel was $40,000 – less than $10 per square foot. Soriano decided to go with steel for the primary structural members – using wood for the secondary elements – because of the ease and speed of construction it offered, and the slenderness of the main structural members that it made possible.

Upon graduation in 1952 Koenig established his own practice in Los Angeles, and built three steel-framed houses in quick succession: the Lamel House, in Glendale, 1952; the Squire House in La Cañada, 1953; and the Scott House in Tujunga, 1953. His public profile in Los Angeles began its upward trajectory, and was helped considerably when the Glendale house was featured in *Arts and Architecture*, in October 1953 – alongside 'A Proposed National Theater' by Mies van der Rohe, and 'A House for Florida' by Paul Rudolph. The Glendale house was published over two pages, with photographs by Julius Shulman. The magazine described the house:

This small steel and glass house takes full advantage of a heavily wooded site by opening to the front and rear with large expanses of glass and sliding doors. Except for the covered passage leading from the carport to the front door, there are no overhangs in order to admit the maximum of light and sun. With the exception of the bath, the house is one large room with sliding doors closing off the bedroom when desired. A storage cabinet serves as the dividing wall between kitchen and bedroom. There are no bearing walls as the cantilevered columns support the roof and take up seismic forces. Columns, beams, roof deck, sliding doors and window frames are all arc-welded. The result is a simple, light and spacious structure.[2]

Significantly, alongside the photographs of the house, the magazine included two photographs of Koenig, one of him bent over his drawing board in the house, the other of him perched on a ladder, attending to a construction detail. Those two images, taken together, perfectly sum up the range of his architectural activities at the time.

The houses Koenig built in the early 1950s were very much 'hands-on' affairs. Building in steel at that time was still in its infancy and there were very few established contractors that could take on such projects; those who would wanted to charge far too much to do it. Koenig, therefore, became both architect and contractor, organizing the site and the sub-contractors in due course. As he remembers it, he often ended up dealing with the apprehensions and concerns of his clients in both of those roles. Through all of this he resolutely maintained his principles for the integrity of the building:

When I started working on my own, I applied some very strict values to what I was or wasn't going to do. I wasn't going to lower my standards, no matter what. I'd starve first – and very often it nearly worked out that way! But I hung in there, despite everything.

Working on small projects to such tight margins meant that the going often got tough. Most of the problems on these and later projects came down to money:

The contractor would want to change a detail, or do something a particular way, for example, just to save money – and the client would often side with him. When you see people making decisions that are wrong it's painful. I know architects who have walked away from jobs in that situation and never came back. Some very good architects in this town won't do private commissions any more because of the impossible obstacles created by contractors and clients. I chose to perservere to have a chance to build my buildings.

To keep the wolves from the door during this period Koenig supplemented work on his own projects with income and experience gained working in various other practices on short-term arrangements. Some jobs lasted a week, others for three months, and he tried to work only with architects whose ethos was sympathetic to his own. Koenig worked short-term in this way for Candreva and Jarrett; for Kistner, Wright and Wright, doing mainly renderings for schools; and for A. Quincy Jones, a prolific architect, planner and educator, who, with his partner, Frederick Emmons, was one of the second wave of architects commissioned for the Case Study House

5 Pierre Koenig, Koenig House #2, 1985. **6** Pierre Koenig, Squire House, 1953. **7, 8** Pierre Koenig at Koenig House #1, 1950.

5

6

7

Program. In addition to Case Study House #24, designed in 1961 but unbuilt, Jones and Emmons undertook some innovative steel-framed commissions, including Jones's own house in Los Angeles. Their multiple housing development for Eichler Homes in San Mateo, 1956, resulted in a prototype steel house, the X-100.

Koenig entered the office while the Eichler Homes project was in development and was able to offer the project architects the benefit of his practical experience of building cheaply in steel; as he recalls 'they had never done steel housing for mass-production before'. Koenig, however, was fast becoming an expert. By now he had four completed steel-framed houses to his credit and had begun his own investigations into steel-framing for mass-production. He developed, for example, a grading system to measure the relative economy of any given frame solution: an I-beam counted as 1, a channel as 0.5, and a column as 2 - the solution with the lowest score was the most efficient. Economy – not only in the use of steel – was a paramount concern in this period, as was the lack of skilled tradesmen in Los Angeles, both of which drove Koenig, and others, further down the road toward prefabrication.

The case for steel had never been stronger. In March 1957 *Arts and Architecture* published Koenig's designs for a 'Low-Cost Production House'. Although he had viewed all his houses to that point as, to some degree prototypical, this was his first proposal for an 'off-the-shelf' factory-made house; or as he characterizes it (paraphrasing Le Corbusier) 'a house made just like a car'. The 1,250 square foot steel-framed house was developed on a long-span module to reduce the number of columns, and employed 10-inch I-beams, and 4-inch columns, to be prefabricated in the factory and assembled quickly on site. Spans between beams were dimensioned to take advantage of maximum spans of profiled-metal decking.

Certain that such a house would find a popular market, Koenig approached Bethlehem Steel – whose mills always suffered a summer down-turn in demand after the spring rush for the automobile industry – to try to persuade them to invest in the project, but they held on to a belief – endemic in industry at the time – that the demand for 'new-fangled' steel homes would be short-lived and that people would return to wood once costs came down. It so happens that history was on their side. Koenig's conviction however, was that he was simply ahead of his time, and that first the architectural profession, and then industry would have to shed their preconceptions, before his proposals could be adopted:

Prefabrication and mass production cannot by themselves produce beauty or ugliness. Good or bad design can come out of handicraft or machine work equally. What is needed in our modern world is for the architect, and especially the architectural student, to accept the premise and the reality of prefabrication and its relatives – mass-production, automation and high-technology – and spend more time dealing with its problems so that we may all enjoy a more beautiful machine-made world.[3]

Although Koenig found his plans for a mass-produced house frustrated, 1957 proved to be a red-letter year nonetheless. He was invited to exhibit at the São Paulo Biennale and his work was brought before an international critical audience for the first time. After publishing many of Koenig's houses in *Arts and Architecture*, John Entenza was finally prompted to invite him to join the Case Study House Program, saying 'Pierre, if you ever have a good house, with some good clients, tell me and we'll make it a Case Study House'.

'Well' says Koenig, 'All of my houses were with good clients, so I just said "I have one now", and that house became Case Study House #21.' This was undoubtedly a great opportunity. By early the following year he had sold his house in Glendale and established an office on San Vincente Boulevard, a location known as the 'Athens of Brentwood', with architects such as Frank Gehry, Peter Candreva, William Jarrett, and Bruce Beckett exchanging shop talk in local restaurants along the Boulevard. He hired draughtsmen and shared a secretary with another architect, and would later hire more assistants as commercial work began to come his way. While Case Study House #21 – the Bailey House – was on the drawing board he completed a new 10,000 square foot broadcasting building for Radio Station KYOR and developed plans for other large-scale projects.

Case Study House #21 was the culmination of Koenig's research on steel construction and the refinement of his detailing vocabulary. For many critics, this elegant, even austere pavilion was the apotheosis of the Case Study House Program. A modestly scaled, 1,320 square foot house for a young professional couple, it exemplified the ideal, affordable, mass-producible and universal house that John Entenza set out to promote in the pages of *Arts and Architecture*. Entenza himself described it as the product of 'some of the cleanest and most immaculate thinking in the development of the small contemporary house'.[4] Like his earlier house in Glendale, the house has only two generic column details. Every part serves two, three or more purposes. As Koenig says, 'it takes a long time to evolve a simple design.'

At a formal level, as Reyner Banham has observed, what distinguishes this house and other steel houses of the Case Study House Program from contemporaneous houses by architects such as Mies van der Rohe and Philip Johnson on the East Coast, is their 'unmonumental manner'.[5] He notes the generally unfussy nature of the detailing, citing Koenig as an example:

The welds are sufficient to their allotted tasks, and within the compass of the welder's craft. Compared with the fine-art weld-laying and subsequent grinding off with emery wheels at the Farnsworth House, this kind of work reveals again the absence of that heroic-style creative *angst* of the European-based Modern Movement and gives an improvisatory air to the whole fabric.[6]

Part of Case Study House #21's great success was the skilled way in which Koenig opened the interior up to nature, providing each of the main rooms with its own outside terrace, and threading a long moat-like pool of water around and through the house, before finally taking it up to the roof and letting it stream back down again. Architecture and nature achieve a unity in this house rarely seen before, or since. Entenza published the house in *Arts and Architecture* in February 1959, by which time Koenig's second Case Study House was already well under way.

Case Study House #22 is perched on what Koenig describes as 'an eagles nest', high in the Hollywood Hills above Sunset Boulevard and the mock-French roofs of the Chateau Marmont. While Case Study House #21 was a brilliantly understated model for mass-production, Case Study House #22 – the Stahl House – is perhaps the ultimate 'one-off', so perfectly adapted to suit this near-impossible site that it couldn't possibly be imagined anywhere else. The house is again a skilful performance. Cantilevered out from its precipitous toe-hold on the hillside, it reconciles not only the extreme structural demands of its location, but offers a seamless transition between inside and outside spaces beneath a sheltering, overhanging roof, and takes spectacular advantage of an unrivalled panoramic view across the city below. Koenig recalls the challenge that the house presented:

> I had only a year to do CSH #22, which I saw essentially as a contextual problem because of the unusual and challenging site. At the time I couldn't see anything other than to create an interior space that was an extension of the exterior. In order to do that I had to minimize what I was doing myself. I had to suppress the idea of building something egotistical that says 'look at me, here I am sitting on top of this hill as a great house'. Like all design processes, after you conceptualize it, you have to constantly hold yourself in range and ask yourself why you're doing something and sometimes fight yourself to keep to your original notion. It's easy to get lost in the process. You constantly have to go back and remember the important things. I think that is what I did successfully in this case so that Los Angeles becomes an extension of the house and vice-versa. The house is just a part of the city.

With Case Study Houses #21 and #22, Koenig showed that it was possible to achieve, with steel, a harmonious relationship with nature and context just as Greene and Greene and Rudolf Schindler had done before him, with wood. The houses in fact, are as much built 'mission – statements' for California-living, like the Gamble House was for the Greenes or the Schindler House.

In what might be seen as a concise summary of the whole Case Study House Program, Koenig has described how his approach to architecture defined not just his two Case Study houses, but his domestic output as a whole:

> As outdoor living became more important, we felt that houses should reflect this. Outdoor space became a continuation of indoor space; buildings moved down to slab-level so that the outside could continue the inside. Glass was used to extend indoor space visually. Kitchens were turned around so that meals could be served directly from the kitchen to the outdoors. The garage went to the front of the house and carports were introduced. Open-planning allowed interaction between the family at the highest level, especially during meal times. Eating, playing, and homework were done in one space rather than in individual rooms. Architecture was a social study then much more than it is today. Now it is considered an art study. At that time the family was the paramount thing.

Getting to know the family – the clients – has always been a key part of Koenig's agenda. Indeed he maintains that he interviews them as much as they do him, to make sure that they are *simpatico*. Once you have established a good rapport with a client, he believes, good architecture can result.

The Case Study House Program demanded that clients open the houses to the public for a period of six to eight weeks after completion. For example, when the Bailey House was published in *Arts and Architecture* the magazine announced: 'This twenty-first project in the magazine's Case Study House Program is now on exhibition to the general public. The house is open on Saturdays and Sundays from 1 to 5 pm through February 22.'[7] To ensure that the houses consistently represented the very best of contemporary architecture and design, they were presented to the public fully finished; none of the clients' old furniture – unless approved by the architect – was allowed. Koenig recalls:

9 Greene and Greene, Gamble House, 1908.

10 Rudolf Schindler, Schindler House, 1922.

11

11 Pierre Koenig, Bailey House (Case Study House #21), 1959.
12 Pierre Koenig, Stahl House (Case Study House #22), 1960.
13 Advert featuring Case Study House #21 in *Arts and Architecture*, February 1959.

12

It was stipulated that the architect should design, build, or select the furniture for the houses and they had complete control over furnishing them. In some cases I designed the furniture, sometimes I selected it and other times I had help from outside. Often furniture companies, such as Knoll or Herman Miller, would put their furniture in the house for the duration of the public exhibition and the clients could buy it afterwards at cost. Usually they did. Most people didn't have modern furniture; often they were moving out of small apartments without a lot of furniture of any kind. The people who moved into Case Study Houses, no matter how much money they had or didn't have, all moved out of apartments. People today don't realize that in those days two bedrooms and a bath was regarded as a normal home. If you had more than that you were considered very wealthy. These homes, which had two bathrooms, were thought of as quite large and luxurious at the time.

This set-up also meant that the architect had to please not one client but two: *Arts and Architecture* was an important and powerful patron. With the magazine also came the photographer and furniture company representatives and a host of advertisers, so there was always pressure to get the houses finished on time, ready for the photographic shoot and the next issue of the magazine. Balancing these demands and keeping the contractor on track often proved to be challenging, and Koenig decided that two Case Study Houses were enough, even though he had more clients and more houses in the pipeline. A letter he wrote to the contractor on Case Study House #22 – Robert Brady – is revealing. It was written on April 19, 1960, and the house was due to be published – complete and furnished – in the June issue of *Arts and Architecture*. Koenig's overwhelming sense of frustration comes through clearly:

Dear Bob
I'm leaving for San Francisco Wed. a.m. and because I have been unable to reach you I must leave this note.
   When I went to the job Mon. I was shocked to see no one there and many things to be done yet. As you know we were supposed to shoot Monday. The deadline has been changed once but it is impossible to change it again. The date is set. Mr Van Keppel is waiting to move furniture in. Shulman comes by the job every day to see when he can shoot. Mr Entenza is shouting for photos so he can print the next issue. The president of Bethlehem is supposed to visit the finished house this Friday. There is to be a press conference this weekend. Not to mention Mr Stahl. This will give you some idea of the pressure being put on. I hope you can act in accordance.
   Also, we have to treat the floors before anything can be placed on them. As I will be gone, I would appreciate it if you can make the arrangements with Mr Forester at Watco-Dennis Gr. 92969 to get this done right away.
   Also, call Mr Van Keppel at ex 31839 and tell him when he may furnish.
Many thanks,
Pierre Koenig[8]

Koenig may have sensed both that the era had changed and that the Case Study House Program was beginning to falter and lose sight of its original vision to provide affordable contemporary housing for the average American family: many of the later Case Study Houses were far larger and more opulent than the norm and were attracting wealthy high-profile clients.

13

Case Study House #28, for example, built in 1966 by Buff, Straub and Hensman provided an enormous 5,000 square feet of space, with five bedrooms and three and a half bathrooms, and suppressed its frame beneath a layer of brick and plaster. It is perhaps no coincidence that this was to be the last house of the Case Study series.

Koenig's career, meanwhile, had taken a fresh turn. In 1962 a new Dean, Sam Hurst, was appointed to the Architecture School at USC, and he set about hiring new staff. He recruited Ralph Knowles, Robert Anderson and Richard Berry and, in 1964, Pierre Koenig.

Koenig's teaching career began as his commercial work slowly began to tail off – although he was still two years away from completing his largest industrial building, the 64,000 square feet EEI Factory and Showroom in El Segundo, California – and he made a conscious decision to maintain his office at a modest size and combine practice with teaching. This has been the pattern of his career ever since.

In the beginning at USC he taught design studio; later he formed an association with Konrad Wachsman which led to his appointment as Assistant Director of the Institute of Building Research, from 1969 to 1971. This was also the start of his long collaboration with Ralph Knowles with whom he worked to establish the School's Natural Forces Laboratory. Koenig characterizes Knowles as 'the scholar' and himself as 'the practitioner' in the partnership; together they pioneered in the School the study of the effects of water, wind, sun and seismic forces on buildings. As part of his research into wind and natural ventilation, Koenig and his students built a number of wind tunnels over the years, the largest of which – at 33 feet long – is still in use.

Professor Koenig is currently Director of the Natural Forces Laboratory of USC's four-year undergraduate Building Science Program, a post he took up in 1980. The Program is a multi-disciplinary course introducing architecture to engineering students. It aims to raise an awareness of structural and environmental issues in architecture, and to direct that knowledge back into student design work, giving students the benefit of a basic methodology.

In 1971 Koenig took up another role in the School, as Director of the Chemehuevi Indian Reservation Planning Program, which allowed him to explore in a real context the development and application of mass-production housing techniques that he had been investigating privately for many years, and to apply them in a way that would bring real improvement to people's lives.

Following his 1957 Low-Cost Production House, which as *Arts and Architecture* noted, used 'every up-to-date building method',[9] Koenig had gone on to apply technology borrowed from the US Army via the aerospace

14 Plans for four patio house combinations, Chemehuevi Housing Project, 1976.

15 Three colour variations for prototype Chemehuevi houses.

industry to the design of a highly insulated house intended for a tract development in Canada. To combat the extreme cold of the winter months – temperatures could fall to below minus 40 degrees – Koenig developed a 'warm' cladding panel – based on aircraft wing construction – which comprised a core of expanded polyurethane foam between pressed metal inner and outer skins. By isolating the steel frame from the panels he was able to solve the problem of thermal bridging and produce an inexpensive factory-made house that could be erected in a single day. The house actually went into production – the panels were assembled in a factory in Detroit – but his client went out of business and no more than six houses were ever built. To add insult to injury all Koenig's documentation for the project was lost in Quebec. Nonetheless it was a good grounding for the Chemehuevi project, having given him his first real experience of the factory.

The environmental problems facing the Chemehuevi project were at the other end of the scale to the Canadian tract housing. The site – the Chemehuevi Indian Reservation – was a plain stretching along Lake Havasu in San Bernardino County, California, where the primary considerations were the extremity of the hot summer sun, sudden weather changes, and the powerful winds that swept down from the surrounding mountains.

The project had a promising start with a Federal Grant of $125,000; USC was appointed as comprehensive planner with Koenig as head of the Program. At the project's peak, Koenig employed forty-eight people, twelve of whom were salaried, the remainder volunteers. Working with a large team of students, Koenig conducted a planning study, in which a variety of housing solutions were developed – including one of his own – and presented to the Chemehuevi Elders. All the schemes were pinned to the wall for the Elders to choose which one they wanted. Koenig recalls:

> The matriarch of the tribe put her finger right on my proposal. They understood the scheme graphically. All the others were conventional houses. The last thing they wanted was a white man's house. Also, in their wikiups they liked to sit on the ground and survey the horizon – mine was the only scheme that had glass starting at ground level so that they could continue this practice. The houses had their backs to the wind and the glazing was oriented towards the view. In the other schemes they would sit on the floor and the windows would be too high.

Koenig and his team went on to produce six basic steel-framed house plans – although more variations were possible within the system – for a planned initial development of more than a hundred units. Variety came from assembling separately developed 'living' and 'sleeping' halves of the plan to face a central covered patio. Working within a 10-foot by 20-foot structural grid, with a framing system similar to that of the Bailey House and other earlier Koenig houses, it was possible to produce an almost infinite number of plan variations for the 'living' and 'sleeping' units, or to arrange smaller self-contained living/sleeping units back-to-back across a shared patio.

Over time the housing units were refined and community buildings designed, and everything from roads and telephone lines to a ferry boat service and marina were planned and implemented. Koenig and his team worked on the project for four years, and then he worked on it by himself for a further two years once funding dried up, trying to overcome Federal political opposition. He recalls making regular trips to Washington, San Diego, Phoenix and San Francisco, each time lobbying a different controlling body, to try to put all the pieces of the puzzle in place. In the end, however, the scheme was defeated by political inertia and the suspicion that: 'The houses we had proposed were too nice. The politicians didn't want the Chemehuevi to have better houses than they had themselves, so they did nothing.'

Looking back, Koenig is proud of the fact that the fabrication system he proposed relied on such a small number of standard details and that each house could be built from only four sheets of working drawings. It was this astonishing level of economy that allowed him to pull off the amazing feat of producing drawings for sixty-five Chemehuevi houses, complete with bathrooms and other details, by himself, in the space of one summer. The story as he tells it not only sums up the man and his determination to win through, but provides a perfect illustration of how prefabrication in architecture can produce the labour savings and economies for which Koenig has argued, for so long:

Everybody had left USC for the summer; my whole crew had gone. Then, just as everybody had packed up, HUD (the Federal Authority) called and said "We need the house plans in three months". I didn't know what to do. I knew I couldn't hire anybody new, it would take too long. Then I thought: I can get a lot done myself. So I got the scissors out – in those days there was no computer – and in three months I had done the job. I had a series of modules that I could put together, including two bathrooms and two kitchens, so by cutting and pasting I could put together all the different plans; and because there were so few construction details I had a full set of drawings for sixty-five houses all ready to go.

Then I went down to the print-shop and used a vacuum photographic press; those drawings came out clear and sharp. They looked like ink. I did the house layouts; I did the tract plan; the streets, the grades, all the engineering on it. Then I bundled the whole thing up and took it to San Francisco.

When I got there, I got nothing but criticism because it turned out they'd tried to play a political game. They wanted to stop the project and figured they could do it and pass the blame onto me if I didn't produce the drawings on time. They didn't believe I could possibly do it in three months, even with my full team. But it can be done. The system works like a charm. And I proved it.

As Koenig has long maintained, his steel and glass houses are almost universally applicable industrial solutions to the housing problems of the twentieth century and beyond. In the early days his houses were mostly custom-built designs which were also clearly prototypical. Over time they have become increasingly flexible and adaptive in response to some very demanding sites, from Case Study House #22 on its cliff-edge to the recent Schwartz House on a tight, steeply sloping lot. He views modern technology as a useful tool in the problem-solving process, and maintains that industrialization offers the freedom and opportunity to create a new kind of architecture which was once believed to be impossible. As the challenges he faces have changed, so too have the solutions; his earlier horizontal designs have given way to vertically organized solutions imposed by smaller sites. His own house in Brentwood, for example, completed in 1985, has a three-storey steel frame, and his latest house project in Laguna has three levels, with the floors suspended from the roof structure. In this project Koenig has stretched the steel frame to its limit, creating volumes and vistas that would not otherwise be possible. He is still exploring; still inventing.

Another major event in Koenig's career was undoubtedly the 1989 Los Angeles Museum of Contemporary Art exhibition 'Blueprints for Modern Living: History and Legacy of the Case Study Houses' which focused enormous media and professional attention on Koenig and generated new interest in his work. As a result of that interest, and ever-ready to explore new technologies, Koenig set up his own website. He sees it not as a vehicle for personal aggrandizement – he is unfailingly modest in that regard – but as a platform from which to fight for the cause of Modern architecture. He views it as his responsibility – as one of the few survivors of the Case Study House generation – to keep the pioneering values of Modernism, and the social agenda of the Modern project, alive for younger generations of architects, particularly students. It is clear that his roles as architect and educator have become inextricably linked, and the web allows him to reach young people far beyond those in his own classroom. Today he finds an audience more willing to listen than ever before.

KOENIG HOUSE #1

1950
Glendale, California
800 sq ft + 200 sq ft carport
Structural Engineer: William Porush
General Contractor: Pierre Koenig

In 1950 Pierre Koenig bought a small residential lot in Glendale and designed and built his first house, while still an architectural student at the University of Southern California. His instructors were supportive of the spatial diagram of the house, but objected to the exposed all-steel structure as inappropriate for domestic architecture, preferring instead wood-frame construction for an open-plan glass house.

Koenig, in keeping with a Modernist agenda, was initially interested in lifting the structure into the air in order to free the ground plane below. Once he faced the realities of the site constraints however, Koenig's attachment to this ideal form was dislodged.

He located a flat 1,000-square-foot area on the site for his one-bedroom, one-bathroom house, intending to maximize the small building's relationship to the exterior. A steep bank, a wash, and a stand of oak trees limited Koenig to a very confined buildable area. Unwilling to sacrifice any part of the oaks' canopy, Koenig restricted his design to one storey. Material limits and tight financial constraints also influenced Koenig's design process. Koenig believed, based on material research and engineering calculation, that a steel structure would minimize construction costs and maximize material efficiencies; he built his idea to prove the point.

1 Perspective sketch of rear elevation.
2 Front of house facing street.
3 Living area furnished with prototypes for mass production.

4 A storage wall separates the bedroom from the kitchen. Steel-framed sliding panels close the bedroom to the living area.

5 Floor plan.

6 Awning-type industrial windows allow views to garden.

7 View from carport to entrance.

A module of 10 feet – the distance 1½-inch steel decking could span between beams – determined the proportions of all rooms and simplified dimensions. Koenig planned multiple 10-foot sliding glass doors to open the rear of the house to the outdoors and changed his specification when he was told by the manufacturer that providing one 20-foot door would cut the cost in half. The steel frame eliminated the need for supporting walls. Infill panels of plywood between the round steel pipe columns form visual barriers.

Koenig used the process of designing and building his own house to experiment with low-cost pre-fabricated materials, utilizing awning-type industrial windows on the front elevation and corrugated steel as siding on the west elevation. He exploited materials manufactured for commercial purposes to create a convincing prototype for affordable housing.

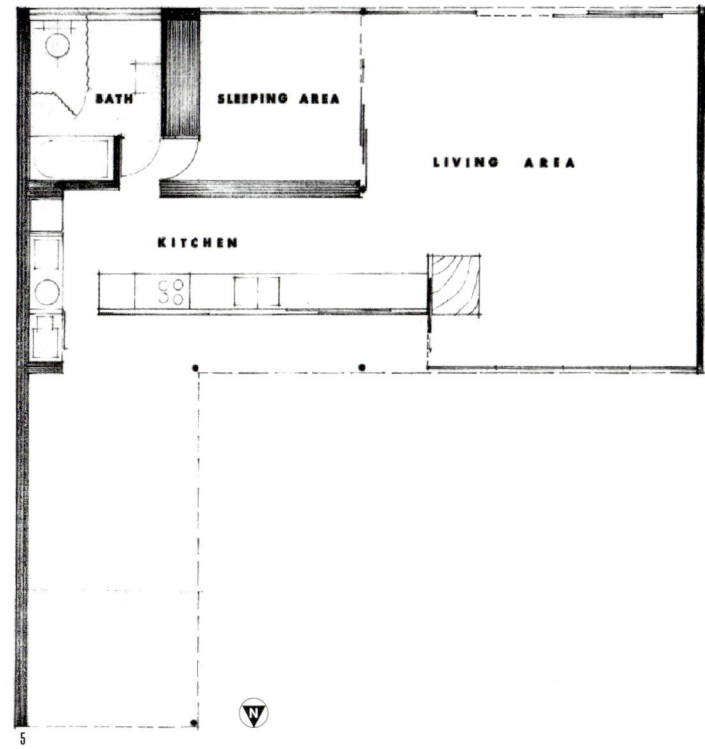
5

6

7

LAMEL HOUSE

1953
Glendale, California
1,200 sq ft + 200 sq ft carport
Structural Engineer: William Porush
General Contractor: Mr and Mrs Lamel

The Lamel House was Koenig's first commission after graduation from USC in 1952. The Lamels bought land on the same street a block away from Koenig House #1. They hired Koenig to design a house similar to his own, on a site with similar constraints. The clients, enthusiastic about building with steel and unconventional materials, asked Koenig to expand the plan for his own house to include an additional bedroom.

Koenig used the same basic materials, details, and components that he had used in the first house. As with Koenig House #1, the availability and properties of materials established the building's proportions: the 10-foot span of steel decking determined the module. Available building materials were still limited, but advances in plastics technology allowed Koenig to use light yellow corrugated fibreglass sheets for screen walls in the entry patio.

Limitations inherent in the site constrained the building footprint to a long, narrow rectangle with a 20-foot frontage. Unlike traditional houses which face the street, the Lamel House's primary orientation is to the side. The long west side acts as the front of the house. A full glass wall opens onto a secluded mantle of oak trees, providing privacy. The oak tree canopy is so thick that the sun shines directly from above only at noon. As a result Koenig could open the west and south walls with glass to allow light in without overhangs. Provisions were made for overhead canvas attachments but they proved unnecessary.

1 House and carport from street.
2 Central courtyard and garden.
3 West elevation (above); perspective view of courtyard from living area (below).
4 Entry stair to courtyard.

5 A screen directs visitors to living and dining areas.
6 Transverse section and details.
7 Central court.
8 Living area.
9 Kitchen and dining area.
10 Floor plan with dry wash along western edge of property.
11 Structural roof plan.

7

8

9

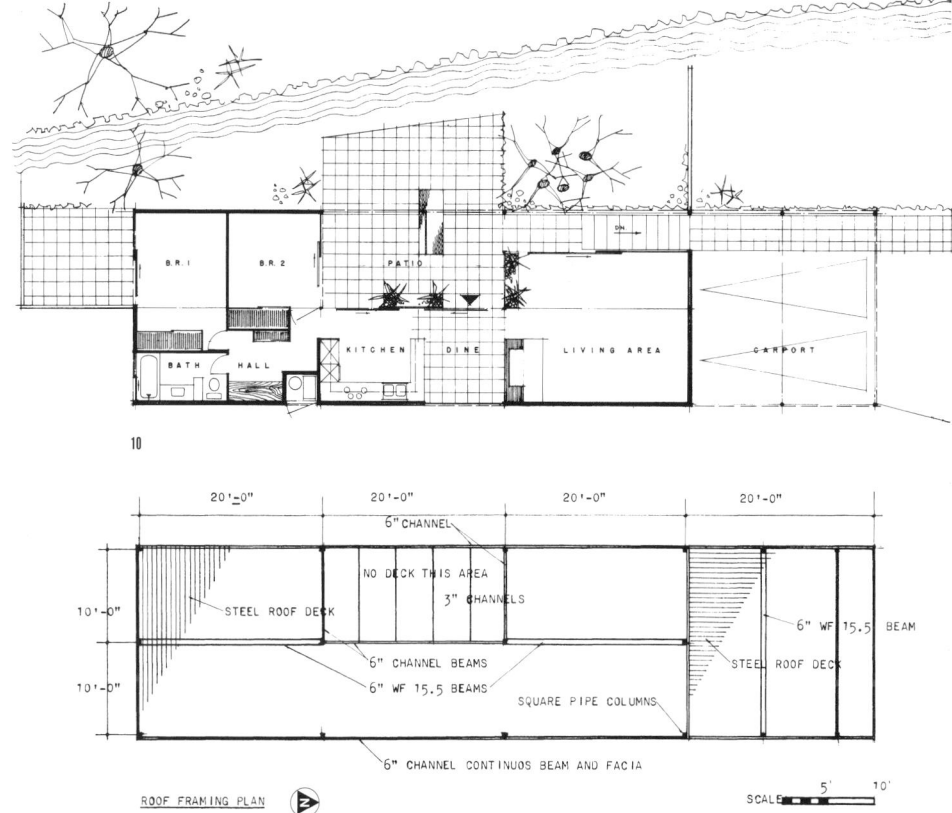
10

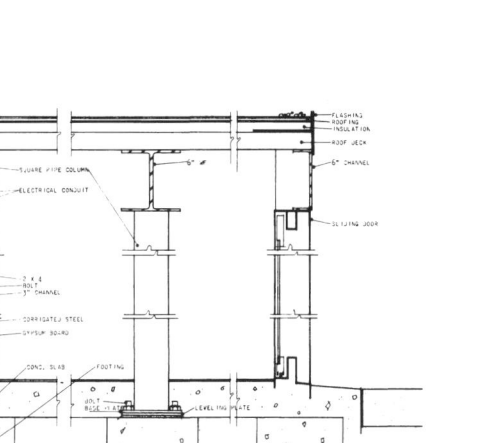
6

11

SQUIRE HOUSE

1953
La Cañada, California
1,400 sq ft + 200 sq ft carport,
900 sq ft patios
Structural Engineer: William Porush
General Contractor: Mr and Mrs Squire

While the Lamel House was under construction, William Squire commissioned Koenig to design and build a 1,400 square foot house, with three bedrooms and two bathrooms, within a 100-year-old olive grove. The house is located in the foothills of the San Gabriel Mountains, with views across a canyon and rugged mountainside towards a national park.

Koenig customarily carefully studied the site to arrive at a design plan. The client stipulated that the house accommodate the existing olive grove, and to achieve this Koenig wrapped glass patio walls around individual trees to create a private exterior court for each bedroom. The patios add 900 additional square feet of exterior space to the house and serve to extend it into the surrounding landscape.

The structural steel framework was devised from the same 10-foot module, and built with the same materials as Koenig's first two houses, although the range and variety of materials was still limited due to post-war shortages.

Despite this, the house was technologically advanced for its time, employing a unique hot air radiant floor slab. In this system, hot air flows through a plenum between the raised double concrete slab to registers around the house.

The house is a variation on a theme that was developing in Koenig's work. It was the first house large enough to allow Koenig some freedom in the circulation and planning of a building. He was able to dispense with the restrictive spatial economy of his first two houses, finding much greater freedom in this more generous programme. The flow from one area to another is more articulate, with varied movement through open space and between privacy barriers.

The approach to the house is intentionally dramatic; the combination carport and entryway leads to a sliding sandblasted glass front door beyond which dramatic views of the San Gabriel Mountains unfold through the living room.

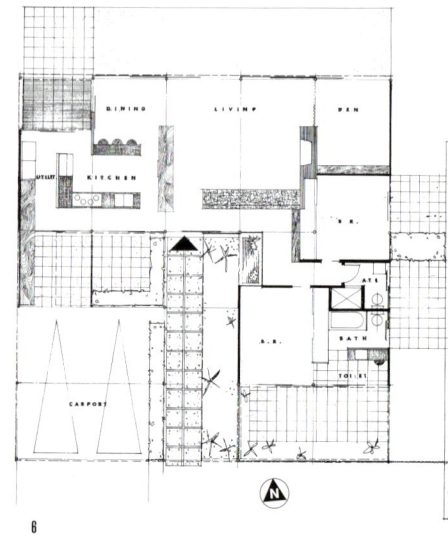

1 View of construction with olive tree in bedroom courtyard.
2 Steel frame ready to receive roof decking.
3 Front entrance between carport and trees.
4 Entry walkway to front door.
5 Obscure glass walls around bedroom courtyard.
6 Floor plan.
7 Perspective sketch of entrance.
8 Perspective sketch of rear elevation.

SCOTT HOUSE

1953
Tujunga, California
1,621 sq ft + 816 sq ft carport and covered area
Structural Engineer: William Porush
General Contractor: Mr Scott

The Scott House occupies a site on the southern edge of the Angeles National Forest adjacent to Little Tujunga Canyon. The north side of the property is surrounded by preserved wilderness, offering spectacular views of the San Gabriel Mountains. Thoughtful planning ensures that the building is still private and protected from the elements. The western sun is blocked by a solid wall with no windows, and a five-foot overhang protects the southern elevation from undesired direct sunlight. The large living room on the south side of the house has extensive views of the canyon. Along the western side, the living room looks through an intermediary outdoor patio to the mountains beyond the dining room. The exposed underside of the steel decking acts as a visual directive; its lines run north–south, carrying the gaze axially through the house to the exterior.

Enclosure walls, positioned under an expansive roof, direct views to the landscape and through the house itself. A low storage wall on the western edge of the carport is topped with clear glass, increasing visibility through the house along the roof's underside.

The wide entrance with a path defined by a line of greenery, is connected to an open carport, creating a spacious roofed outdoor room. Large sliding glass doors lead to an L-shaped circulation hall. A concrete-block fireplace wall buffers the internal circulation spine, as does storage space, a bathroom, and a laundry room. A hall door connects the kitchen to the carport, and sliding glass doors link the laundry room to the outside at the northern wall of the carport.

The dining room area expands with a 10 foot wide sliding glass door opening onto a roofed outdoor patio for indoor or outdoor meals. Although the dining room appears to be contained within the middle of the plan, Koenig opened the room to the landscape by allowing views through the roofed outdoor patio and the living room. The kitchen and both bedrooms open to the north with large glass walls. Two bathrooms were included in the design, a very unusual feature at that time.

Koenig's choice of materials is minimal, expanded only with the use of slate tile on the floor of the entrance area, the kitchen and dining areas, and the adjacent outdoor patios. He used wood panels as an interior wall surface in this, 'a transition period', when clients could not yet accept the white walls he favoured. This was Koenig's first domestic experiment with a hot water radiant heated slab, a forgotten technology in Los Angeles before Koenig pioneered its second wave of popularity.

A year after the house was completed, a hurricane struck Los Angeles generating 100 mph winds in Tujunga. High winds tore apart a new tract of wood post-and-beam houses, lifting their roofs off with the beams and posts connected, depositing shards of debris across the landscape. The Scott House remained perfectly intact, demonstrating the efficiency of the structure.

1 Floor plan.
2 View from living area looking out to patio.
3 Perspective of living room.
4 Entry elevation.

BURWASH HOUSE

1 South elevation through the carport. **2** Rendering of rear of house.

BURWASH HOUSE

1957
Tujunga, California
1,250 sq ft + 450 sq ft carport and storage
Structural Engineer: William Porush
General Contractor: James A Stottlemeyer

The Burwash House, like all of the Koenig houses, is a direct response to the environment of Southern California. Here Koenig was able to reconsider his concept of the efficient structural system, this time including climate control for extreme weather conditions. Tujunga, on the northern tip of the Verdugo Mountains, is a hot and arid area where daytime temperatures can often reach more than 100 degrees Fahrenheit for six months of the year. Koenig convinced his clients that the house could be ventilated and shaded naturally, emphasizing the ecological implications of such an approach. The house is oriented so that its longest elevation faces south; by extending the overhang on this southern side he doubled the annual three-month period of shade that the property received.

Prior to this project, Koenig had maximized the efficiency of the steel beams by running them in the longest direction of the plan. In this case, he positions the steel I-beams across the shortest direction in order to cantilever a wide eaves over the southern glass wall.

There are no columns or load-bearing walls within the perimeter of the house. Koenig endeavoured to reduce the structure to as few component parts as possible. All of the living spaces fit within five bays of 10 feet by 25 feet. Dividing walls that do not reach the ceiling are introduced to address the new orientation of the beams. A low, concrete block fireplace serves both the living area and the den and has a round steel flue similar to the one that he designed for the Lamel House four years earlier.

The house has two bedrooms and two bathrooms. The carport has a generous storage area. An L-shaped concrete walkway leads to a concrete block wall extending from the interior of the house and directing the visitor inside. On the west side of this wall, Koenig extends a long landscape element southward, providing a more private patio for the den and a backdrop for the fireplace. Large sliding glass doors on the north and south elevations allow efficient cross-ventilation and extensive views. All of these features are indicative of Koenig's desire to dissolve the visual barriers between interior and exterior.

The Burwash House was a challenging project and marks a turning-point in Koenig's building philosophy. Until now he had relied on a simple numbering system devised for gauging the amount of steel he would need for the most efficient execution of a structure. Invariably the scheme that required the smallest number of steel components was selected. This system worked but was not suitable for the Burwash commission. Koenig pursued a rigorous, yet flexible, thinking in this house, and the solution is very much influenced by the demands of the site.

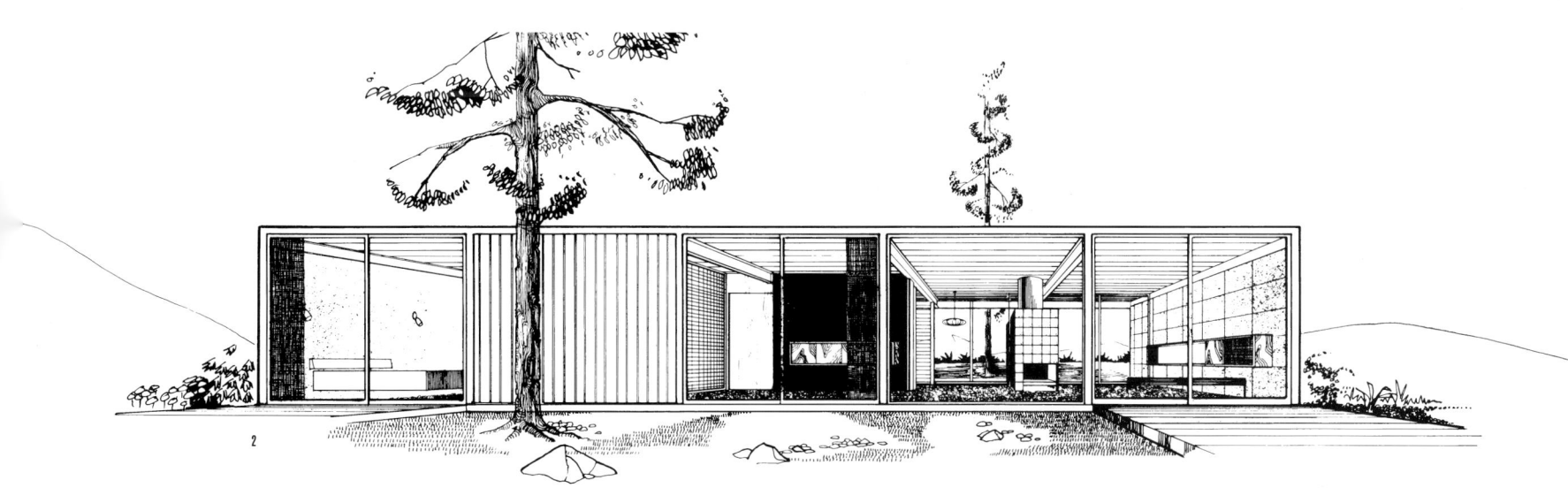

3 Floor plan.
4 Perspective sketch of den.
5 South elevations with five-foot overhangs.
6 Den with refrigeration cork on west wall.
7 View from garden to den.
8 Living area with northern view.

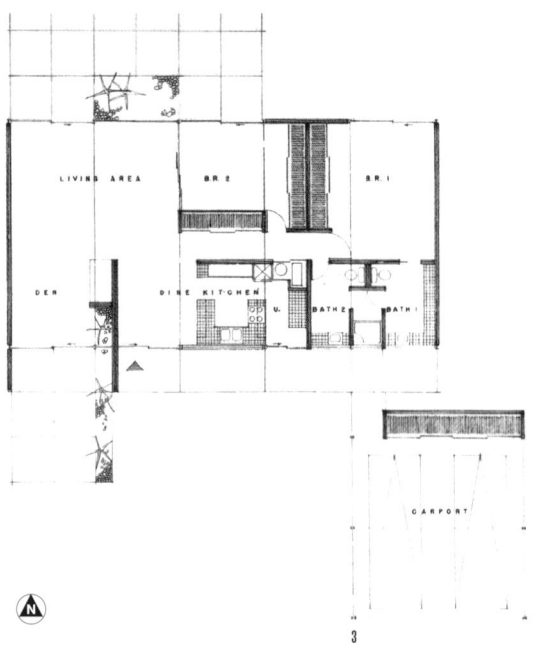
3

5

6

4

7

8

1 Entry elevation. 2 Ground floor plan. 3 Upper floor plan. 4 Perspective drawing of entry elevation.

RADIO STATION KYOR

1958
Blythe, California
10,000 sq ft
Structural Engineer: William Porush
General Contractor: Robert Bruce Inc

A previous client recommended Koenig to the president of Imperial Broadcasting System, who wanted to build a new radio station. This project was Koenig's largest commission to date, although he had already worked on various commercial remodelling schemes.

Koenig chose a combination of steel frame and concrete block for the structure of the building, the frame providing stability for the north and south block walls. A steel beam running along the length of the building, braced mid-way with a steel column, supports the studio floor above and connects the front steel frame with the rear wall. The steel framework is visible in the front elevation, but remains mostly concealed throughout the rest of the structure.

The lower floor of the building contains commercial rental space, while the top floor houses the broadcasting studio, control room, station manager's office, reception area and tape storage space. Ahead of its time, the floor is elevated, so that removable panels may be lifted for access to the repair cables. The absence of loadbearing walls on the lower floor creates an open and unimpeded space that can be treated a number of ways. Potentially, the ground floor space can be evenly divided into two sections, both with street frontage. The toilets, at the rear of the ground floor, are accessible from outside the rear elevation.

This commission coincided with Koenig's growing fascination with acoustics. There are no windows on the upper floor to comply with soundproofing and insulation requirements, deliberately creating an introspective studio environment. The gypsum-board walls are attached to the framing with resilient clips that provide an acoustic rating equal to that of an 8-inch concrete block. The lack of windows emphasizes the function of the structure: the upper solid floats over the void below, and the resulting front elevation is Mondrian-like in its organization. Inside, glass walls allow viewing from the reception area into the studio and from the studio into the control room. The triple-glazed stairwell, at the southeast corner of the front elevation, allows natural light into the building from the east.

METCALF HOUSE

1 Upper floor plan.
2 Lower floor plan.
3 Southern elevation facing Silverlake Reservoir.
4 Southeast corner of house overlooking Silverlake Reservoir.
5 Northeast corner of house showing carport and entry.
6 Perspective view of entrance.

METCALF HOUSE

1958
Silverlake, Los Angeles, California
2,600 sq ft + 1,600 sq ft carport and covered areas
Structural Engineer: William Porush

Arnold Metcalf worked in the steel business and was Koenig's fellow student at USC. He commissioned Koenig to design a house for himself and his wife after purchasing a piece of hillside property overlooking the Silverlake Reservoir.

Koenig and Metcalf proposed a new building system, as yet untested, to address the challenges of the hillside site. Koenig continued his interest in the steel frame, but considered the steel decking in a different way. This time he would invert the decking and use it as a permanent form for concrete. The shape of the inverted steel decking locks into the concrete and eliminates the need for the reinforcing bars used in raised-slab construction. In addition, Koenig believes that the system is ideal for museums and homes, as the underside track of the inverted deck can be used to suspend artwork.

Metcalf's steel company supplied the decking material for the full-scale experiments which Koenig made. He built and tested two model panels, one of which now serves as the bench outside the Bailey House (Case Study House #21).

Between the street and the house is a combined entrance and two-vehicle carport bridge. The front door is recessed into the middle of the plan, with a balcony on either side. The balcony offers views of the sky and the hillside below, made possible by reveals in the roof and floor decks. Koenig effectively brings light and air into the middle of the house with this arrangement. The sliding glass front door leads to an entry area and beyond it to a central stairway to the lower floor. None of the walls dividing the interior living spaces are full height – the stairway, fireplace and storage closet help to define room boundaries without obscuring the view. All of the living areas on the upper floor open onto a 40 foot wide glass wall facing the reservoir.

A 12 foot wide sliding glass door on both balconies provides ventilation for the entire house. The side elevations, panelled with steel-siding, are without windows to ensure privacy from neighbouring properties.

On the middle level, the family, dining and kitchen areas are open to each other and all are open to the view. For ventilation, both bedrooms have access to a hillside terrace running along the entire elevation. Sliding doors on both sides of one bedroom connect it to the family area, the terrace and hillside, and provide the views. A circular stairway on the balcony leads to outdoor play areas shaded by the house above. The slope and the landscape of the hillside beneath the house remain untouched.

The house had many innovations for its time, including solar panels and low voltage controls. Metcalf abandoned the project when he divorced, and the house was never realized.

'THE STYLE THAT NEARLY'
THE GENESIS OF THE CASE STUDY HOUSE PROGRAM

Because most opinion, both profound and light-headed, in terms of post-war housing is nothing but speculation in the form of talk and reams of paper, it occurs to us that it might be a good idea to get down to cases and at least make a beginning in the gathering of that mass of material that must eventually result in what we know as "house – post-war".

Agreeing that the whole matter is surrounded by conditions over which few of us have any control, certainly we can develop a point of view and do some organized thinking which might come to a practical end. It is with that in mind that we now announce the project we have called THE "CASE STUDY" HOUSE PROGRAM.
The Editors, *Arts and Architecture*, January 1945

The Case Study House Program was announced in the January 1945 issue of *Arts and Architecture* magazine, and was addressed to a war-weary audience of Californians tired of sacrifice, struggle and uncertainty, and quite willing to be shown the way towards a bright new future. As a regional flowering of the well-established principles of the Modern Movement, it promulgated housing issues by illustrating real demonstration units in a way that can be seen as analogous to much earlier experiments, including the Pavillon de l'Esprit Nouveau by Le Corbusier at the Exposition Internationale des Arts Décoratifs in Paris, 1925, the extremely influential *Weissenhofsiedlung* in Stuttgart, 1927, and the exhibition houses produced by Albert Frey and Gregory Ain for the Museum of Modern Art in New York, which became so closely identified with the International Style through the exhibition of the same name curated by Philip Johnson and Henry Russell Hitchcock in 1932.

While the Case Study House Program may have had many precedents, what made it effective was the foresight of the magazine's publisher, John Entenza, in using houses that had been designed in the most part for real clients and, by publishing the results, making fantasy believable. Rather than happening *de novo*, however, the Case Study Program was the logical extension of a continual commitment by Entenza to make what had once been a regionally focused magazine – formerly entitled *California Arts and Architecture* – which he bought in 1938, into an international voice for architectural change, as indicated by the ideological position of its editorial board. As Esther McCoy, who was a member of that group, commented: 'No one single event raised the level of taste in Los Angeles as did the magazine, certainly nothing could have put the city on the international scene as quickly.'[1]

The thirty-six Case Study projects that were designed and recorded (with a chaotic, non-sequential numbering system reflecting the high excitement and improvisational quality of the Program), fall roughly into two categories: mixed materials, including wood, prior to 1952; and steel and glass pavilions afterwards. In each case the houses were offered as prototypes for modern living in Southern California. Sized for modest middle-class budgets, they were intended to replace the labour-intensive houses of prewar America with an easy-maintenance, carefree vision of the future. Entenza's motives were not entirely altruistic, however. Like his European counterparts, he had total faith in the ability of modern architecture to change popular aesthetics; he had a specific group of architects whose work he wanted to promote; and he wanted to sell more magazines. He alone managed the difficult task of marshalling all of the necessary resources together to put an idea – the 'postwar house' – then being widely talked about, into action. Reyner Banham relates how Charles and Ray Eames' house – Case Study House #8 – came to personify the entire effort for European observers, largely because of the combined impact of both building and furniture, the latter being 'modern' yet able to embody perfectly the pervasive spirit of the time: suggesting a relaxed, informal way of living, in and out of doors. Banham uses the word 'confirmation' to sum up the importance to Europeans of the Case Study Houses, especially in their later steel phase, in that they brought the ethereal and virtually uninhabitable residential visions of Mies van der Rohe – designed in the most part for a super-rich clientelle – accessible to the ordinary middle-class family, while still upholding a fundamental belief in 'clarity, honesty, and unity'.[2]

Banham's perception about the impact of the furniture is interesting because it highlights an important aspect of the Program: its emphasis was consciously on the entire living environment provided by the houses, and not just their envelope. In this brave new modern world to which war veterans

1

would be returning, everything was intended to support a progressive lifestyle that used the concept of total design promoted so effectively by architects such as Frank Lloyd Wright and the leaders of the International Style. Other than Richard Neutra, William Wurster, J R Davidson and Eero Saarinen, the majority of the architects chosen by Entenza to contribute Case Study Houses were little known outside of California at the beginning of the Program. Other, better-known, names – such as Rudolf Schindler – were excluded for various reasons, including certain clients' refusal to allow the public visits deemed necessary to get the modern message across. At this remove, however, their collective achievement can be seen as a remarkable act of will, guided by a visionary with exceptionally good timing, and all the more impressive because of its near twenty-year duration.

In retrospect, it should come as no surprise that Los Angeles, as the context for the Case Study House Program – and for Pierre Koenig's life's work – should have become the focal point of America's post-war optimism, and the symbol of national aspirations. As Peter Schrag has observed in his book, *Paradise Lost*[3], California has long been for America what America once was for the world at large, a place of promise and a cornucopia of plenty. For the post-war generation California was 'America-plus', the brightest national beacon of a better way of life.

The 'Golden State' has always had this status. California was regarded as El Dorado – and as remote for most Americans as the end of the rainbow – even before the gold rushes of the mid-nineteenth century. The mythical journey west to a better way of life was deeply planted in the American psyche long before John Steinbeck chronicled the journey of 'Okie' farmers fleeing the dustbowls of Depression-era middle America in *The Grapes of Wrath*.

California's population began to grow almost exponentially from the 1920s – accelerating rapidly after 1945 – and when, in 1962, it finally overtook New York as America's most populated state, having grown from 6.9 million in 1940 to 15.7 million in 1960, there was a tremendous sense of optimism. The State Governor at the time, Pat Brown, described it as, 'the greatest mass-migration in the history of the world'.[4] That optimism was based in hard reality: jobs were plentiful, and the entertainment and aerospace industries were booming. Largely on the back of this economic miracle there was an ambitious investment in infrastructure projects. In the 1960s, for example, the Brown administration undertook the radical extension of the freeway network (Pierre Koenig's first house in Glendale would ultimately disappear beneath the Glendale Freeway) and raised the astonishing sum of $1.75 billion to fund the California Water Project to serve the growing population.

Much of this postwar transformation can be traced to the impact of the war years on California's economy and in particular to the explosive pattern of industrialization that occurred in response to Allied demands for transportation, aircraft and armaments. The aviation industry, for instance, which had been nurtured in Los Angeles in the 1920s, grew to full strength in response to President Roosevelt's immediate call for 50,000 aeroplanes; national levels of production that had seemed impossible at the outbreak of war were easily being exceeded by 1945, most of the output coming from the aeroplane manufacturers concentrated in Southern California.

The hundreds of Liberty Ships mass-produced in Henry Kaiser's shipyards in Los Angeles Harbour also represented an unprecedented feat of industrial organization and prefabrication that was instrumental in keeping open the vital convoy lifeline between Europe and the United States. In many ways, the Liberty Ship effort can be seen to presage the technologically focused, mass-production mentality that dominated the discussion of post-war housing provision which led in turn to the Case Study House Program.

At the end of the War, the ingenuity and organizational skills that had made such feats of production possible were channeled into the idea of a better life. The hardship that American soldiers had experienced in Europe and the Pacific (which those at home had largely escaped) gave rise to a determination to make the future more secure and comfortable. The house for the ordinary working family became the object of that resolve. The GI in Europe and the Pacific had fought to defend democracy; returning home he longed for a tangible improvement in his way of life and resourceful housing developers sought to target this potential market. The experimentation with new materials and technologies that had made the war-time aeronautical revolution possible was now transferred to techniques and materials for housing construction, as well as the furniture and appliances needed to fill them; this 'technology transfer' became a national imperative.

With the War's end, national magazines, such as *House Beautiful*, began to run articles about the ideal house for the returning veteran. The May 1946

1 Charles and Ray Eames, Eames House (Case Study House #8), 1949.

2 Ludwig Mies van der Rohe, *Werkbund* exposition, *Weissenhofsiedlung*, Stuttgart, Germany, 1927.

issue, for example, was dedicated almost entirely to 'the first postwar house', which was actually built in Los Angeles and involved over a hundred suppliers, each of whom then advertised in the issue. Thomas Hine has determined that there are four times as many references to California residential construction between 1945 and 1947 in the Readers' Guide to Periodicals than to any other state, activity fuelled in part by the fact that 'the entertainment industries, heavily concentrated in Southern California, were creating new money to build houses at a time when most other regions were stalled'.[5]

John Entenza sensed the explosive potential of the housing market. The Servicemen's Readjustment Act was passed by Congress in 1944; it allowed returning veterans advantageous loan terms provided they lodge their applications within two years of their homecoming (or within two years of the War's end, whichever was the longer). Within three months of this Act passing into law, Entenza announced the Case Study House Program.

Esther McCoy, who regularly contributed to Arts and Architecture throughout Entenza's tenure as Editor, remembered the period just after the War as a time of tremendous pent-up energy when:

There was something electric in the air, a particular sort of excitement that comes from the sound of hammers and saws after they have been silent too long. Architects had endured a sobering wait during the thirties while building came to a virtual standstill and there were few opportunities throughout the war years to design anything except subsistence structures. Young architects were drawing military maps in Europe, designing jigs in airplane plants, building barracks in the Pacific while they marked time. Techniques and materials in their infancy at the outset of the War were undergoing an emergency development.[6]

Entenza's talent was his ability to maintain an objective, visionary view of the chaotic changes taking place around him and to channel those forces into a cause – better housing for a postwar society – which he believed had historical consequences in the region. Implicit in that intention was a Modernist's belief in the necessity of progress, the advances brought by new technology and the conviction that social inequities and difficulties could be successfully addressed by architects. By 1940, Entenza's reconstruction of the newly retitled Arts and Architecture was complete. The word California had been dropped from the masthead as were any regional references to the Mission style that Chamber of Commerce 'boosters' had promoted in the 1920s to lure American immigrants from the East Coast and Midwest toward a rapidly growing symbol of a new, non-agrarian lifestyle. The noted graphic designer Alvin Lustig joined Charles and Ray Eames in the re-design effort.

Lustig, along with Lester Beall and Paul Rand, was one of the leading editorial designers in the United States after the War. He had spent time in Frank Lloyd Wright's community at Taliesin, and Wright's geometric discipline is evident in Lustig's highly original typography. Between 1942 and 1944, Ray Eames designed more than half the covers for Arts and Architecture incorporating Lustig's new condensed sans serif masthead. Special issues of the magazine were laid out by guest designers; the September 1946 issue, for example, devoted to the work of Charles and Ray Eames was designed by Herbert Matter, a Swiss, who had worked in the Eames studio from 1943–6, and went on to design all the advertising for Knoll furniture, a job he took over from Lustig.

Later John Follis, a friend of Entenza's, joined the team as the in-house designer charged with maintaining and further developing the sleek new image of the magazine. By 1943, the editorial advisory board had expanded to include Dorothy Liebes, Gregory Ain, Sumner Spaulding, Grace Clements, Peter Yates and Richard Neutra.

Under Entenza's editorship, Arts and Architecture encompassed all aspects of contemporary culture from architecture and design to music and the theatre. Entenza believed in integrating all the arts. He was also socially motivated and began to use the magazine as a platform from which to promote his own views and ideals. His monthly editorial – 'Notes in Passing' – was as likely to address political issues or human rights as it was to dissect the niceties of design.

Entenza, like most who have had a profound impact on the architecture of the city, was not a native Angeleno. Like Charles Eames, he was born in the Midwest, in Michigan, and came to architecture indirectly, via the movie industry. He had worked in a short-lived MGM experimental film unit, which was closed down during the Depression. His interest in architecture was ignited when his father's partner – an attorney – commissioned, and

3 Alvin Lustig's masthead on Arts and Architecture, March 1960. Cover design by John Follis.

4 J R Davidson, Case Study House #1, 1948.

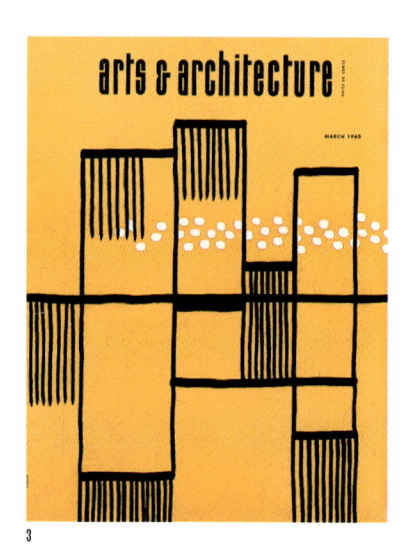

rejected, a house by Harwell Hamilton Harris. Impressed by what he had seen of Harris's work, Entenza commissioned him to design a house for himself in Santa Monica Canyon, in the International Style, which Harris completed in 1937.

Entenza's association with Charles Eames began in a business partnership in a manufacturing concern – The Plyformed Wood Company – which exploited Eames's expertise in forming plywood into complex furniture components to produce medical splints and aircraft parts for the war effort. It ended acrimoniously in a law suit in the early 1950s.

As Editor, Entenza positioned *Arts and Architecture* as a champion of both new technologies in the building industry and the drive for mass-production techniques to be applied to house construction in anticipation of post-war housing shortages. In August 1943 the magazine announced a competition – 'Designs for Postwar Living' – with a brief to design a small, low-budget family house, whose construction would be sponsored by a roster of twenty-two materials and component manufacturers, including the American Rolling Mill Co, the Harbor Plywood Corporation and the Pacific Portland Cement Co. First prize was awarded to a scheme by Eero Saarinen and Oliver Lundquist from Washington DC; second prize went to I M Pei and E H Duhart of Cambridge, Mass; and third prize to Los Angeles architect Raphael Soriano. Saarinen and Soriano would both be prominent contributors to the coming Case Study House Program.

That initiative was followed in July 1944 by a long feature on prefabricated housing, with contributions from Buckminster Fuller, Eero Saarinen and Charles Eames, and the magazine continued to promote pioneering developments in architecture. In November 1947, for example, it published the 'House of Industry', by Konrad Wachsmann and Walter Gropius, a design that relied on a patented system of load-bearing standardized panels intended for factory mass-production by the General Panel Corporation of New York.

Announcing the Case Study House Program in January 1945, with a roster of architects that included Eames, Saarinen, Ralph Rapson, Richard Neutra and J R Davidson, the magazine revealed that it had commissioned an initial batch of eight houses, declaring:

> Architects will be responsible to no one but the magazine, which having put on a long white beard, will pose as 'client'. It is to be clearly understood that every consideration will be given to new materials and new techniques in house construction … we have been promised fullest cooperation by manufacturers of products and appliances who have agreed to place in the hands of the architects the full results of research on the products they intend to offer the public. No attempt will be made to use a material merely because it is new or tricky. On the other hand, neither will there be any hesitation in discarding old materials and techniques if their only value is that they have generally been regarded as "safe".
>
> Each architect takes upon himself the responsibility of designing a house which would, under all ordinary conditions be subject to the usual (and sometimes regrettable) building restrictions. The house must be capable of duplication and in no sense be an individual "performance".[7]

The intention was for each house to be completed, fully furnished and opened to the public for a period of six to eight weeks, in order to show the 'average American' the best of contemporary architecture and design.

The first house to be showcased, in the February 1945 issue of the magazine, was by J R Davidson. Like all the first Case Study houses, it was designed speculatively. It was not to be built until three years later, in modified form, on a site in North Hollywood. The house was atypical of those that followed in that it had two storeys, but otherwise it set a standard. It was sized at 1800 square feet, intended for a husband and wife who 'were both professional people with mutual business interests, the family consisting of one teenaged daughter away at school and a mother-in-law who is an occasional welcome guest'.[8] Based on a two-foot module, the rectilinear house was oriented on an east–west axis, with a garage on the eastern end and bedroom-bathroom cluster on the west, bracketing a living, dining, kitchen zone in the middle of the plan flowing seamlessly out to a patio. Davidson is remembered most for his efficient space planning and Case Study House #1 strikes a balance between inside and outside in this central zone that was to become the norm. His reliance on hard-wearing, contemporary materials was also prescient. He used buffed and polished concrete floors in the living area, asphalt tile in the kitchen, laundry and bathrooms; and plywood, painted insulation board, glass or translucent plastic for interior walls. Built-in furniture and storage components were used wherever possible, including bookshelves, bureaus, desks, closets, storage units, and even a built-in piano in the living room.

Once construction began in 1948, the house was altered to a one-storey plan with guest quarters on the ground floor separated from the main living area. In its final form, Case Study House #1 consisted of standard wood frame construction on an on-grade concrete slab with aluminium siding, plasterboard or plywood sheathed interior walls, Formica counters in the kitchen, and gas appliances. Davidson's consistent use of built-in furniture and acceptance of a changing, more casual lifestyle set the tone for the projects to come.

The architectural sensibilities embodied in the Case Study House Program – the unity of interior and exterior to increase contact with nature; the amplified use of contemporary materials such as steel, glass, plastics, and aluminium; and the exploration of the efficiencies made possible by prefabrication – may seem to have miraculously appeared as an act of will of John Entenza. In fact the Case Study House Program represents a logical extension of an established tradition in the Southern California region, rather than a revolution. The extent of that tradition of innovation must be described in order to appreciate more clearly Pierre Koenig's achievement and the Case Study House Program's place within it.

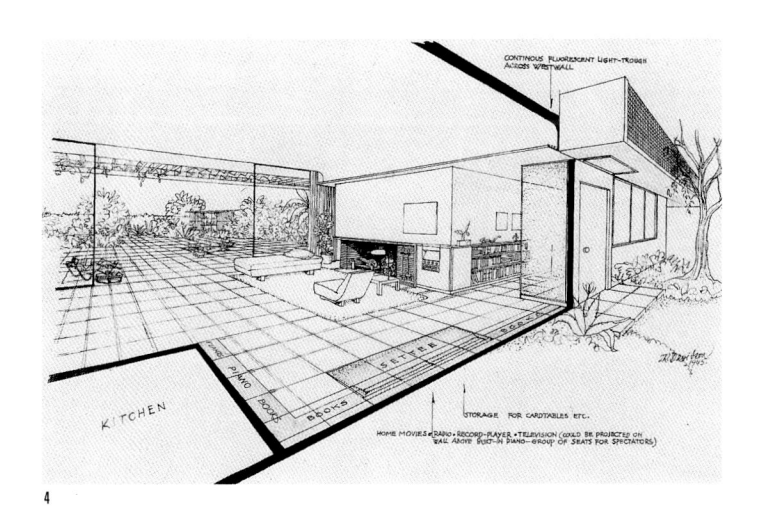

4

5 Rudolf Schindler, Schindler House, 1922. Patio courtyard – outside room.

6 Richard Neutra, Lovell Health House, 1929.

The ideas of a spatial relationship with nature and the honest expression and efficient use of materials first emerged in California in the work of Charles and Henry Greene, and are perfectly summarized in their Gamble House in Pasadena of 1908. While only one of many houses they realized throughout California, the Gamble House epitomizes their commitment to Arts and Crafts ideals first propounded by John Ruskin and William Morris in England. Morris anticipated the ethos of the German Bauhaus that would follow three decades later. He called for:

A new guild of craftsmen, without the class distinctions which raise an arrogant barrier between craftsmen and artist. Together let us conceive and create the new building of the future, which will embrace architecture and sculpture and painting in one unity and which will rise one day toward heaven from the hands of a million workers like the crystal symbol of a new faith.[9]

The love of craft evident in the attention to detail given to each wooden member in the Gamble House extends to the hand sanding and polishing of most of them; while this would not seem to qualify it as a Case Study House precedent there are striking indications of a common ancestry on closer examination. The Greene brothers are generally acknowledged to have been influenced by traditional Japanese architecture, as were other California architects after them including Frank Lloyd Wright, Rudolf Schindler and Charles Eames. Modularization is a salient characteristic of the Japanese system, so much so that Sigfried Gideon, in his attribution of the historical influences of early Modernism, singled out the reaction that Bruno Taut had when first seeing the Katsura Palace: he was impressed by its elemental contemporainity conveyed through minimalism, standardized elements and its true expression of materiality.

Frank Lloyd Wright, who was deeply immersed in the transcendental branch of Arts and Crafts philosophy through Thoreau and Emerson, was also more influenced by Japanese art and architecture, than is generally realized. He first travelled to Japan with his wife in 1895, when it was still difficult to do so. He came to California to work on an arts complex for Aline Barnsdall, located on Olive Hill at Sunset and Vermont built between 1917–19, and subsequently established an office there to realize a series of modular 'textile' concrete block houses – the Millard, Ennis, Freeman, Storer and Sturges residences – which were designed and built between 1920 and 1924. The Barnsdall House was regarded as anomalous in his Californian work in comparison to the relatively systematic constructional approach he later took in the textile block house series. However, Wright attempted to reconcile the sensibilities he brought with him from the Midwest – of the Arts and Crafts movement underscored with what he called 'the machine', or industrial production – and the specific climate of Southern California. In his commentary on the Barnsdall House, Wright remarked on his reaction to Los Angeles as a place of extremes, where ocean, mountains and desert meet. The four elements – earth, air, water and fire – are represented symbolically in the house, coming together in front of the living room hearth.

Significantly the Barnsdall House possesses a relaxed attitude towards nature and the 'out of doors' lifestyle encouraged by the seemingly endless sunshine. Wright opens up the plan to invite a series of easy transitions between inside and outside spaces, and roofed and unroofed 'rooms'. Indeed, the focus of the plan is not an internal space, as one might have expected from his earlier 'Prairie' houses, but an open central courtyard, from which all the ground floor rooms and a series of roof-top terraces can be accessed. Wright's visceral reaction to the climate of Southern California as a sensitive newcomer helps to illustrate a fundamental paradox about Los Angeles that has important implications for the new directions that were determined there after the War. Simply put, that paradox is the way the natural environment in Southern California initially seems utterly benign to most outsiders until the first torrential rains, wind-driven brush fire or earthquake hits. Then an alternative, malevolent character is unforgettably exposed. Wright himself quipped that the torrential rain that can fall on the city had 'surprised the roofs' of the Millard House as water gushed in. The search for a suitable architecture to address the paradoxical Southern California environment has focused the minds of succeeding generations of Los Angeles architects.

Subsequent émigrés, following in Wright's footsteps, also did much to advance the cause of an environmentally responsive architecture in the city and to set the stage for acceptance of the idea of modular design and industrialized construction methods. Chief among them was Rudolf Schindler. He came to Los Angeles in 1918 from Wright's office in Wisconsin to pacify Aline Barnsdall at a critical point in the construction of the Olive Hill house, while Wright was on site in Tokyo building the Imperial Hotel. Schindler tried his best to rationalize the American timber construction process. Using a system of measurement based on the standard units used by the lumber industry, he attempted to eliminate the waste he routinely saw in carpentry, which generally involved a disregard for standard cut lengths.

Schindler's own house on Kings Road, Hollywood, of 1922 stands as an eloquent testimony to his success in developing systems that maximize timber components, while simultaneously exploring newer, more inventive constructional techniques. The Schindler House – built in collaboration with the structural engineer Clyde Chace to house his and Schindler's families – also remains one of the clearest expressions, after the central courtyard of the Barnsdall House, of the ideal California synthesis of inside and outside.

Schindler's reading of the role that shelter serves in reconciling the individual (as part of a wider social framework) with nature is lyrical. While the Barnsdall House establishes a direct visual and physical sense of connection between inside and outside through wide opening walls of glass, Schindler provides clearly articulated outdoor 'rooms', complete with fireplaces, for each of the major internal zones of the house. Schindler responded to the climate, light and landscape, creating a house that formed a backdrop for an informal, bohemian way of life. He even encouraged sleeping on the roof in canvas-covered 'sleeping baskets' until lack of privacy and winter rains curtailed the enthusiasm of all concerned. The innovative 'tilt-slab' construction method that Schindler used for the outer shell – reinforced concrete panels cast *in situ* in formwork laid on the floor slab and then hoisted vertically into place when cured – extends a technique pioneered in California by Irving Gill. Schindler described the house as 'a simple weave of a few structural materials which will retain their natural color and texture throughout. It is the beginning of a building system which a highly developed technical science will permit in the future.'[10] The panels also echo Wright's attempt to simplify the building unit in his textile block houses – where individual blocks were cast on site using local aggregates – and prefigures the focus on standardization and technological innovation in the Case Study houses to come. By the time the Program started Schindler had demonstrably moved away from the simplicity of the early statement of the Schindler House; thus John Entenza's decision not to include him reflected the theoretical distance Schindler had travelled.

The ethos of prefabrication and a renewed relationship between indoor and outdoor living space can also be seen in Wright's Usonian House series, which began with the Herbert Jacobs House in 1935, and further in the Case Study House Program, through both its early wood and later steel phases. Aspects of the Schindler House can almost be regarded as the 'DNA' for the Case Study houses, featuring as it does, many of their principal characteristics: a floor slab level with outside terraces; sliding glass doors opening onto those spaces; a flat roof with deep sheltering overhangs; movable internal partitions and purpose-designed fitted furniture.

Schindler continued to advocate advances in building systems, and in 1942 he produced a thirty-four point argument in favour of prefabrication envisaged in this instance in wood rather than steel, but with a set of principles that could be applied equally to either option. In what he called the 'Panel-Post' house, he foresaw a modern mass-produced dwelling, framed rather than loadbearing, composed of factory-made building units, lightweight to permit easy transportation and capable of construction by an unskilled labour force, with the minimum of specialist finishing on-site.

It would remain for other architects such as Koenig to pick up this baton and carry it forward into reality, largely in steel. There can be little doubt, however, that Wright and Schindler both significantly advanced the theoretical constructs of Arts and Crafts in the region, effectively grafting them onto an emerging *zeitgeist* of outdoor living in California in readiness for the Case Study House Program.

Esther McCoy, *Arts and Architecture*'s chief architecture critic and principal chronicler of the critical period in the history of California architecture in which Pierre Koenig participated, accurately placed him in what she termed 'the third generation' of architects building in Los Angeles. Richard Neutra and Raphael Soriano, as the progenitors of the first and second generations respectively, had already broken important new ground toward a shift from timber frame to steel construction, and Koenig credits them both as having had a significant influence on his work. Neutra's Lovell Health House of 1929 – the first major Modern Movement steel house in Los Angeles – can perhaps be regarded as the 'first Case Study House', not just because of its steel pedigree, but because of the publicity it garnered. It was undoubtedly a watershed in that architect's career and an achievement that he never approximated again. Steel construction was the most feasible approach for the precipitous Lovell site; but Neutra determined to use steel frame in a polemical, as well as strictly functional way in response to the challenge that the topography presented. Structural elegance rather than aesthetic scale was the main vehicle of that polemic. The columns do not exceed the four inches necessary to carry their load and the open-web joists are also extremely slender. This thin frame acts as a cage through which sections of the elevation project, thereby forming large partially enclosed balconies that facilitate the kind of outdoor life that the climate of Southern California makes possible.

Frank Lloyd Wright may, albeit in a primitive way, have prepared the ground for acceptance of the idea of prefabrication in his textile-block houses, but the Lovell Health House, as Neil Jackson has observed,[11] brought the prefabrication ethos of the European Modern Movement intact to America, transplanting it in California where it almost immediately began to flourish. Furthermore Neutra, by introducing the steel frame, can be credited with creating a new regional vernacular, employing a structural material more suited to the developing architecture of Southern California than the ubiquitous timber frame.

The highly visible public profile of Neutra's client, Dr. Philip M Lovell, who was well known for his column on health and fitness in the *Los Angeles Times Sunday Magazine*, was more effective in broadcasting the architect's Modernist viewpoint than the sleek profile of the house itself, on its then secluded hillside site. In 1929 Lovell extended an invitation to all his readers to visit the house in the December 15th issue of the newspaper, and over the next two weeks hundreds of people participated in tours personally conducted by the architect. Much was made of the notion that the house was constructed of pre-assembled shop-fabricated parts welded together on site and the fact that the entire steel skeleton took less than forty hours to erect. The Lovell Health House – exhibited by Hitchcock and Johnson in the 1932 Museum of Modern Art exhibition, 'International Architecture' – brought its architect, and Los Angeles, international acclaim, to an extent not achieved by Neutra again. Yet, his approach in carrying forward ideas engendered in the Lovell Health House was always in the spirit of showcasing prototypes, an attitude that was also to underscore the Case Study House Program.

Neutra's most significant project after the Lovell Health House bears this out. His own home and studio, named the Van der Leeuw Research (VDL) House after the industrialist who partially funded the enterprise, was completed in 1932 on a small site overlooking the Silverlake Reservoir. In a strategy reminiscent of John Entenza's tactics a decade later, Neutra solicited the latest building materials from manufacturers on the premise that they would receive extensive advertising by doing so, but due to his restricted budget, Neutra was limited to a wood rather than steel frame. Putting a positive spin on financial constraints, Neutra characterized remaining within a modest budget as an experiment, and put much emphasis on the precast concrete floor joists on which the wooden frame rested. Expanding on Schindler's socialist sensibilities as exemplified in the equality of the planning of the Kings Road house, Neutra wanted the spaces in the VDL House to be as flexible as possible so that it could be easily adapted to additional occupants and later uses. This mostly unspoken, and still largely unexplored political agenda behind a majority of the early Modern architecture in Los Angeles, sheds a different light on the notion of flexible planning that is now seen as one of its critical hallmarks.

Raphael Soriano had been exposed to Neutra's philosophy of prefabrication and the use of the latest technological advances in architecture as a student at both USC and the Academy of Modern Art, which existed only briefly in Los Angeles in the early 1930s. Soriano worked in Neutra's studio on the Rush City Project during the last part of 1931 and into 1932 and returned after a hiatus working with Schindler after graduation, before opening up his own office in 1933. The Depression made it a difficult time to begin a career, but nonetheless, Soriano was able to advance the vision of physical lightness and large clear spans in steel that Neutra had achieved in the Lovell Health House. In spite of the obvious evolution in the application of steel construction that can be seen in the work of these two architects, Soriano himself noted that it was Neutra's skill as a logical space planner – working within the discipline that steel framing imposed – that was to influence his own approach to architecture, rather than Neutra's use of steel *per se*.

Soriano's rational acceptance of the higher levels of restriction in tolerances, fabrication and construction that steel structures demand rather than choosing to build in the material for aesthetic or stylistic reasons, is critical to an understanding of how steel construction would be taken up by the next generation of architects, particularly Pierre Koenig and Craig Ellwood. As Koenig says, 'Steel is not something you can take up and put down. It is a way of life.'

Soriano's first steel-frame home, the Katz residence, was completed in 1947, three years before the one house he was to contribute to the Case Study Program, but such enlightened clients – who would adopt modern principles and build in steel – were rare, which goes a long way toward explaining why the Case Study houses were initially commissioned with the magazine as 'client' and why of the first batch of eight designs, ultimately, only four were built for real families.

Case Study House #4, designed in 1945, is a notable case in point. Ralph Rapson's design for what he christened the 'Greenbelt House' was the most polemical of the series and also the most controversial. Instead of continuing the idyllic image of the industrial pavilion in Arcadia, Rapson broke the pattern with a hypothetical proposal for a residential solution to urban blight, a house intended to capture and protect nature, rather than be a mechanized counterpoint to it. Rapson's choice of 'Greenbelt' as a title was a conscious attempt to portray the solution as a microcosmic prototype, claiming in the August 1945 issue of *Arts and Architecture* that 'Greenbelt … represents a return to a simple, basic kind of living … It seems fundamental to bring nature within the house – not in small, pretty planted

7 Charles and Ray Eames, Eames House (Case Study House #8), 1949.

areas, but in a large scale that will do it justice.'¹² As a rectangular central courtyard of green space, flanked by enclosed bar buildings on each side, the house logically lent itself to public–private separation without convoluted circulation patterns.

A 'commuter' helicopter seen hovering over the Greenbelt House, in one of Rapson's sketches, and a Jeep in the driveway are a graphic reminder of the direct link between the forced development of new technologies during the Second World War and the impetus behind the concept of an industrialized post-war house; they were both potent symbols of pragmatic, ingenious adaptations of divergent technologies, meant to solve problems of mobility and quick response on the battlefield. It should come as no surprise that Pierre Koenig, freshly returned from combat, first became aware of the technological possibilities open to him in contemporary architecture when he saw Rapson's renderings of the house in *Arts and Architecture* in the San Gabriel Library before he enrolled in the architecture programme at USC. Rapson's sketches – amounting to a visual manifesto – struck a chord.

While Rapson envisaged the house in wood post-and-beam construction, the design never evolved far enough for structural materials and details to be specified because a client could not be found for it. Had it proceeded, Rapson's emphasis on modular organization and prefabrication in his extremely descriptive freehand sketches would have allowed the design to be easily adapted to steel; his notes which indicate natural plywood panels, Cemesto Board inserts in primary colours, and opaque glass, presage Case Study House #8, the Eames House, designed that same year.

Case Study House #8 by Charles and Ray Eames for themselves and House #9 by Charles Eames and Eero Saarinen for John Entenza began the steel phase of the Program in earnest. Significantly, they were also the first houses in the Program to have specific clients, and actual sites – in a high, secluded meadow in Pacific Palisades, overlooking the ocean. In that respect, they mark a dramatic transition in the series from idea to built reality. Both houses – their progress monitored in the pages of *Arts and Architecture* – were to have a profound effect on the international direction of Modernism at the beginning of the 1950s. That influence was arguably caused most by House #8, which began as a steel X-frame bridge projecting out perpendicular to a steep slope at the back of the site into the tree sheltered meadow, allowing long views towards the ocean far below. The perpendicular placement of the Eames House ensured privacy by positioning the blank end of the rectangular bridge toward the Entenza House, but was intrusive in the meadow that the Eames' had come to love. After visiting an exhibition of Mies van der Rohe's work at the Museum of Modern Art in New York, where he saw a similar *parti* sketched by the German master, Eames was confirmed in his belief that a different approach was needed. Eames consequently decided to swing the rectangular box of the house around in a 90-degree arc and fuse it to a retaining wall that he cut into the slope, placing the house behind a stand of mature eucalyptus trees. Nature thus became a more integral part of the concept than it had previously been in the Program.

The eucalyptus foliage offered a natural screen for the long east facade which looked out onto the Entenza House and the early morning sun. This elevation was further defined by an open courtyard inserted between the living and working portions of the house, and by details such as the strategically located solid panels, inserted into the predominantly glass facade, which are painted white or vibrant primary colours. The De Stijl palette of pure red, blue and yellow (or more accurately in this case, gold) had made an appearance before in the Program – most recently in the Thornton Abell interiors of Case Study House #7 – but not in such a purposeful architectonic way. Such tactics were not only used to ensure privacy, but to modulate the patterns and shadows of sunlight during the day, as well as to frame selective views towards the trees, ocean and sky. The message that this compelling and quirky set of compromises between technology and topography, solid and void, light and shade, personal preference and minimalist obligation, ultimately conveyed was that Modernism could be principled and still have an attractive human face.

The Eames House seems to visually embody the prefabrication ethos. It was based on a lightweight steel frame of 4-inch H-columns and Truscon open-web joists. *Arts and Architecture* noted that the frame, which was erected in a day and a half, had in its unclad state, 'an aesthetic quality one would like to preserve'.¹³ Attached to the frame were factory-made windows, doors, roof decking and other elements straight from building suppliers' catalogues. Proof of the inherent flexibility of such a system – and its wide range of potential applications – was provided by Eames himself and his last-minute decision to reconfigure the building long after the steelwork had been ordered. He was able to replan the house, working within the discipline of the specified beam and column lengths, and to optimize the building's volume accordingly, so that, in the end, no materials were wasted.

The fact that a steel-frame system is quick and easy to erect on site has long since become a high-tech article of faith. Pierre Koenig's thinking – evinced by the steelwork erection sequence drawing he produced for his own house in Brentwood in 1985 – professes that quick construction has not only become accepted as proof of the efficacy of prefabricated construction systems, but an end in itself, as time on site is money.

In contrast to the Eames House, the Entenza House was far more reticent in proclaiming its prefabricated pedigree, much of its steel frame being concealed by cladding. Edgardo Contini, who acted as structural engineer on both houses has referred to the Entenza House as 'anti-structural' in stark contrast to the Eames House which was 'structurally assertive'.¹⁴

The degree to which the technologically articulated details of House #8 reverberate against the solid square foil of House #9 is now impossible to appreciate due to the extensive remodelling carried out in 1995, but the initial intention of balance or dialogue was obvious. Eero Saarinen has frequently been credited as the source of rhetorical restraint evident in the Entenza House. The house represents a thoughtful attempt at matching the personality of architecture and client. The stability inherent in the square 42-foot plan, the selective articulation of the exterior, and a limited palette of elegant materials all reflect some of the characteristics of the owner. This match extended to the house's internal arrangement, purposefully left as open and flexible as possible to accommodate Entenza's busy and variable social life. Despite this, Esther McCoy asserts that Entenza, a life-long bachelor, never really liked the house, and he eventually moved to a Neutra-designed apartment in Westwood.¹⁵

Unlike the Eames house, the Entenza house proclaimed its reliance on the spatial freedom that steel framing can provide by its larger uninterrupted spans, openness and careful coordination of its furnishings, rather than in the exuberant display of structural elements. The main living-entertainment space features a rectilinear area at ground level with a freeform sofa built into a platform raised up two steps behind it, the precursor of the 'sunken' living rooms that were to become so fashionable in houses during the 1950s. The ground level portion of the living area, adjacent to the external glass wall, connected to an outside patio, partially covered by a continuous, cantilevered brow that reinforced the notion of inside–outside space.

Taken together, as they were intended to be, Case Study houses #8 and #9 clearly represent all of the goals that Entenza had initially sought to

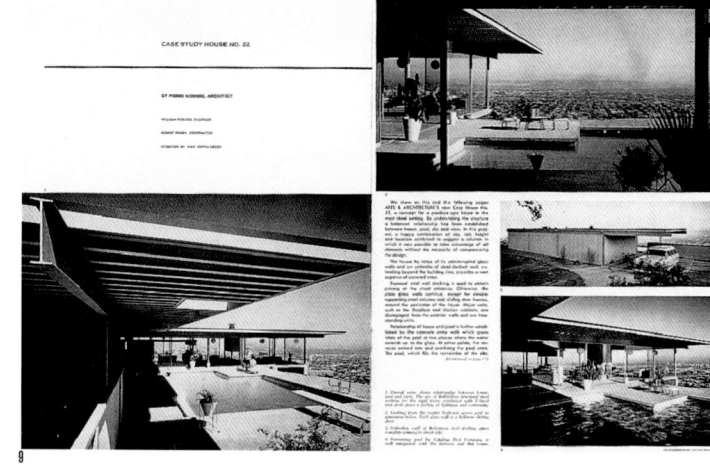

8 Case Study House #21 in *Arts and Architecture*, February 1959.

9 Case Study House #22 in *Arts and Architecture*, June 1960.

achieve in advancing the Modernist agenda. A complementary pair, they proclaimed the cost-conscious freedom allowed by new materials and constructional techniques, flexible planning and a *rapprochement* with nature. While the Eames House demonstrated how technology can transform nature, the long spans and broad overhangs of the Entenza House showed how new materials can allow far greater access between the rational inside, and the natural outside realms.

The Eames and Entenza Houses represent the apotheosis of the programmatic attempts at inside–outside integration of the Case Study houses that precede them. From this point forward in the Program until Pierre Koenig's contribution with Case Study Houses #21 and #22, the only manifested refinement of the message was an increase in the size of structural steel members, or further exploration of the artificial versus natural equation. These interim Case Study House projects offer on the whole few surprises or innovations; many are by earlier contributors to the Program.

One exception to this rule is Craig Ellwood. Koenig's fellow youngster in the Program – Ellwood completed his first Case Study House at the age of thirty – he appeared on the architectural scene in Southern California as a technically innovative designer in the early 1950s. His greatest interest was to advance construction techniques using steel, gradually refining his methodology case by case, house by house.

In the nine years between the completion of the Eames House and Pierre Koenig's design for Case Study House #21, Craig Ellwood introduced the only discernible variables in what had, by the beginning of the 1950s, started to become a rather formulaic exercise. Case Study Houses #16, #17 and #18 were assigned to Ellwood in 1952, 1954 and 1956 respectively, having previously been allocated to Rodney Walker; by then the arcane numbering system operated by *Arts and Architecture* was intelligible to only a few insiders, and probably not even to them.

During this time Koenig was establishing his reputation as an architect. Koenig's first house for himself in Glendale, 1950, and the Lamel, Scott, Squire and Burwash houses that followed, between 1953 and 1957, are all exquisite spare pavilions which precisely illustrate the Case Study ideals and further refine them. These houses brought Koenig to the attention of John Entenza who, in 1957, designated as Case Study House #21 the house he had been commissioned to design for a young psychologist and his wife, Walter and Mary Bailey. Designed seven years after Koenig's first experiment with steel, the Bailey House was the result of constant refinement of a structural system as the tectonic expression of the ethos that he had begun to explore in his own house.

Case Study House #21 was designed for a level site in the Hollywood Hills. The couple were childless and their requirements were for a small house with an open plan and materials that would allow for easy maintenance. Koenig responded with what John Entenza later described as 'a design that is beautifully articulated in steel and represents some of the cleanest and most immaculate thinking in the development of the small contemporary house.'[16]

Case Study House #21 was first published in *Arts and Architecture* in drawing form in May 1958, and completed at the end of that year, at the same time as the Seagram Building in New York by Mies van der Rohe and Philip Johnson was announced to the press. With characteristic economy of means, Koenig divided living, kitchen and bedroom areas by using a freestanding service core that contains two bathrooms and a mechanical room, making the interior of the house seem much larger than its 1320 square feet. To balance the unrelenting constructional logic of steel (here employed in bays of 10 by 22 feet) Koenig surrounded the house with a reflecting pool, bridged by terraces intended to connect interior and exterior space, and join the house to nature. As Esther McCoy has said: 'Koenig handles basic industrial materials with unusual spareness to achieve mobile perspectives. His dispassionate examination of steel is accompanied by an inventiveness of plan and detail, a sensitivity to proportions, and in Case Study House #21 a sensuous feeling for water.'[17] The pools are a novelty in the Case Study House series in that the water in them is recirculated onto the roof into perimeter gutters and cascades down the sides through projecting scuppers. The mirror-like quality of the water softens the otherwise hard edge of the building and provides continual changes of mood and character throughout the day, while the sound of falling water permeates the house.

When *Arts and Architecture* published the finished house in the February 1959 issue, the editors were prompted to suggest that:

> Case Study House #21 represents a form of culmination of
> development of the steel house, as it represents the epitome

of architectural refinements in planning and execution, in a material heretofore considered experimental. By utilizing readily available steel shapes and products in a carefully conceived manner, a finished product comparable to any other luxury home is achieved minus the excessive cost usually associated with quality and originality.[18]

It appeared that with his first house for the Case Study Program, Koenig had gone straight to the top of the league. The aesthetic of expressing the steel structure between the panels that form the external skin was extended to great effect by Koenig in this house, and as Neil Jackson has observed,[19] his attitude towards prefabrication was quite different to Ellwood's and closer, in fact, to that of Charles Eames. In Case Study House #21, Koenig relies on ready-made products and materials, rather than specialist prefabricated systems, bringing it closer to the initial spirit of the Case Study House enterprise.

In sharp contrast to the delicate, Oriental, pavilion-like quality of Case Study House #21, Koenig's second house in the series, Case Study House #22, completed in 1960, has a more substantial, broad-shouldered feeling to it, due mainly to its high ceilings, wide spans, and overhanging eaves. The owners, Carlotta and C H (Buck) Stahl, were sensitive to the potential of the site, and wanted an unencumbered 270-degree view. Framing the house in steel, Koenig used 20 foot wide bays with columns spaced at 20 feet to maximize the amount of glass, providing uninterrupted views of the whole city spread out below.

As with all the Case Study houses, *Arts and Architecture* followed the progress of the house in its pages. The drawings were published in May 1959, and it was featured under construction in February 1960. Photographs of it taking shape show to dramatic effect the 20-foot clear spans and 8-foot cantilevered over-hangs designed to provide cover for outdoor activity by the pool and to protect the interiors from direct sun during the hottest part of the day. As the editors noted: 'The concept of a free-floating roof shelter oriented to an expansive and spectacular panorama begins to take form.'[20]

While Case Study House #21 was hailed as a prototype, Case Study House #22 seems inevitably unique, by virtue of its extraordinary site, which perhaps explains its rather muted initial presentation in the June 1960 issue of *Arts and Architecture*. The magazine oddly confined itself to a functional description of the house, and the engineering feats that made it possible.

But the house may seem more remarkable today than it did then. As the curators of the 1989 MOCA exhibition, 'Blueprints for Modern Living: History and Legacy of the Case Study Houses', noted 'For #22 Koenig exploited to the maximum the potential of steel to open up space, constructing a minimal cage spanned by sheets of glass.'[21]

In fact the house seems to be *all* space: the only elements that might be regarded as rooms in the conventional sense are the bedrooms and utility rooms that hug the blind, roadside wing of the L-shaped plan; but even the bedrooms have an entirely glass wall looking out over the pool. In the living room which forms the major, projecting branch of the 'L', architecture is dematerialized: there is only the platform of the floor and the sheltering plane of the roof; the rest is mile upon mile of uninterrupted view.

In one of those rare instances when a photograph manages to distill the essence of a certain time or place, Julius Shulman's photograph of Case Study House #22 captured not only the physical envelope but the end of an era as well. As architectural critic Paul Goldberger has described the photograph:

The house is sleek and white, and its glass walls are cantilevered out over the hills; two elegantly dressed women lounge inside as the lights of the vast sprawl of the Los Angeles basin twinkle below. Modernity and elegance, privacy and openness – things that so rarely went together in the older cities of the east coast – here become one, bound together in a way that epitomized the seductive power of Los Angeles in the first years of its heady postwar growth.[22]

Shulman's photograph of Case Study House #22 has continued to have such enduring resonance and iconic power. Taken on the eve of America's involvement in Vietnam it records the last glorious moments of American post-war hegemony and self-confidence and its unquestioned belief in the benefits of progress and technology.

Case Study House #22 became a national icon, marking a critical moment in the collective American psyche. Unfortunately, at the time, this wasn't enough to convince the United States' building or financial establishment to support prefabricated steel construction as the answer to the housing shortage. Reyner Banham characterized the Case Study House Program as 'The style that nearly',[23] because it was almost, but ultimately not quite able to provide a solution to the post-war housing question, not so much due to resistance from the construction industry, although that was undoubted, or a conspiracy to continue time consuming union practices, but mostly out of apathy and fear of the unfamiliar on the part of the great mass of ordinary house-buying Americans. It is interesting to note also that the completion of Case Study House #22 came at a moment when the provision of new single-family housing in the United States dropped to its lowest level since 1947, although California continued to buck that trend. Only five more Case Study houses would follow Koenig's masterpiece.

Banham records that when he first arrived in Los Angeles in the early 1960s – a visit that was to lead to his seminal book *Los Angeles: The Architecture of Four Ecologies* – he was told that all the 'steel and glass' architects were in dire straits generally, and that neither Koenig or Ellwood had any work in their offices.[24] As might have been expected, news of their demise proved premature, but it was a fact that by 1963 the Case Study House Program had run out of steam. So too had *Arts and Architecture*.

The magazine had never really been profitable, largely due to Entenza's selective approach to advertisers, and his refusal to broaden the magazine's readership by loosening his editorial belt. When, in 1960, Entenza was offered the directorship of the Graham Foundation, and left Los Angeles for Chicago, the magazine entered a terminal decline. Two years later he sold the magazine to David Travers who struggled to keep it afloat, launching new initiatives such as the Case Study Apartment Program in 1963 in an attempt to broaden its appeal, to no effect. The magazine appeared for the last time in September 1967, as advertising revenue finally dried up.

The spirit of the Case Study House Program lives on, however; and, to many outsiders – like Banham – Los Angeles still 'cradles and embodies the most potent … vision of the good life in a tamed countryside'.[25] That observation, made from a viewpoint at the end of the 1960s remains compelling, despite the painful social upheavals that have characterized Los Angeles in the 1990s. Now, perhaps more than ever, images such as David Hockney's 1968 'A Bigger Splash' – which Banham took to illustrate his point – have become iconic of the fabled California, a place of sunshine and easy living. It is, of course, no accident that the backdrop for Hockney's pool, and the 'splash', should be a Case Study House, its simple steel frame offering a kind of shorthand notation for all that is good in Los Angeles architecture.

BAILEY HOUSE

Case Study House #21
1959
Hollywood, Los Angeles, California
1,320 sq ft
Structural Engineer: William Porush
General Contractor: Pat Hamilton
Interiors: Viki Stone for SM Furniture Co,
Jerry McCabe

For many critics, Koenig's Case Study House #21 – the Bailey House – represents the high-water mark of the Case Study Program. In February 1959 *Arts and Architecture* hailed it as representing 'some of the cleanest and most immaculate thinking in the development of the small contemporary house'. For Koenig it represented the culmination of several years' careful development of the steel house prototype, honing and refining his vocabulary until it was reduced to only two steelwork details and an effortlessly economical plan: it is seen as a seminal single-family house by architects worldwide.

This was Koenig's first house in the Case Study House series and resulted from earlier work which was published in *Arts and Architecture* leading to John Entenza's invitation to join the Program 'when you get the right house and the right client'. The clients in this case were a professional couple, a psychologist and his wife, Walter and Mary Bailey who commissioned Koenig in early 1957. The site was in the Hollywood Hills, and the problem was to design a 1200 to 1300 square foot house with two or three bedrooms and two baths on a level lot. As a childless couple, the Baileys had an informal lifestyle, which dictated the relative openness of the plan and fluid spatial design.

Koenig's site planning, as always, was skilled. He identified the southern orientation as the most important; a steep slope blocked the western view, and the main access road was to the east. He therefore opened the house up on a north–south axis and put solid walls on the east and west, bracketing and compressing an L-shaped plan.

The house is a 30-foot by 44-foot rectangle and the roof structural system extends another 30 feet to encompass the entry and carport. By compressing

1

1 South elevation.

2 Carport with entrance beyond. Steel roof decking continues through the house.

3   A channel of water circumscribes the house.

4-6   Steel frame placed in position.

7   Steel frame with decking partially installed on wall and roof.

8   The house in the surrounding environs.

9   Bird's-eye perspective of the proposed house.

the plan, Koenig was able to establish a linear progression from the carport and main entry at the northern end of the site, through a transition zone into the living room area and out to the garden at the southern end of the axis. In the living room area is a deep pile carpet with furniture grouped to define a conversation area. Pure white vinyl tile surrounds the carpeted area and defines a circulation path.

The openness of the plan is accentuated by Koenig's decision to concentrate the services – bathrooms and mechanical rooms – in a solid rectangular core along the north–south axis. The social and private areas of the house are divided by a bathroom and mechanical core which in turn opens on to an interior court, open to the sky. The kitchen-dining area and living room opens up to the court, while the bedrooms are hidden behind the core to the west.

The core is faced with grey mosaic tile and is divided by an open courtyard, with plants and a small pool with a fountain, which are part of Koenig's strategy for the integration of nature within the house. The core effectively allows natural light and air into the centre of the house.

Commenting on the dichotomy between the manufactured and the natural, Koenig landscaped the garden, and surrounded the house with reflecting pools. Paving bricks, inset in steel frames bridge the water at every opening, serving each interior space.

Water is used as part of an innovative environmental control system. The circulation system pumps the water up to the gutters at the edge of the roof where it falls back through the scuppers into the pools. This strategy is both pragmatic and lyrical; the water has some cooling properties and the hard building edge at ground level is softened

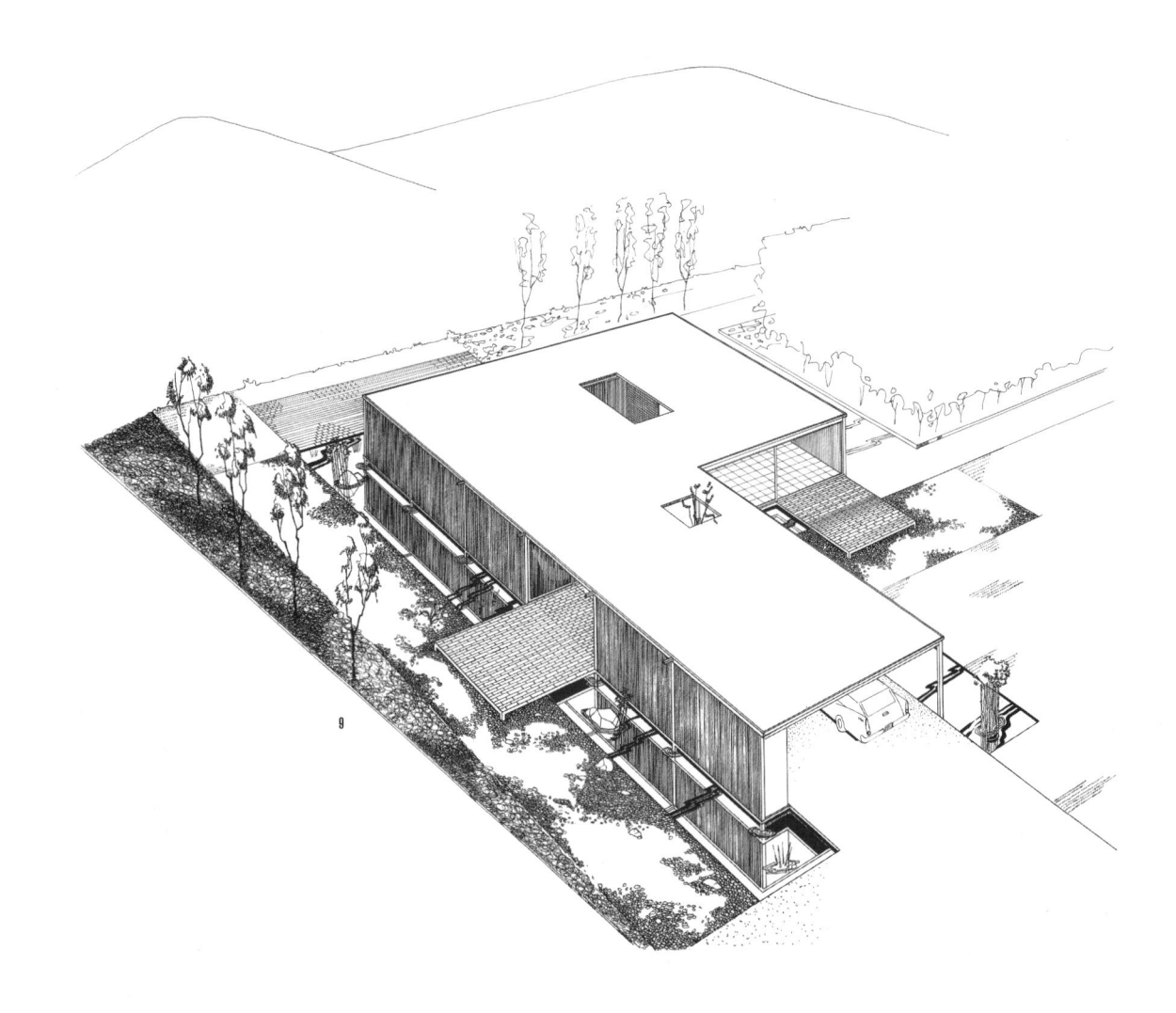

10

11

12

13

10 Front entrance hall and living room beyond. 11 Front door and brick terrace. 12 Kitchen and living area from central patio. 13 Reflecting pools and gravel constitute a large part of the landscaping.

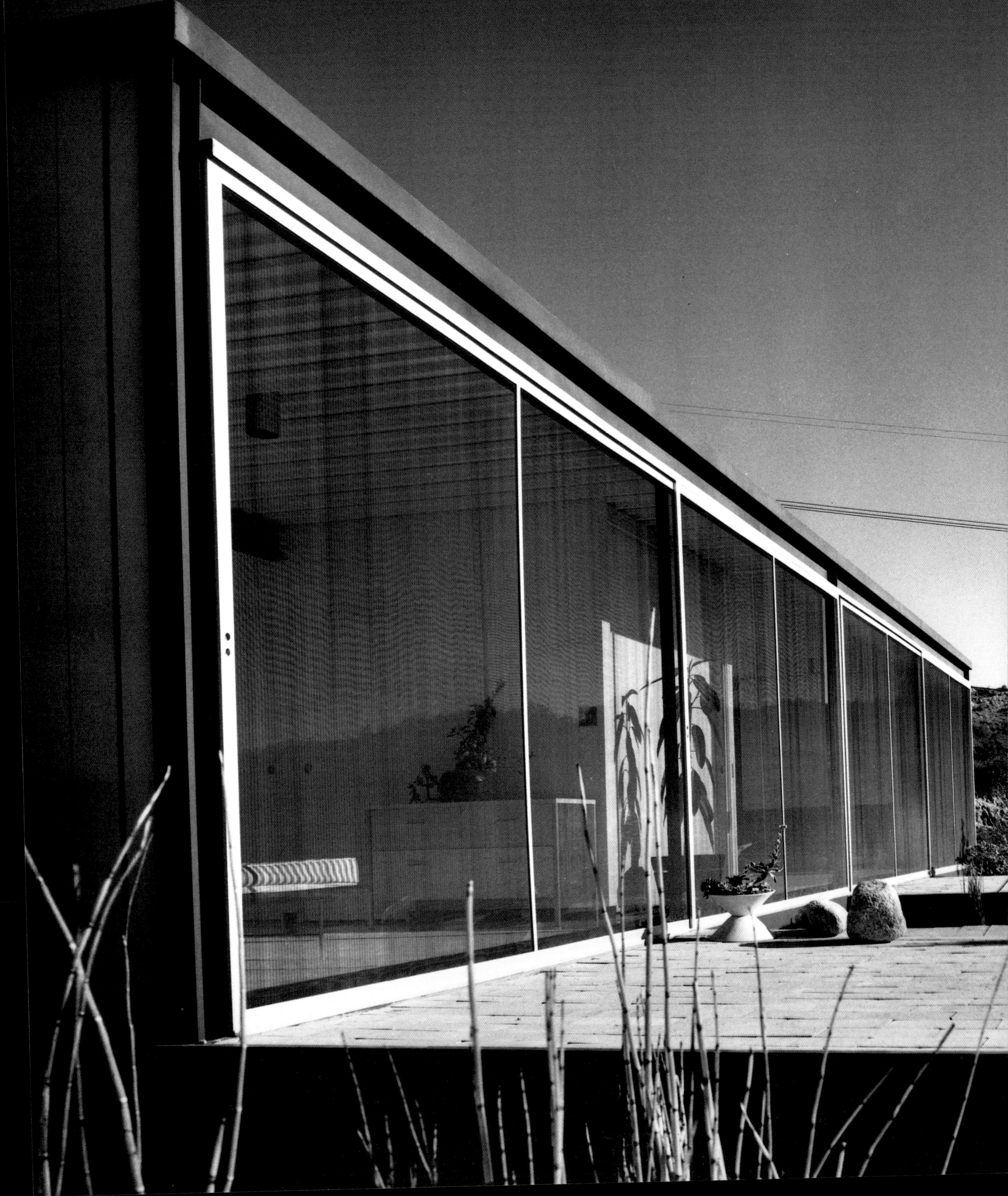

BAILEY HOUSE

14 South elevation with Koolshade sunscreens.

15 Sketch of interior courtyard patio.

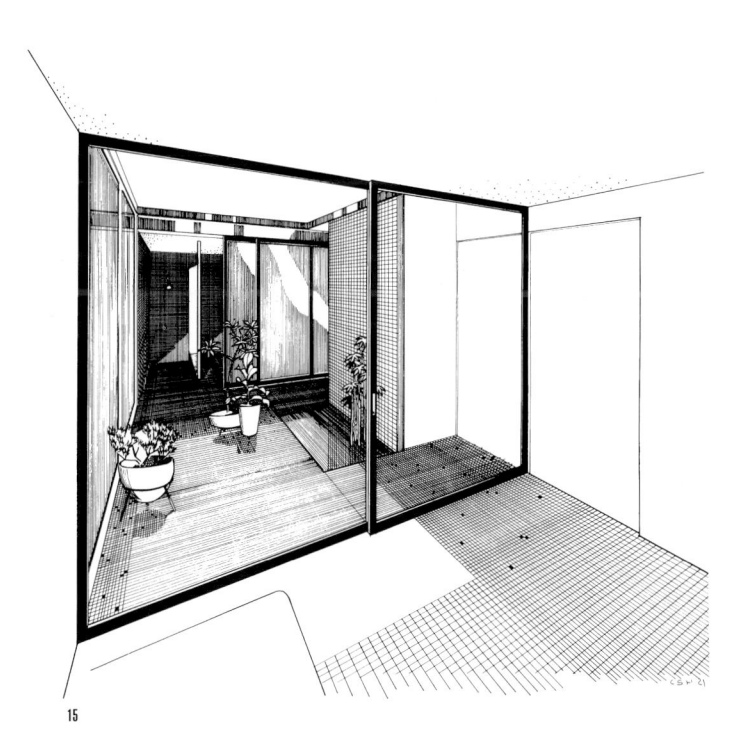

by the reflective surface of the water, while the rippling fountain-like sound that can be heard through the house engenders a sense of calm. The circulation system replaces the need for chemicals so that fish and plants can be grown in the water.

The kitchen originally had a charcoal grey and white palette with mustard-yellow steel cabinets, and Koenig specified a General Electric combination sink, range and dishwasher with a stainless steel countertop and a wall-hung refrigerator. High-level cabinets mounted in a steel frame between the kitchen and the living area surmounted a reach-through counter. A high degree of integration between architecture and interior design, using manufacturers' products was one of the essential aims of the Case Study House Program. A water heater and furnace were located in a cupboard adjacent to the central court which facilitated ventilation and acoustic separation. Heating ducts led from the furnace to floor grilles at the base of the glass walls.

Externally, the smoothness of the exposed steel frame acts as a striking visual counterpoint to the panels of profiled steel decking. The effect of the dark steel frame and lighter panels is especially striking on the east and west elevations, where the frame runs horizontally along the base and cornice. Rather than use overhangs to provide sunshading Koenig used gliding and removable Koolshade sunscreens on the glazed elevations on the south to allow the maximum amount of sunlight into the house in the winter months.

Throughout the development of the house, Koenig investigated various structural patterns with an evolving floor plan, until settling on a 22-feet by 10-feet structural module. This final arrangement is efficient in both planning and structural terms; by forging the bathrooms and interior court into a single freestanding structural element, disengaged from the external walls, Koenig was able to simplify the perimeter condition to either solid infill panels or sliding glass doors, all of a standard size.

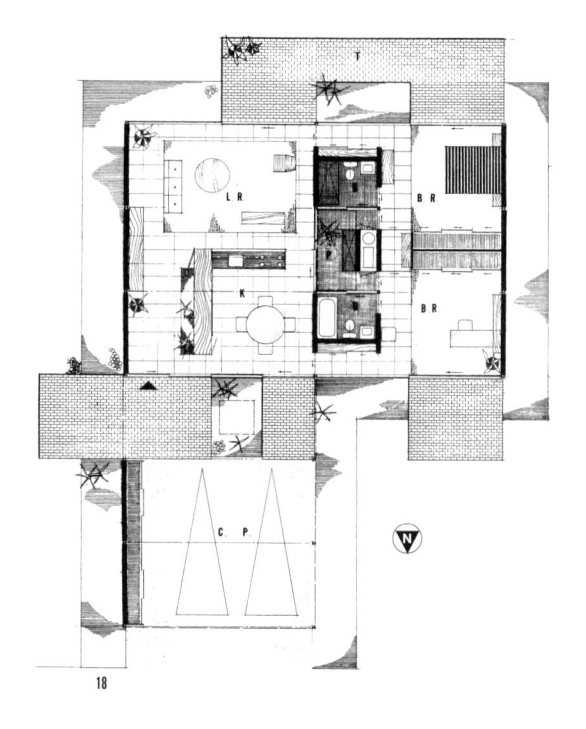

BAILEY HOUSE

16 Bedroom seen from outside. **17** The bedroom opens to an external terrace. **18** Floor plan. **19** Terraces bridge the reflecting pool.

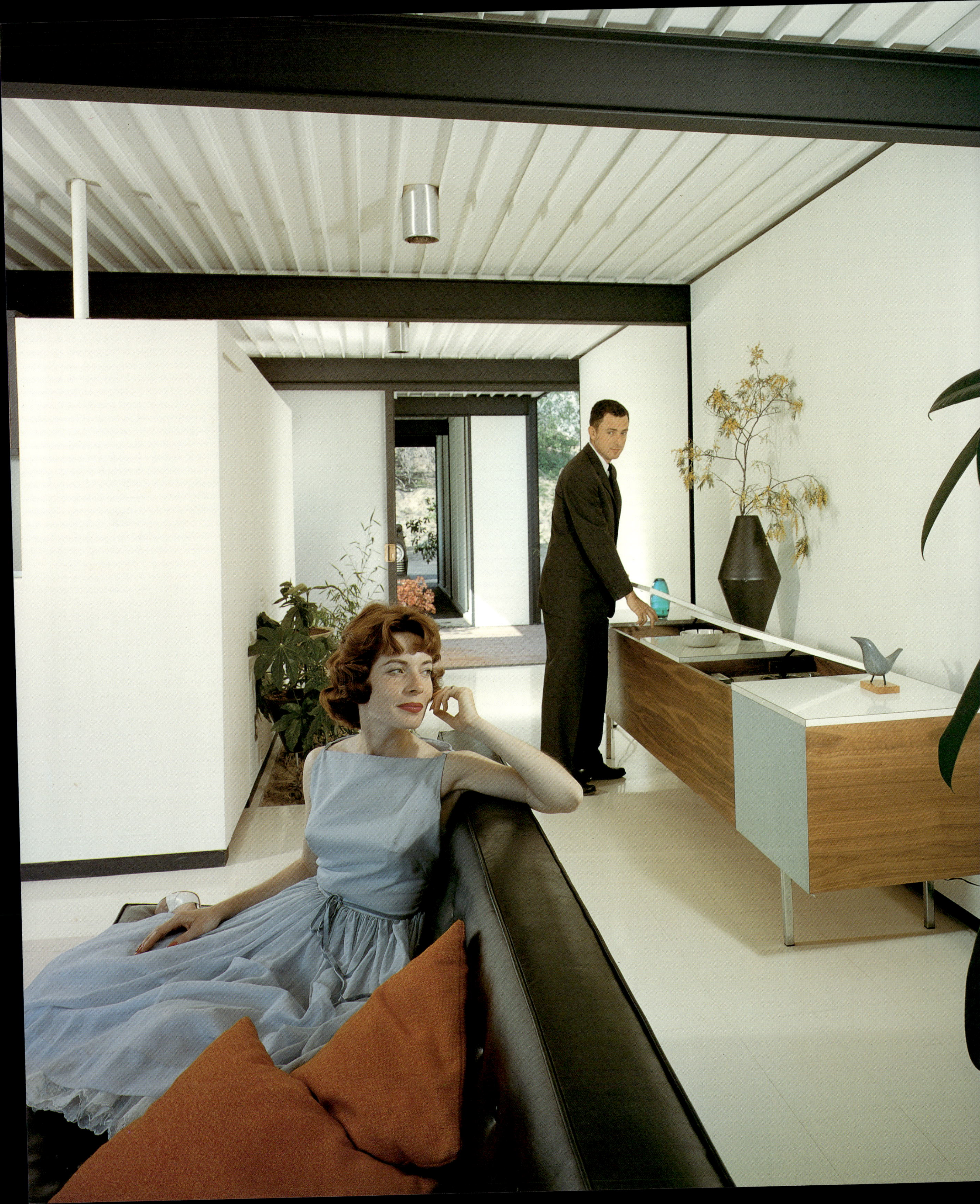

The entire framework, as well as the roof deck was arc-welded using what was then a relatively new technique; rigid connections, left exposed, were welded and ground smooth. Each steel bent was prefabricated and delivered to the site in one piece. Each steel bent provides lateral stability in the east–west direction. The steel deck spans 10 feet between beams, and the soffit is left exposed internally. Resistance to seismic forces and wind loads in the north–south direction is provided by rigid bents formed by channels welded to the top and the base of the columns. It is these channels that can be seen running continuously around the building, tying it together both structurally and compositionally.

Koenig considers this to be one of his most successful houses. The design resulted from a five-year period of exploration of houses for mass-production and so it can be considered the culmination of a series of houses. Koenig recalls being surprised at some of the 'hidden extras' he discovered when the house was built:

You know, when you've solved something and everything's working well, you get pleasant surprises. Some of the vistas I saw after the house was built, I never dreamed would be there. That's the benefit of a well-organized plan. If you don't get that then there's something wrong – not at the end of the process, but way back in your early thinking. When things are really spinning along though, there are little bonuses.

In 1997, Koenig was asked by the new owners to restore the house to its original condition after many years of neglect and ad-hoc alteration. Restoration was completed in the summer of 1998, and Case Study House #21 can now reclaim its place as one of the great Los Angeles houses.

20 Pierre Koenig pictured with a model in the living room and entry way.
21 Eating area with external terrace and carport beyond.
22 Prefabricated built-in kitchen units.
23 Kitchen with eating area.
24 Living area.

1 An original photograph of the house which appeared in *Arts and Architecture* magazine in June 1960.

2 Rendering of the 'helicopter view' of the south elevation.

3 (overleaf) View from master bedroom overlooking Los Angeles.

STAHL HOUSE

Case Study House #22
1960
Hollywood, Los Angeles, California
2,300 sq ft
Structural Engineer: William Porush
General Contractor: Robert Brady
Interiors: Van Keppel-Green

Writing in his seminal book on the city, *Los Angeles: The Architecture of Four Ecologies*, Reyner Banham characterized perfectly Pierre Koenig's architecture: 'This is, *par excellence*, an architecture of elegant omission that takes Mies van der Rohe's dictum about *Weniger ist Mehr* even further than the master himself had ever done.' The acme of Koenig's drive to out-reduce the great reductivist must surely be Case Study House #22 – the Stahl House – completed in 1960. Perched high in the Hollywood Hills above Sunset Boulevard, with a pool and panoramic view across the city spread below, it is perhaps the archetypal Southern Californian 'good-life' house; it is also undoubtedly emblematic of American architecture in that halcyon age between the end of World War II and the Kennedy assassination.

The clients, Carlotta and Buck Stahl, had purchased the site several years before they actually commissioned Koenig to design the house. Buck Stahl was conscious of the fact that the view was the site's one great asset, and wanted a 'contemporary' house that would exploit the view to best advantage. He had approached a number of architects in Los Angeles, but each in turn had been confounded by the clients' demand for a 270-degree unobstructed view and by the steeply-sloping site. The Stahls wanted a spacious house, with two bedrooms and a large swimming pool, but they had limited funds, which further challenged the architect.

Close inspection of the plan reveals how Koenig took maximum advantage of the positive aspects of the house's highly problematic and restrictive location. By utilizing rigid frame construction and caissons in lieu of continuous footings, he placed one leg of the L-shaped plan along the east–west axis to secure a foothold on the small area of solid land available.

Locating the carport at the extreme western end of this leg – accessible via a steep driveway – he established the doorway from the carport as the main entrance into the family's private realm. A processional route leads from there past the master bedroom and across a sequence of footbridges into the kitchen core; here the route turns sharply right into the longer north–south leg of the 'L' towards the living room and the view.

The master bedroom wing, placed behind the house's one solid wall facing the street, also contains a large children's bedroom – with its own shower and WC – which can be subdivided into two smaller rooms, by means of sliding partitions. The master bedroom has its own en-suite bathroom which backs onto the main service core in the crux of the 'L'. A continuous line of storage cabinets mounted high on the solid wall lining the street, effectively lowers the scale of the space at that point, providing a second ceiling above the beds. Both bedrooms have unobstructed views across the swimming pool to the vast expanse of Los Angeles far below.

Ironically, the house, perceived as luxurious today, was considered economical at the time. Like Case Study House #21, many of the other houses in the Program were built in the hills in Pasadena or Hollywood. The soil there was considered poor and the land difficult to build on, and such sites were, therefore, relatively affordable for the first-time house builder. Koenig recalls:

Young middle-class couples, or families who wanted a custom-built house but didn't have a lot of money were forced to buy lots that were substandard. These were mostly in

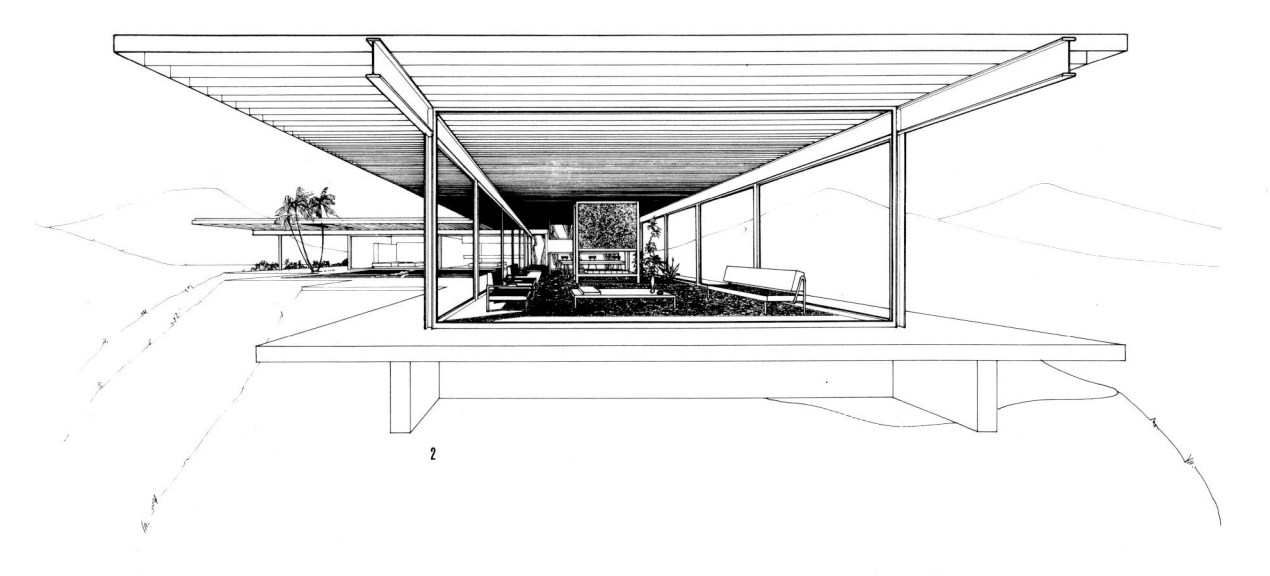

2

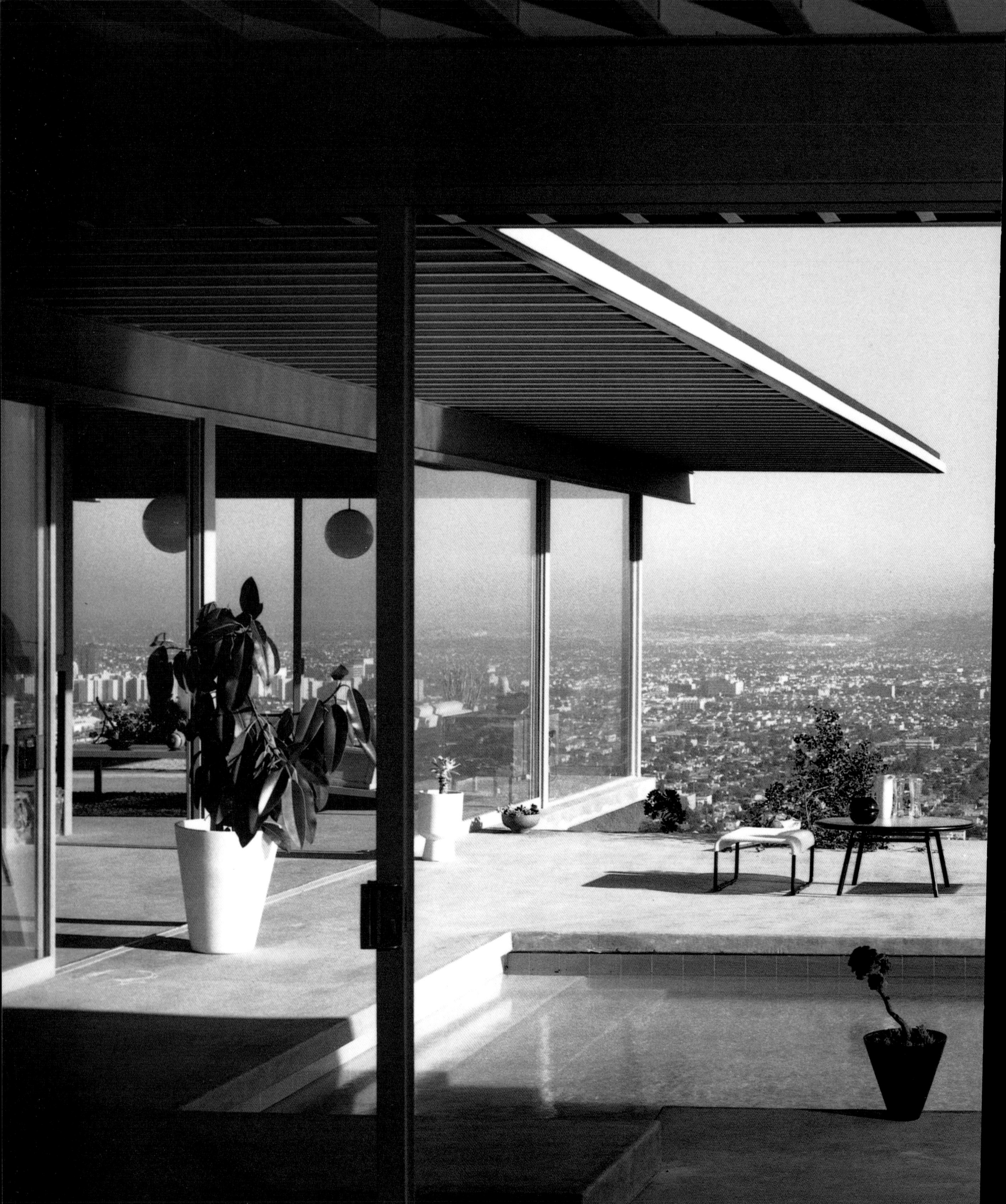

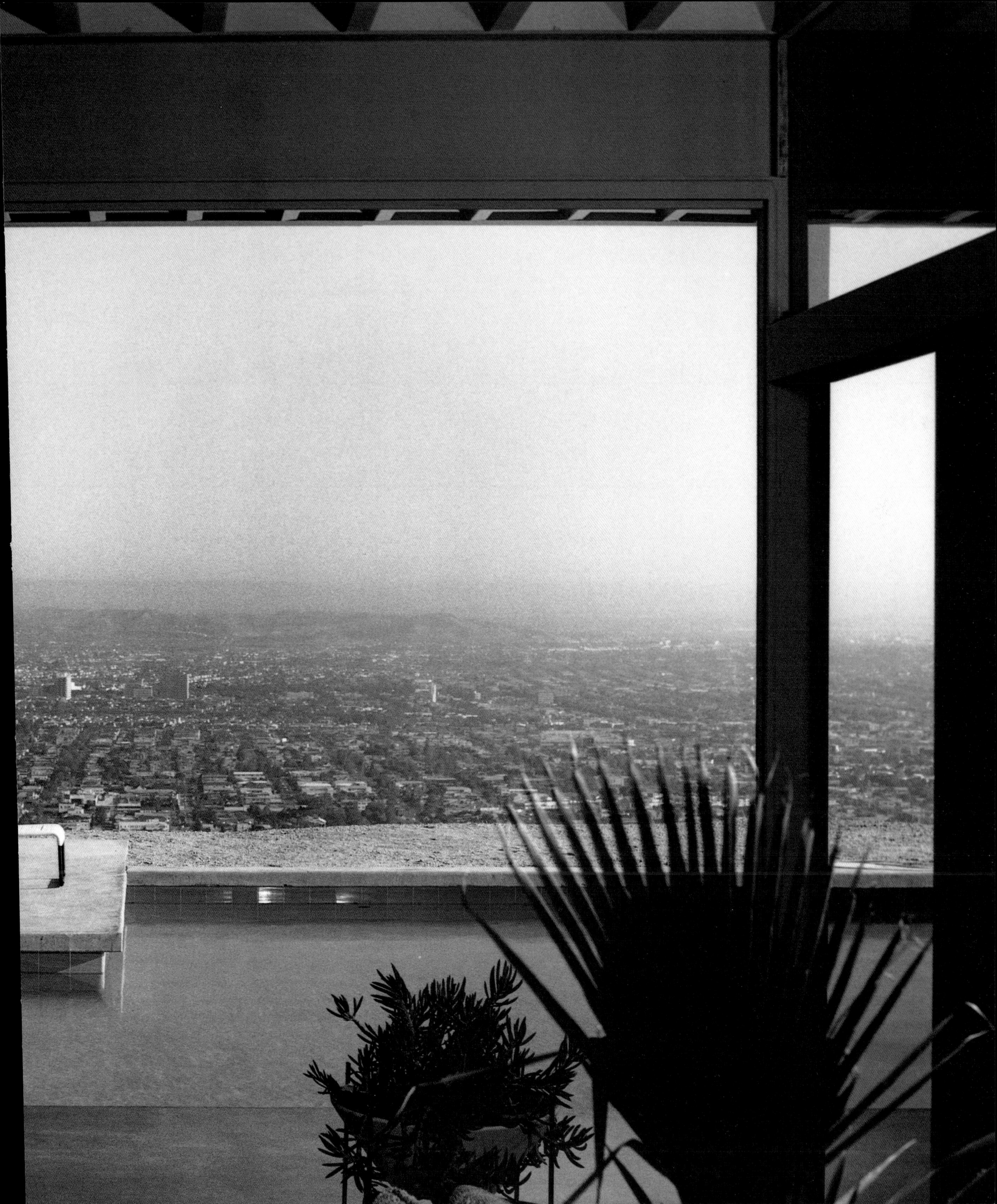

4 Partial framing plan.
5 Partial roof plan.
6 Floor plan.
7 Structural frame with fireplace ready for installation.
8 Structural frame seen from above.
9 House under construction with cladding in place.
10 Perspective rendering of house looking over bridges towards front door.

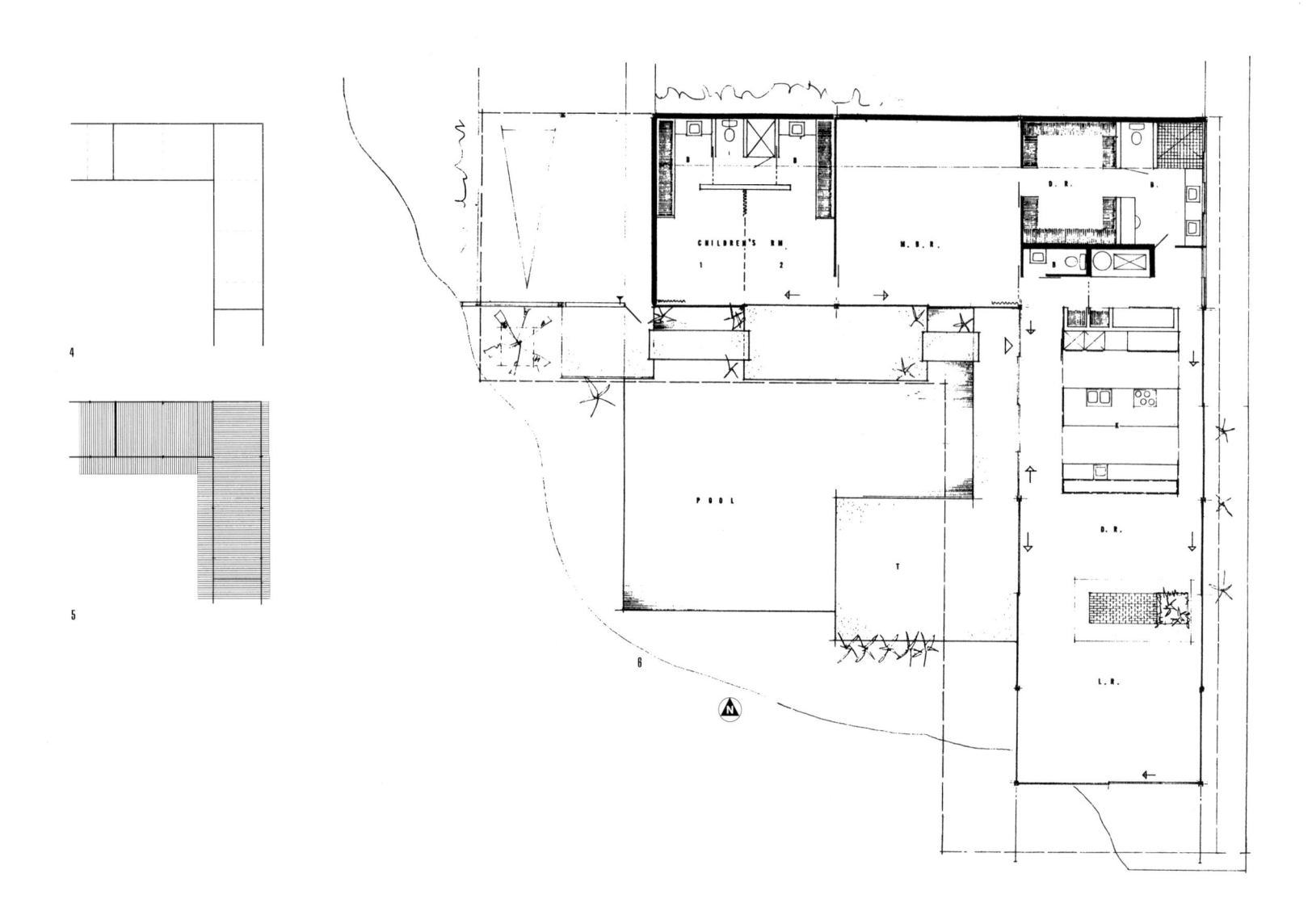

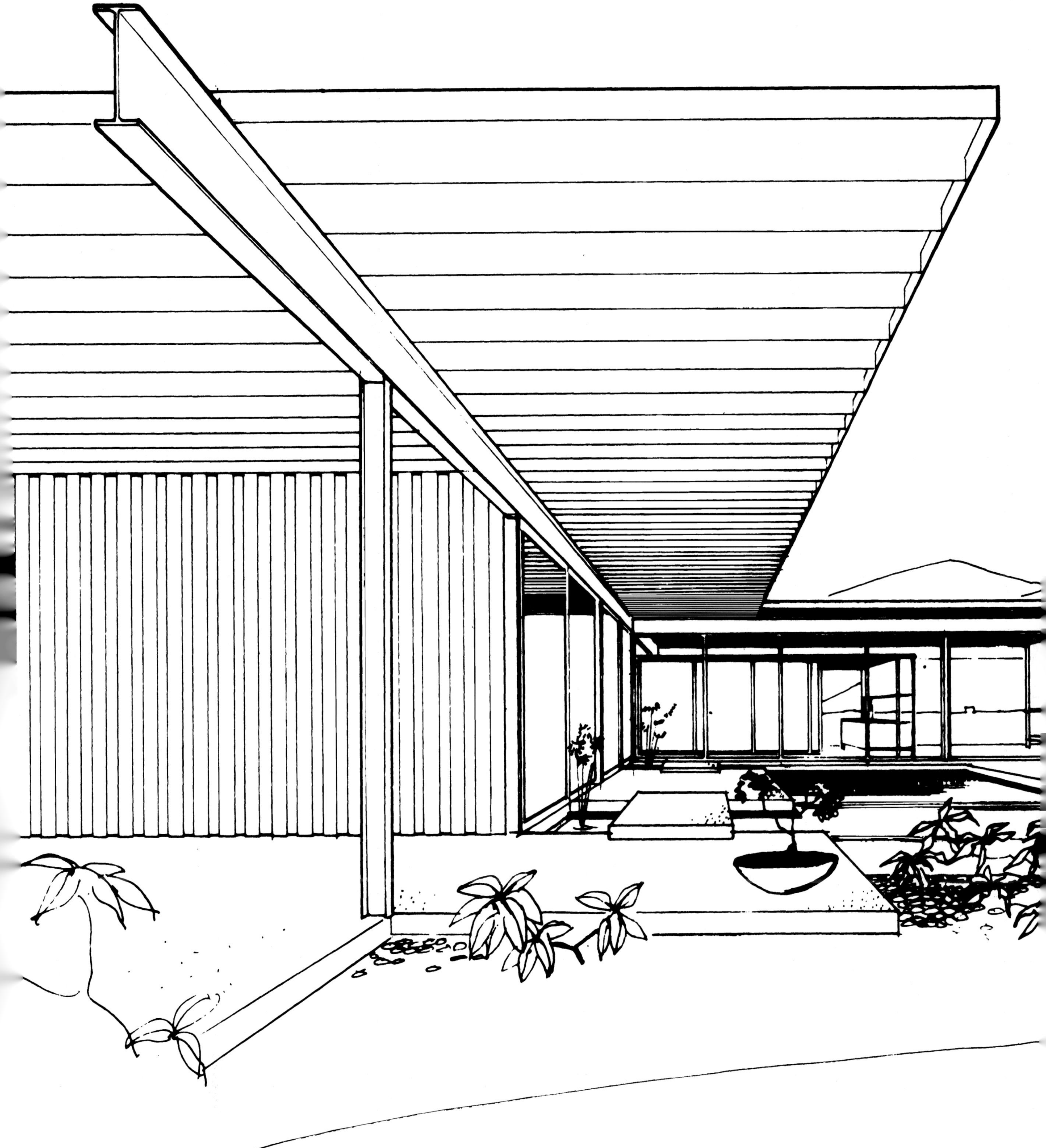

11 The house as it is currently.
12 View from kitchen overlooking pool.

the hills, and there were fewer restrictions in the hills as far as style went. Fortunately there was more freedom to build or design whatever you wanted without fear of antagonizing your neighbours.

The house is entirely steel and glass perched on concrete caissons. Koenig's characteristic unified kitchen consisting of prefabricated cabinets, two stainless steel ovens and a stainless steel sink was planned to preserve sight lines to the view. In order to further maintain the view of the city, Koenig designed a steel frame fireplace that is open on all four sides.

The decision to build the house was risky as traditional banks were reluctant to finance such an experimental structure. Koenig therefore approached banks that he knew to be 'architecturally aware' and was able obtain a satisfactory loan for the Stahls. The family's continuous occupancy of the house, from its completion until today, is clear testimony to their satisfaction with it. It is now a highly sought-after residence, and the regular scene of countless fashion and film shoots.

Buried beneath the cantilevered wing of the house is a series of large reinforced concrete beams, 30 inches deep, which are supported by up to 35 feet deep concrete caissons. The steel frame and roof deck are all welded, and all the steelwork connections are moment-resisting. Non-loadbearing walls allowed the architect to provide the clients with their desired 270-degree view of the city. Steel beams with the columns attached and the prefabricated fireplace were trucked to the site and the steel frame was erected in one day, as usual. The large structural module generates an expansive feeling of space and also reduces the number of caissons.

Insulation board, composition roofing and gravel provide a finished roof on the steel decking. The exposed underside of the decking forms the finished ceiling, adding considerably to the economy and beauty of the system. The linear quality of both the beams and the decking help direct the eye toward the view. A similar steel decking to that used for the roof, but with a shallower profile, forms the external walls, which are lined on the inside with insulation and gypsum board. Hot-water radiant heating pipes in the floor slab heat the house. Solar panels on the roof heat the pool water.

The land, sloping away precipitously on three sides, and the small area of level site, dictated the layout of the house. By placing the house along the northern and eastern edges of the property, there is room in the centre for pool placement. The building is considerably higher than several houses to the south and east. By placing a solid wall on the street

12

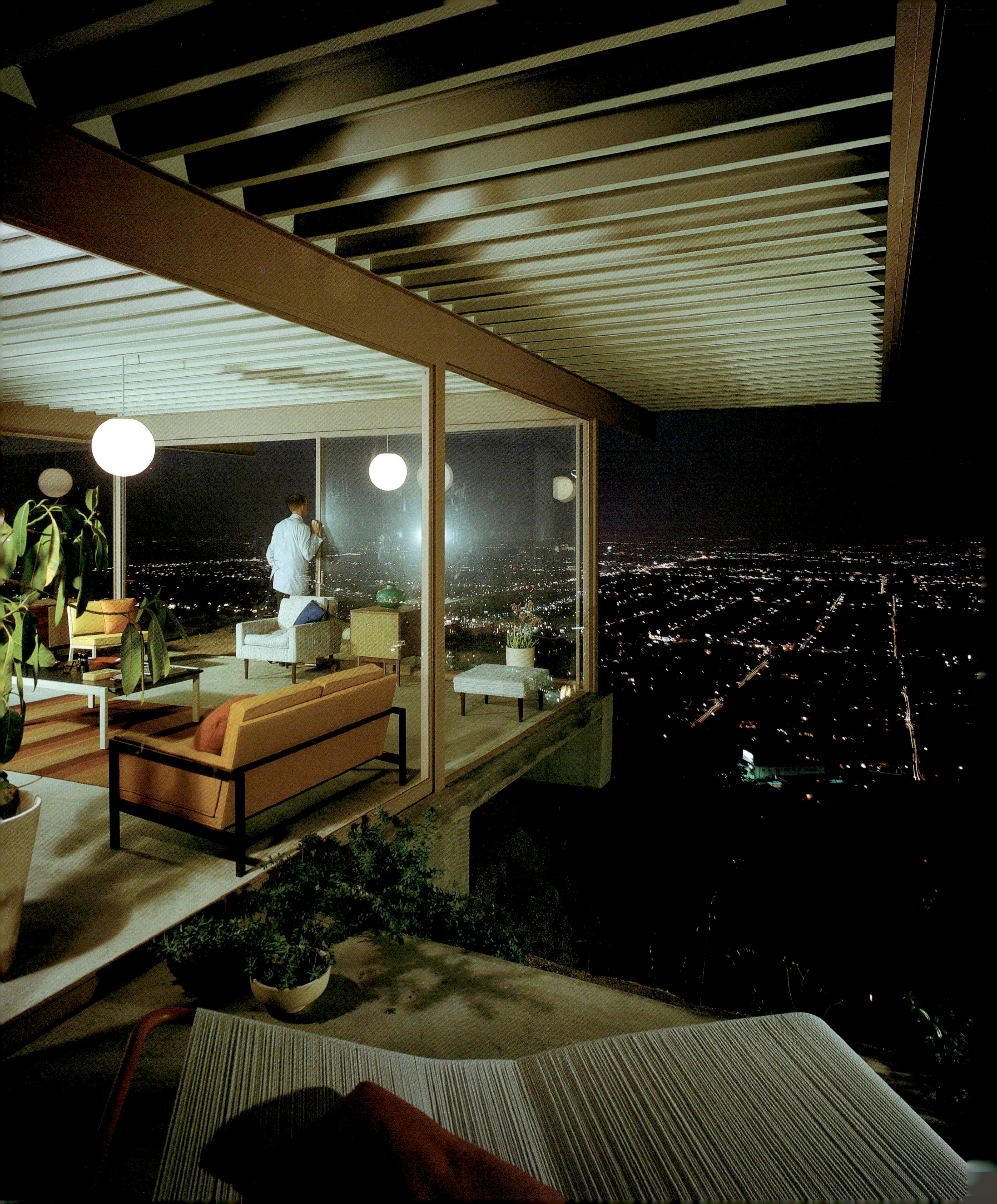

13 Night-time view of the Stahl House (Case Study House #22) with the lights of Los Angeles below.

14 Large sliding glass doors open the house to the exterior.

south, east and west, Koenig was able to maximize privacy and take full advantage of sunlight and view. Cross ventilation within the house is facilitated by 10 foot wide sliding glass doors on three sides of the perimeter. Along the southern and western exposures, Koenig provided an 8 foot deep overhang extending the roof area to almost double that of the enclosed floor plan – protecting the interior during the hottest part of the year, and giving ample shelter for pool-side activities. The overhang prevents the higher summer sun from penetrating the house, whilst the low winter sunlight is able to shine through the glass to warm it.

In 1989, a full-scale walk-through model of the house was built as part of Los Angeles MOCA's 'Blueprints for Modern Living' exhibition. The exhibit offered a complete history of the Case Study House Program, and brought Koenig's work to a wider architectural audience sparking a new wave of interest in the early Modern Movement.

15 Living room showing original furniture supplied by Van Keppel-Green.

16 Section drawing of prefabricated fireplace.

17 Elevation of prefabricated fireplace.
18 View of the kitchen showing both the cooking island and the bar island.

19 The dropped ceiling in the kitchen encloses the lights, fans and the electrical supply.

20 Master bathroom with expanded metal lath under sink.

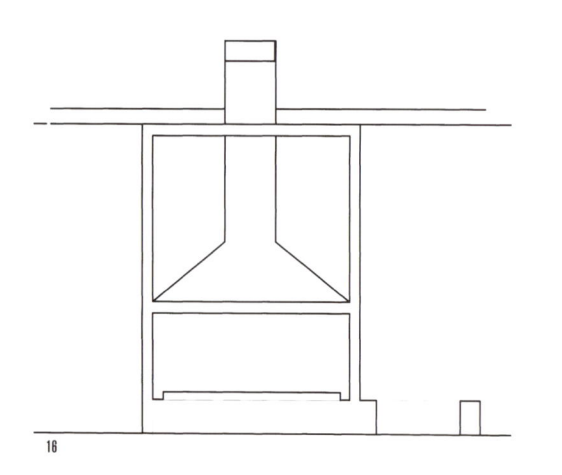

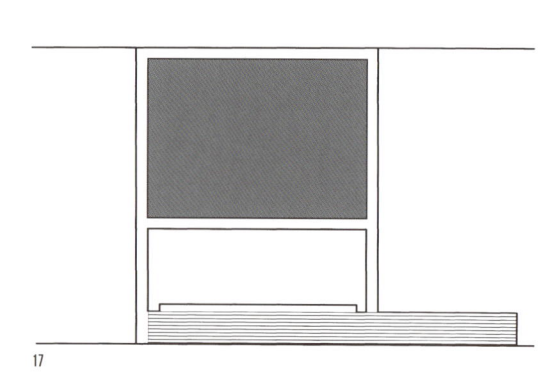

18

19 20

BEIDELMAN HOUSE

1 East elevation of Scheme 2.
2 West (front) elevation of Scheme 2.
3 Bird's-eye view of Scheme 2 showing central patio.
4 Model of Scheme 1.
5 Upper floor plan of Scheme 2.
6 Lower floor plan of Scheme 2.

BEIDELMAN HOUSE

(Schemes 1 and 2)
1961
Los Angeles, California
1,750 sq ft + 1,050 sq ft carport and covered area
Structural Engineer: William Porush

Koenig developed two schemes for the Beidelman House, although neither was ever realized. The projects were significant, though, because he learned important lessons from the design processes and from the cost analyses, which informed his decisions on subsequent projects. Koenig describes these lessons as 'very educational'. He learned about foundations, and developed his theory that 'an outdoor space ideally should equal the indoor space it serves to make it useful. People don't use three to four foot balconies except to stand and look at the views.' The Beagles house, built in 1963, is a direct beneficiary of this lesson.

Scheme 1 proved to be too costly, as the structure was complicated. The plan was to include twelve columns, far more than usual for Koenig, and a substantial foundation to counteract the poor soil on the site. Koenig developed a long bar-shaped plan. The entrance is on the southern side of the house and opens onto a landing that leads both up and downstairs. On the upper floor a long hall runs east–west leading to two bedrooms, a bathroom, an open kitchen, a dining room and a living room. All of the rooms have access to a balcony beyond the glass wall on the northern elevation. On the lower floor is a bedroom, a bathroom and a utility core with the carport on one side and an open area shaded by the house on the other.

Scheme 2 has a more compact plan. It uses only four columns, reducing the foundation expense immeasurably. In this project the balcony from the previous scheme was eliminated in favour of an exterior centralized patio, to be used as an outdoor room. The house is elevated and its upper floor cantilevers from four steel columns. Koenig describes it as 'up on stilts, up in the air'. Glass is used extensively and yet the building retains its privacy from the street. Access to the house by car is from beneath the building. From the street it is reached via a bridge.

The upper floor has two bedrooms that occupy two corners of the house, with a bathroom in between. This level has an open kitchen, dining room, den and living room surrounded by glass with access to the central patio. The lower level has two bedrooms, a bathroom and a utility room. Habitable space occupies less than half of the space below the first level.

Koenig uses this second scheme as an opportunity to expound upon his ideas about circulation: 'Circulation has to be unfettered – free circulation. There mustn't be any interference with other functions. Bypass when you can. The uses have to be separate where they can be. If the many uses take the same circulation path, then that needs to be taken into consideration. The materials on the floor should be picked for the purpose of multi-function.'

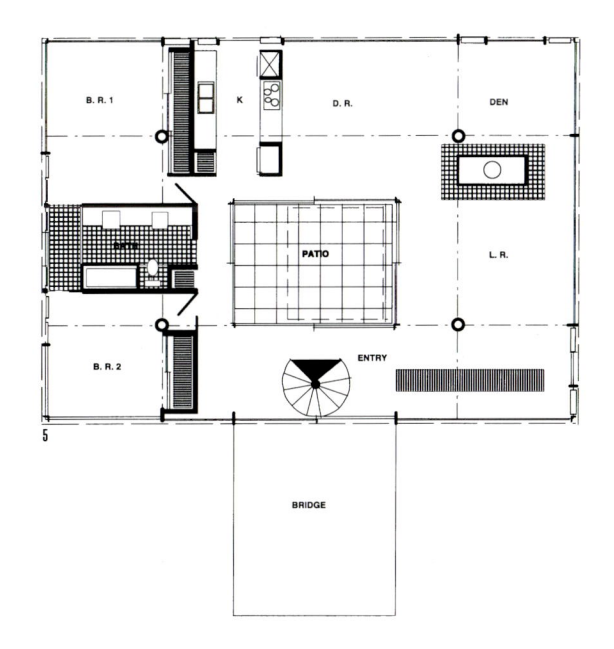

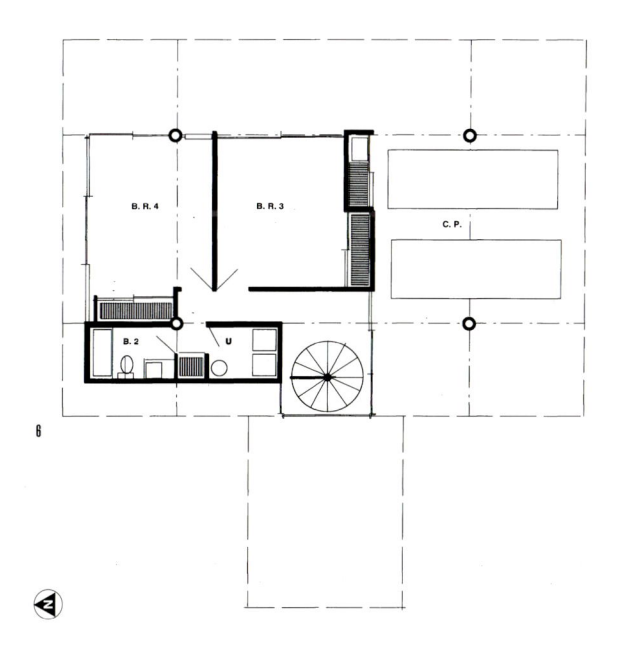

SEIDEL HOUSE

1960
Brentwood, Los Angeles, California
1,680 sq ft + 480 sq ft covered area
Structural Engineer: William Porush
General Contractor: Tom Seidel Associates

Rollé Addition I
1984
2,700 sq ft + 1,000 sq ft covered area
Structural Engineer: Dimitry Vergun
General Contractor: Tom Seidel Associates

Rollé Addition II
1994
3,844 sq ft + 1,000 sq ft covered area
Structural Engineer: Dimitry Vergun
General Contractor: R G West Corp

In 1959 Tom Seidel commissioned Koenig to design a house for a pre-levelled site he owned in Mandeville Canyon. The plot was hewn from a rocky cliff and the resulting long, narrow site with poor, loose soil seemed initially unsuitable for building. To stabilize the structure Koenig used concrete caissons, reaching 15 feet into the ground to anchor the house to the bedrock. Keeping construction costs to a minimum, Koenig used the same type of long-span steel decking that he used in Case Study House #22, but with a deeper dimension that allowed for 33-foot spans.

Although zoning and grading laws determined the maximum footprint of the house, Koenig created an open, airy plan that accommodates its natural setting. A dense band of trees on the east side of the house provides privacy from the road twenty feet below. The north and south elevations provide a panoramic view of dense greenery up and down the canyon. Typically, Koenig ensured that every interior space extends towards the outside, both visually and physically.

The house is composed of three modules with patios in between. An arcade of continuous galvanized T-type roof decking visually ties together the modules and provides shelter over the walkway leading from the carport to the entrance. The entrance is central and provides the connecting link between the living and sleeping areas. The rigid steel-frame construction provides for large expanses of glass and non-structural walls.

In 1983, Mr and Mrs Rollé commissioned Koenig to design a first-storey extension and a pool. The first addition included a new master bedroom, a den and two more bathrooms over the southernmost module of the original house.

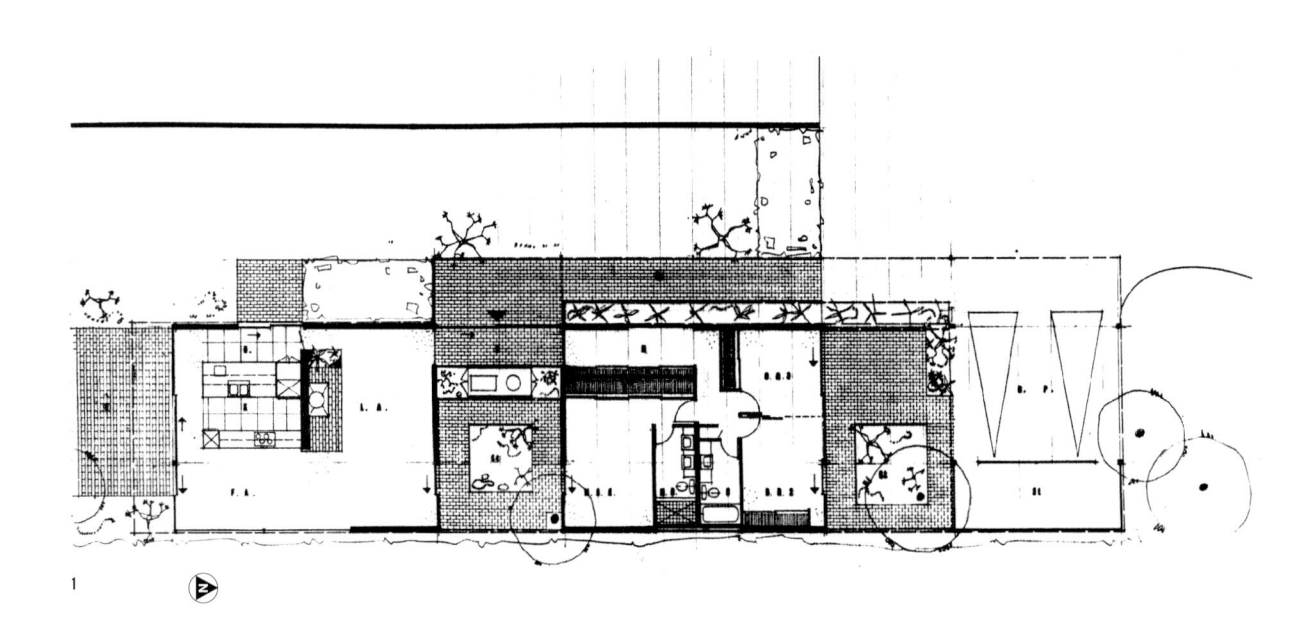

1

1 Plan of original house showing carport and entry as constructed in 1960.

2 West elevation with overhang for sun protection. Kitchen and dining area have direct access to the garden through sliding glass doors.

3 (overleaf) Children's bedroom with sliding partitions which can divide the large room into smaller sleeping areas.

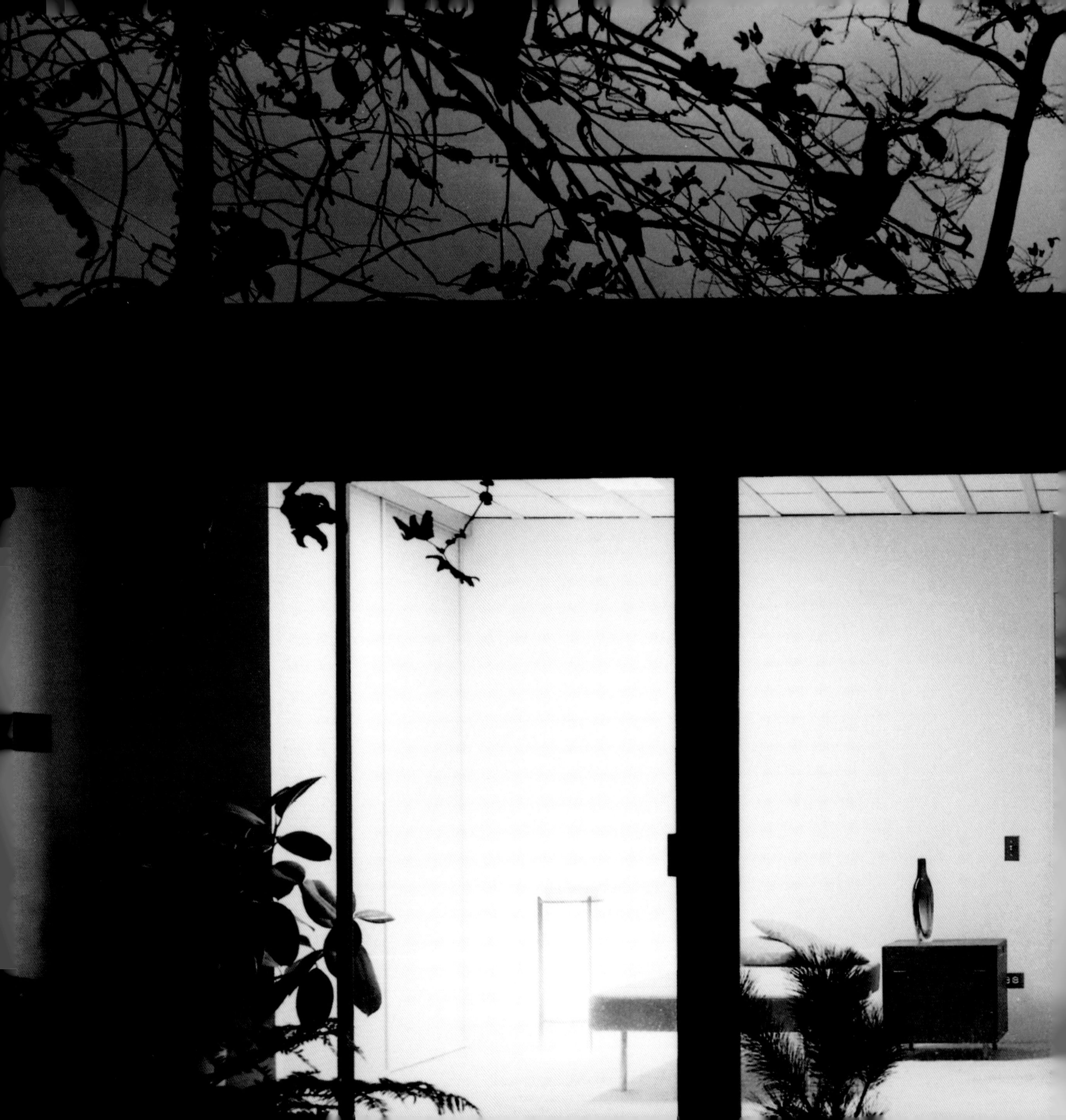

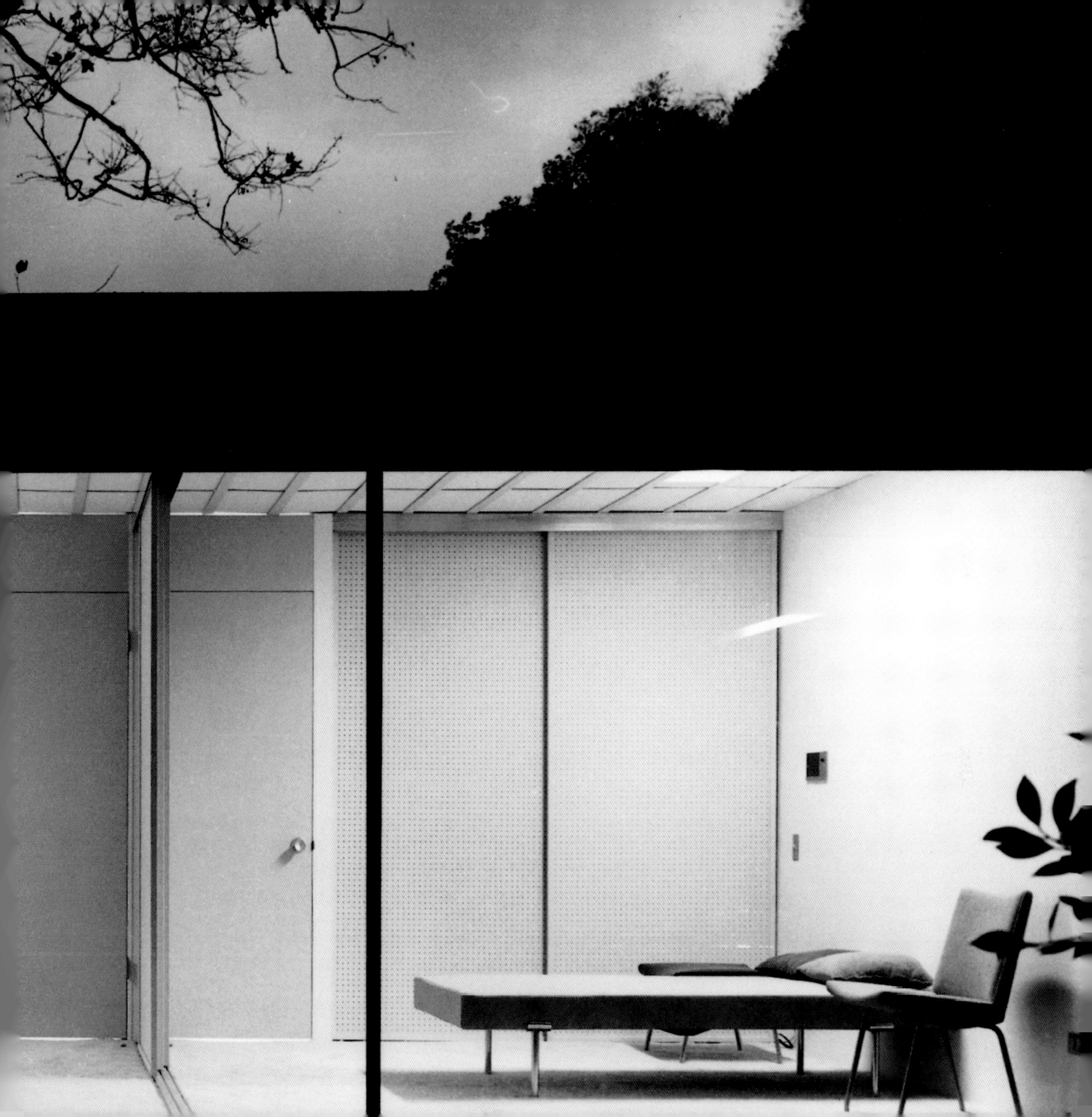

4 Original living area.
5 Original kitchen.
6 Exterior view of kitchen and dining area, c. 1960.
7 Plan of first-storey addition.
8 Original plan.
9 Perspective of original entry drive and carport.
10 Perspective of original western elevation and patio.

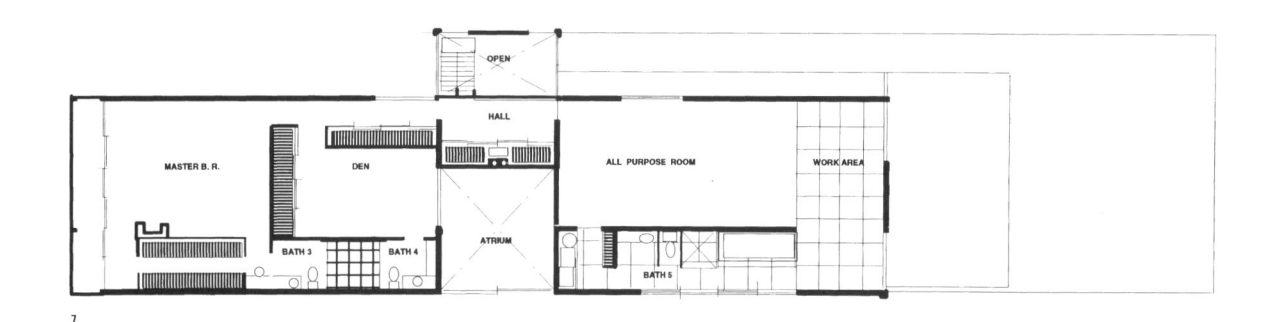

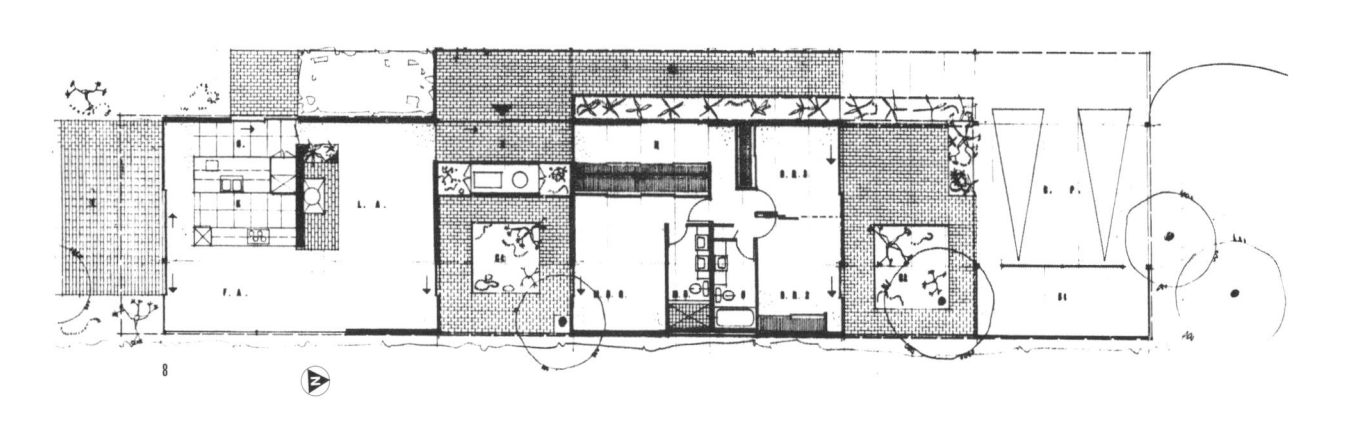

SEIDEL HOUSE/ROLLE ADDITIONS

9

10

Koenig designed an essentially independent steel-framed module that would fit over the existing structure. This unit slips down over the first floor with a half-inch space between the new beams and the old roof. This space is sealed in, with the new columns covering the existing ones. The module has its own floor beams, joists, walls and floor system, all supported by four 20 foot long steel columns rooted in independent concrete pads just outside the original building. The final result is a complete integration of the old and the new structures.

In 1993 the Rollés asked Koenig to expand the house again, this time on the north side. The second addition, over the bedroom module, included a large all-purpose room, a large bathroom and laundry facilities. The same construction process used in the first addition was applied here. A space between the two second-storey modules was glassed-in to create a 25 foot high atrium with a glass roof.

All the beams of the house are painted with a soft grey coating while the exposed steel roof decking ceilings and all the interior walls are painted a flat white. The original steel kitchen cabinets were repainted to match the beam colour.

11 Addition II includes a glassed-in atrium.

12 House with additions as seen from parking area.

13 First storey addition over bedroom module.

14 Original entry and carport.

12

13 14

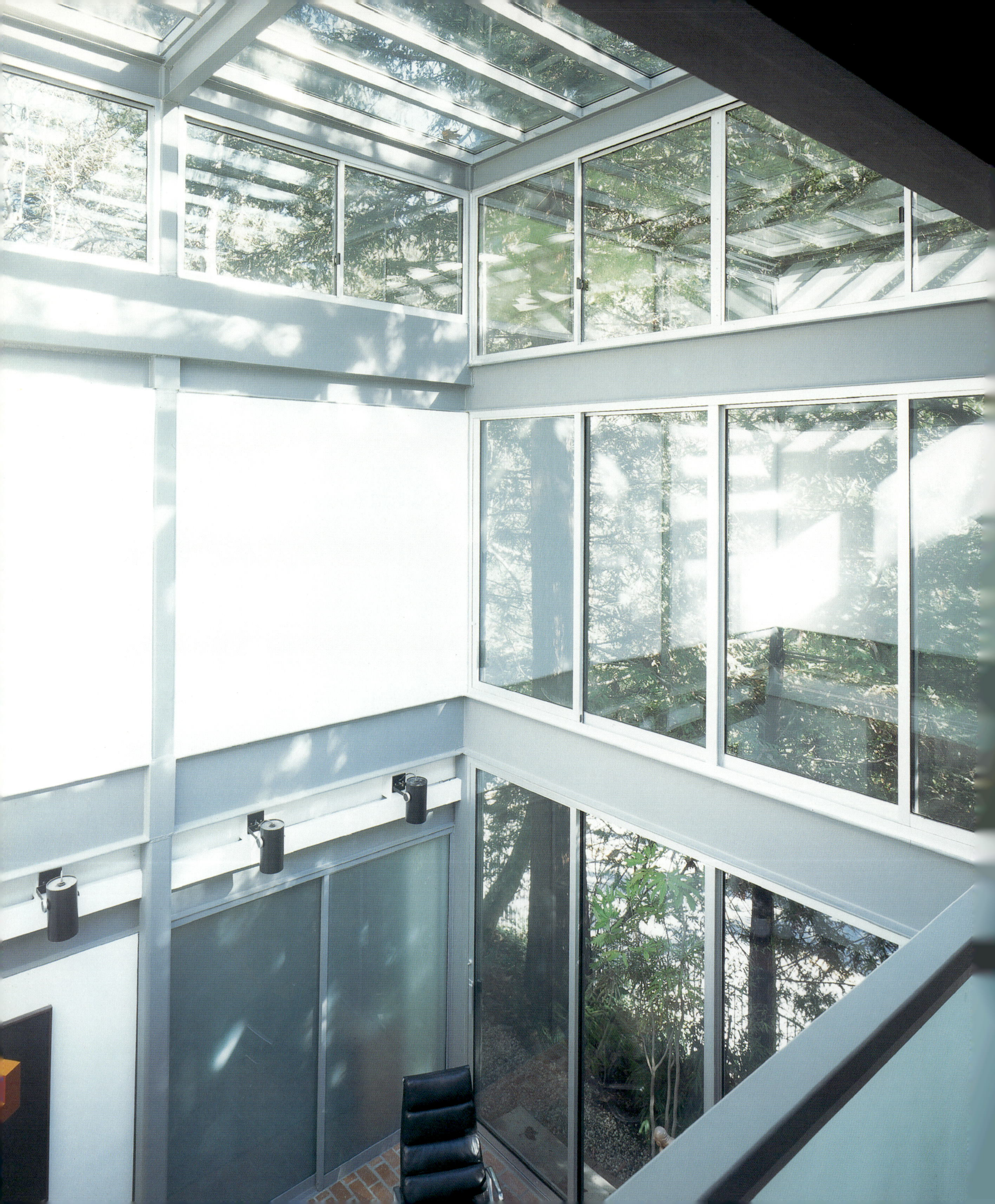

SEIDEL HOUSE/ROLLE ADDITIONS

15 Interior of atrium with sliding glass doors and glass roof above.   **16** Interior stairs leading to first addition.   **17** Interior atrium.

1 Compact kitchen-dining-living area designed for beach lifestyle.   **2** The efficient plan fits neatly inside the small lot.   **3** North and east elevations shelter the house from the Pacific Coast Highway.   **4** The south elevation faces the Pacific Ocean.   **5** (overleaf) The ocean can be seen through wall-to-wall glass doors from the living area. The Seidel family relaxes on the balcony.

SEIDEL BEACH HOUSE

1961
Malibu, California
1,000 sq ft
Structural Engineer: William Porush
General Contractor: Tom Seidel Associates

In 1960 Tom Seidel bought a small plot of land near Ventura County Line. He commissioned Pierre Koenig to design an ocean-front weekend retreat for his wife, the actress Jean Hagen, and his two children. The house was designed to comply with a restrictive construction budget, and by simplifying the form and detailing Koenig maximized the ocean view. The wood frame house is supported by six wood piles. There are no shear walls and Koenig used a cable X-brace for the first time to stabilize the frame and the wall-to-wall glass beach elevation.

The relatively large living area is the focus of the house, receiving the southwest light and seeming to extend into the seascape. Three perimeter walls, with few apertures, contain the interior space, while the fourth wall comprises a 20 foot wide expanse of floor-to-ceiling glass with central sliding doors providing the view and opening onto a wooden outdoor deck. The sliding glass doors are made of aluminium, painted to protect the metal from the elements.

Koenig's concept was of a compact plan where the bedroom and living spaces surround an internal utility core consisting of an enclosed bathroom and an open kitchen. As a cost- and space-saving measure, only one plumbing wall is used. Storage space is located opposite the bathroom in a dressing area outside each bedroom. Bedrooms are left free, apart from a door and a light slot on the northern wall.

From the Pacific Coast Highway, a wooden pathway wraps around the east side of the house leading to the front door situated in the middle of the plan. Near the front door, stairs descend to the sand of the beach below. Due to seasonal changes that effect the shoreline, the house can be suspended as much as fifteen feet in the air in the winter, with waves crashing beneath its back bedrooms. However, in the summer, the sand may rise to only two feet beneath the house.

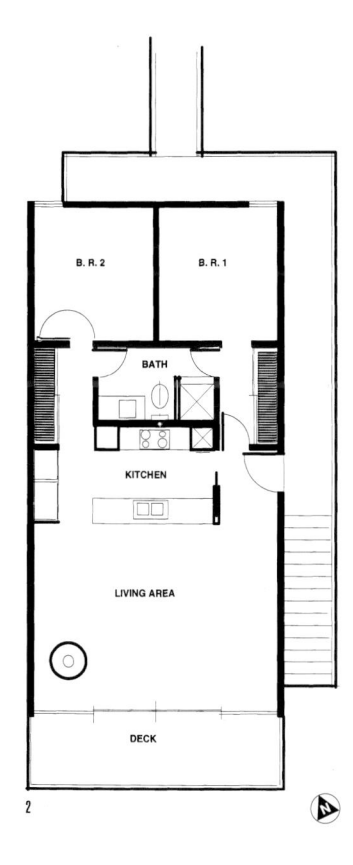

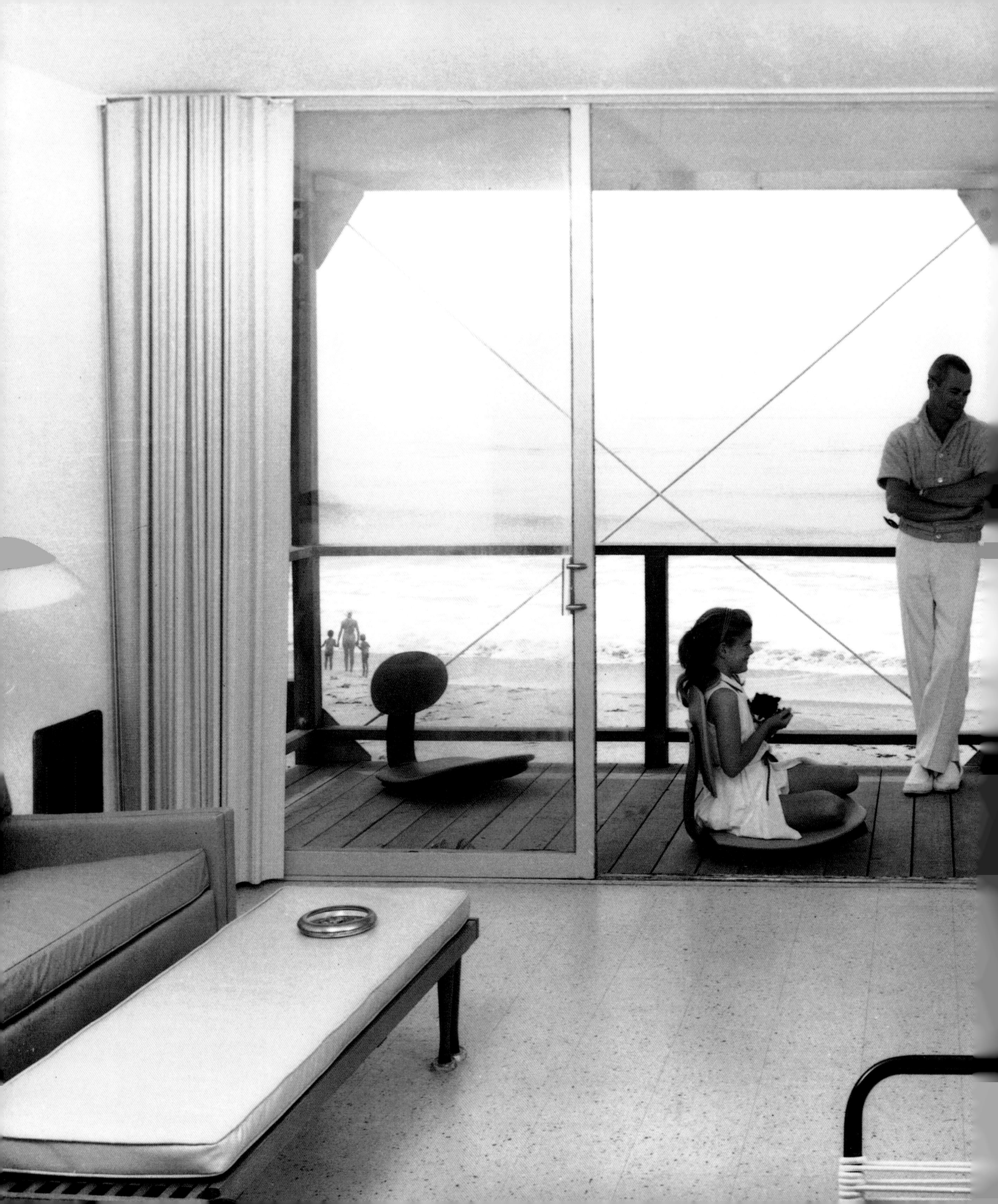

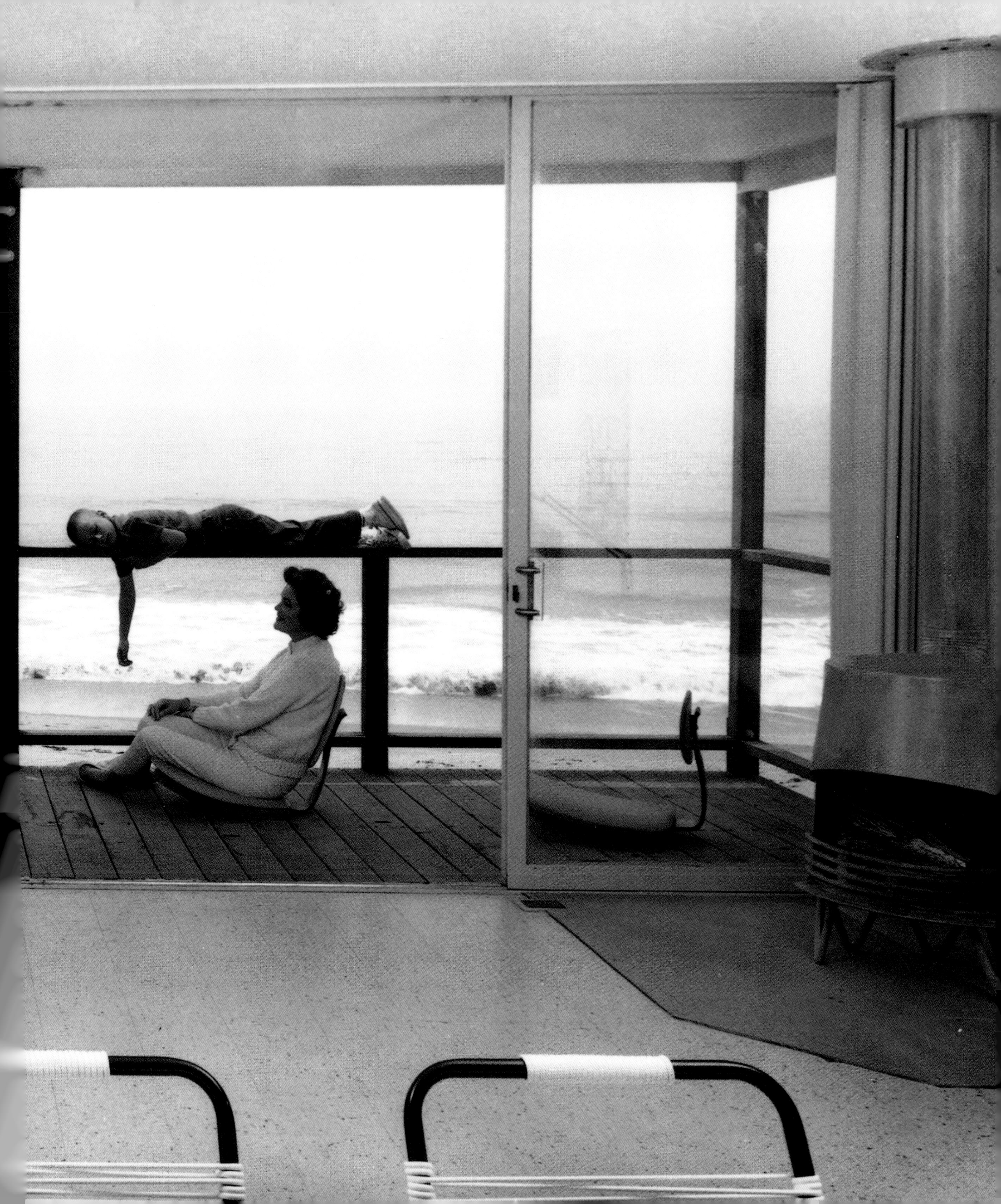

JOHNSON HOUSE/RIEBE ADDITION

1,2 Johnson House under construction in 1962.
3 Detail showing installation of steel sliding glass door frame.
4 Johnson House under construction.
5 Floor plan of original design.
6 North elevation.
7 View from entrance towards living area.

JOHNSON HOUSE

1962
Carmel Valley, California
2,800 sq ft + 1,200 sq ft carport and covered area
Structural Engineer: William Porush
General Contractor: Charles R Strathmeyer

Riebe Addition
1989
3,800 sq ft covered area
Structural Engineer: Dimitry Vergun
General Contractor: Roux & Co
Interiors: Cynthia Riebe ASID
Landscape Architect: Garrett Eckbo

The Johnsons were familiar with Koenig's work from *Arts and Architecture* magazine and commissioned him to design a steel and glass 'pavilion in the trees'. The site covers one and a half acres of oak-covered rolling hills in the Carmel Valley, ten miles from Carmel on a dirt road off the main highway. Koenig located the building on a slight incline so that there are views through the trees to the rolling hills on the southern side of the house. The sun sets early behind a mountain on the west side of the house reducing the need to shade the western elevation with a deep overhang. Overhangs of 7 feet in length are used to provide the eastern and southern sides of the house with shade.

By 1962, steel-decking spans had doubled in length, and Koenig doubled his former building module accordingly. The house is pristine in its geometry: Koenig uses a square 20-foot module with clear spans of 20 feet in each direction and columns 20 feet on centre. Sliding glass doors in the house are 20 feet wide by 9 feet high and these are operable, so that entire walls seem to dissolve. The living area has one solid wall on the western elevation, and Koenig recalls that this concession was realized because the Johnsons wanted 'a background for their furniture', despite the fact that for Koenig, 'furniture belongs in the center of the room'. Nevertheless, the solid wall protects the room from the western sun. The kitchen, dining, and generously proportioned living areas are open to each other, with no dividing walls, the whole occupying a cumulative space of 20 feet by 60 feet. The kitchen design follows the standard Koenig formula: only the steel frame for the wooden cabinets touches the ceiling, leaving the steel roof deck to continue uninterrupted above. The fireplace helps to define the living and dining areas and is open on all sides, with the flue hovering above.

The house effectively functions as a T-shaped plan, with the carport and workshop serving as the western wing that balances the eastern bedroom wing. Adjacent to the detached two-car carport is a workshop with an outdoor work area on the west side of the entry court. In plan, the entry is carved out from the overall T-shape, so that entry is possible in the intermediary space between the carport and the house. In the middle of the house, at the point where the three wings hinge, Koenig places a large utility room to house the heating system and provides a laundry room with a generous work area. This is the core of the house, the most internal space, and from here the remainder of the house extends into the landscape. As Koenig says, 'It's like living outside.'

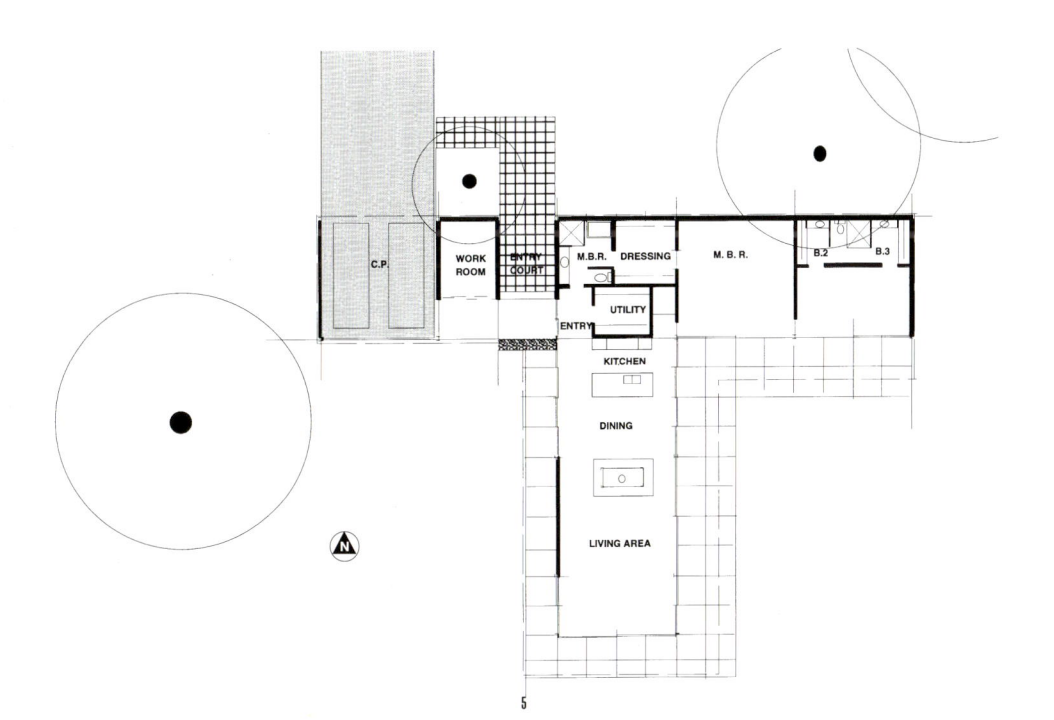

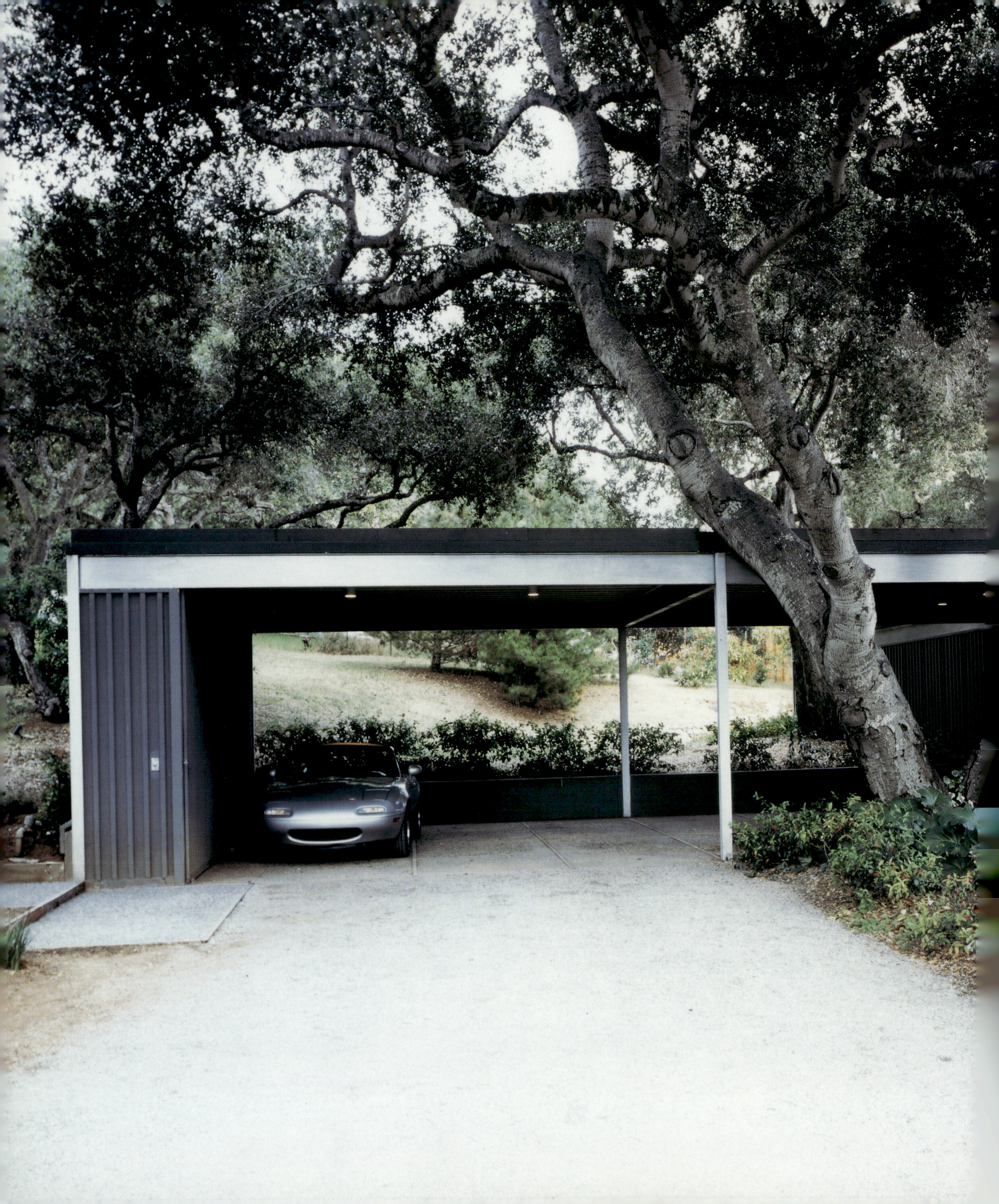

8 Riebe addition: new carport and entrance wing.
9 Panoramic view of house and oak trees.
10 Night view of living-dining area.
11 South elevation.

14

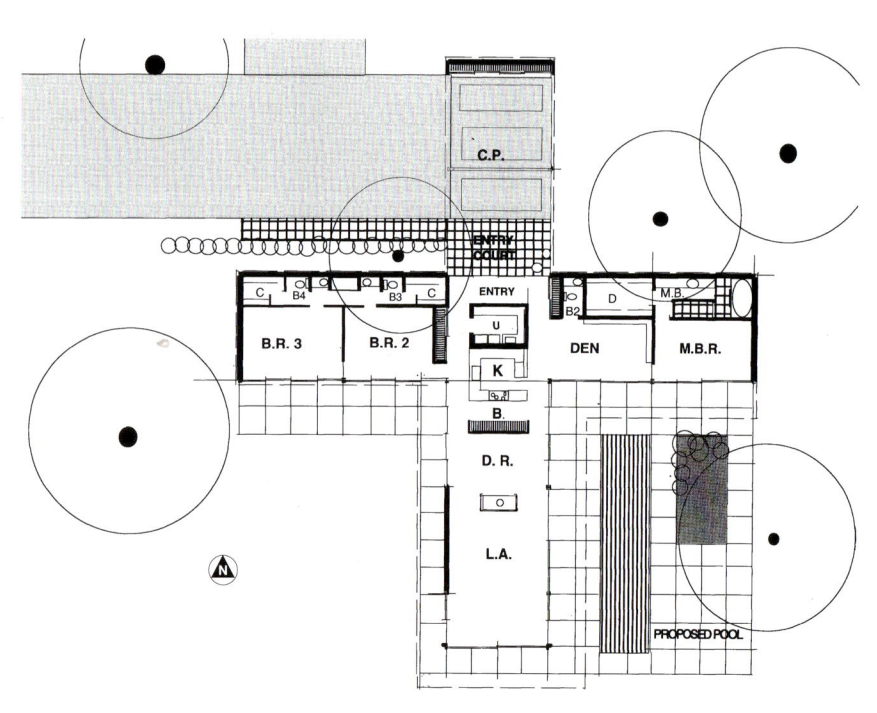

12

13

15

JOHNSON HOUSE/RIEBE ADDITION

16

12 View to living area from kitchen on left.

13 Floor plan with addition.

14 Covered entrance is an extension of carport.

15 Breakfast bar looking north with master bedroom and office on left.

16 Kitchen-breakfast bar looking south with children's rooms beyond.

IWATA HOUSE

1963
Monterey Park, California
12,000 sq ft including carport and pool house
Structural Engineer: William Porush
General Contractor: Colletta & Edgle
Landscape and Pool: Pierre Koenig

'Houses of mine, up until this period, were all prototypes for mass production. This is not; it is a unique experiment.'

The Iwata House, located on top of a high ridge running along the north side of Monterey Park, has dramatic views of the San Gabriel Valley and Mountains. The site is 'pie-shaped' with its narrow end on the street. Koenig places the house as far from the street as possible to maximize the amount of level land available for the pool and parking. A separate building encloses the poolhouse, patio, and four-vehicle carport.

The structure of the house is a cantilevered steel frame with a secondary structural system of wood and plaster room modules placed in this steel frame. Each of the three levels is a separate structural unit with its own floor and roof.

For sound isolation and mechanical access, there is a space of three feet between the top of one level and the bottom of the next. As the building rises from the ground, it gets larger; the modular progression is 1–2–6, so that the floor area increases as the need for private space increases. Koenig located space for group activities and individual privacy by dividing the house vertically into three major zones. The ground floor, with the smallest area, contains the fewest, largest, most flexible spaces for indoor and outdoor play. The first storey accommodates specific public functions with divided spaces for cooking, eating and entertaining. The top floor is the largest in area and has the most highly defined amount of smaller spaces for sleeping and study. The entry is placed in

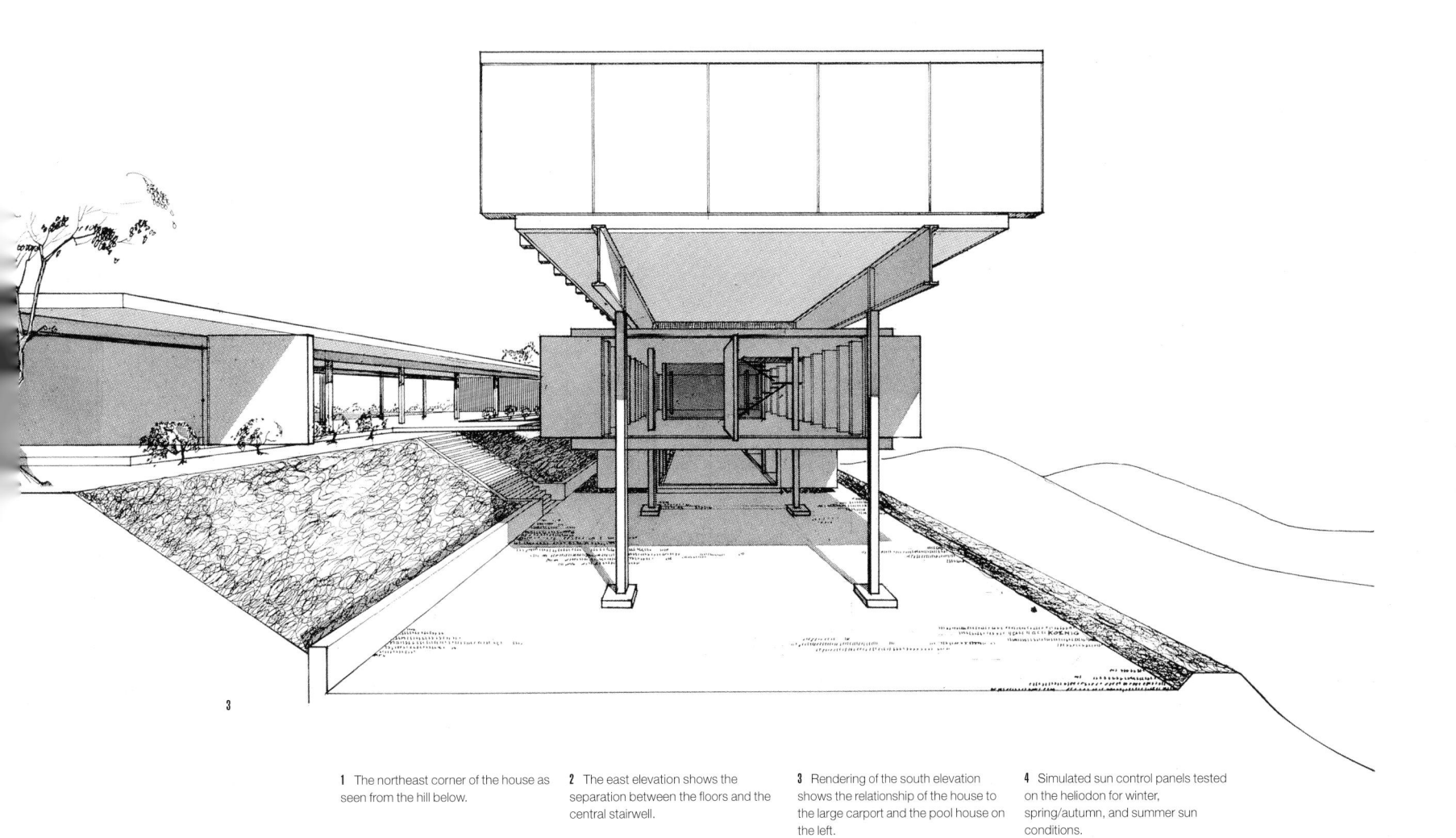

1 The northeast corner of the house as seen from the hill below.

2 The east elevation shows the separation between the floors and the central stairwell.

3 Rendering of the south elevation shows the relationship of the house to the large carport and the pool house on the left.

4 Simulated sun control panels tested on the heliodon for winter, spring/autumn, and summer sun conditions.

5

6

5 West elevation with pool and parking area in the foreground.
6 Perspective drawing showing two bridges leading to house.
7 Sun control fins casts shadows at the entry.

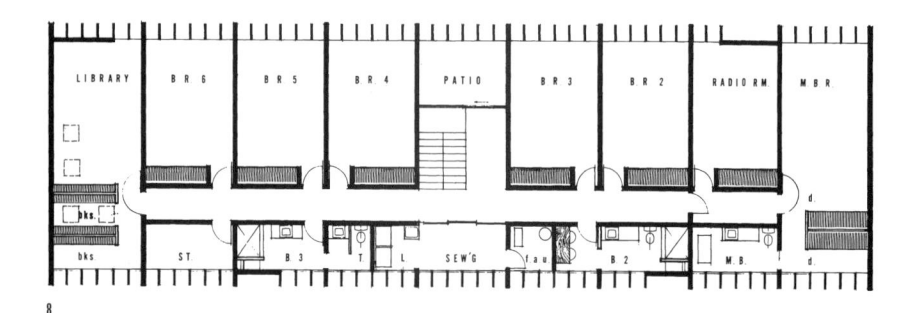

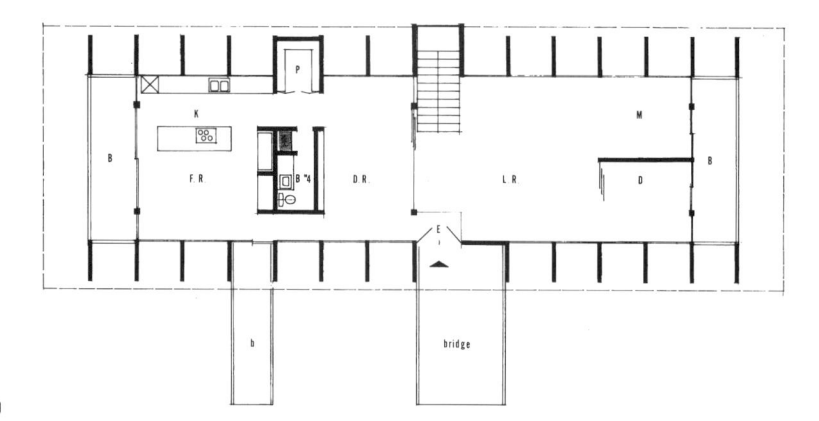

the middle of the three levels, to reduce the amount of travel up and down stairs.

All of the main structural steel is exposed. The structural 'tree' is supported by 27-inch wide-flange girders under the first floor and 21-inch wide-flange girders under the second floor with 16-inch wide-flange beams spanning across the girders. The six steel tube columns (8 by 8 by $^3/_8$ inch) cantilever from large concrete pad footings and are designed to resist lateral loads.

The horizontal plane of the overhanging floors, along with the vertical sun-shade fins, provides equal shade on each level. Two furnaces provide a forced air heating system throughout the house with provisions for future air-conditioning installation.

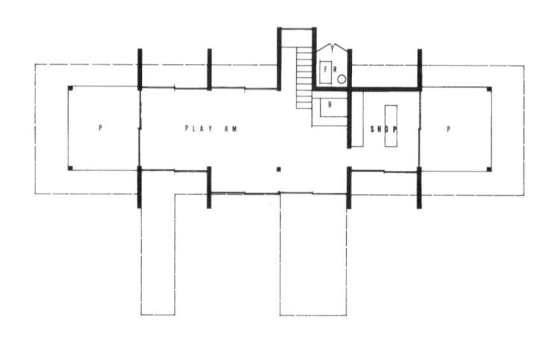

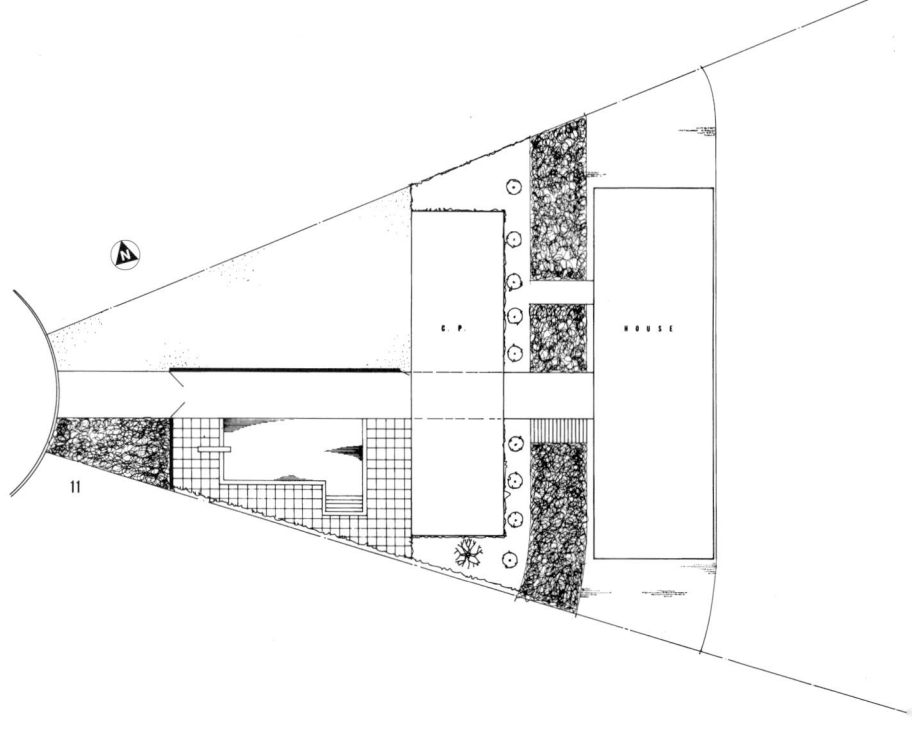

8 Second floor plan.
9 First floor plan.
10 Ground floor plan.
11 Site plan.
12 The effectiveness of the sun control fins is evident in the shaded living room.
13 Living room facing dining area and kitchen beyond.

MOSQUE

MOSQUE

1963
Hollywood, Los Angeles, California
10,000 sq ft
Structural Engineer: William Porush

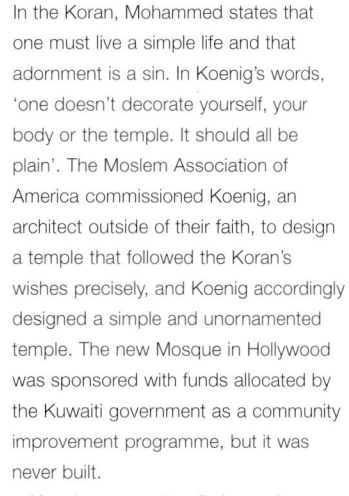

In the Koran, Mohammed states that one must live a simple life and that adornment is a sin. In Koenig's words, 'one doesn't decorate yourself, your body or the temple. It should all be plain'. The Moslem Association of America commissioned Koenig, an architect outside of their faith, to design a temple that followed the Koran's wishes precisely, and Koenig accordingly designed a simple and unornamented temple. The new Mosque in Hollywood was sponsored with funds allocated by the Kuwaiti government as a community improvement programme, but it was never built.

Koenig prepared preliminary plans for a pre-cast concrete structure that satisfied the city's requirements for the construction of assembly buildings. Koenig, favouring prefabricated systems, planned to construct the building from pre-cast, pre-stressed elements. The post-and-beam structural frame is made of reinforced concrete with brick infill walls. Koenig articulates the difference between a steel building and a pre-cast concrete building system: 'For the concrete, the connections are quite elaborate. They are steel connections, really. It takes a long time to build even a pre-cast building because the truck can only carry one of the concrete beams at a time, whereas a truck could carry the whole building at once in steel. That figures into the cost. I didn't want to do formed-on-site concrete. That's handicraft work. I wanted to avoid that.'

Other religious facilities are used solely for religious holidays, tending to remain vacant for the rest of the time, but the mosque is a centre of constant activity, used for classes and social gatherings in addition to religious observances. Koenig planned to include vertical sliding walls to divide the interior space into four areas for classrooms or religious services. Exterior sliding glass walls can be opened to accommodate larger crowds on special occasions.

Around the perimeter of the building is a colonnade that shades and defines the outdoor overflow space. This covered walk provides shade on the south side of the building, and solar screens on the glass provide protection from the sun on the west side. The entrance court serves as a visitor's area and can be converted into an outdoor room if necessary. Water is revered by Moslems for its cooling properties and scarcity and Koenig included fountains, pools and sprinklers as dominant features.

On the main floor, a community kitchen, library, baths and a mortuary are contained within the religious centre. In accordance with the Koran, the rounded *mihrab* in the mosque faces east. There is also a modern minaret with an elevator that climbs to the top. In the southeast corner of the plan there is a complete two-storey residence for the Ahmen who runs the Mosque and lives on site.

1 Main floor plan.
2 Apartment on first floor.
3 Forecourt at entry of mosque.

OBERMAN HOUSE

1962
Palos Verdes, California
1,810 sq ft + 820 sq ft covered area and patio
Structural Engineer: William Porush
General Contractor: Mr and Mrs Oberman

The Oberman House is Koenig's only 'all glass house'. Glass walls line its entire perimeter, with the only solid walls on the interior, forming a core. The site is a levelled lot on top of a gently sloping hill in Palos Verdes that has a broad view to the Pacific Ocean and Santa Catalina Island. The clients were musicians who appreciated the geometrical nature of Koenig's previous houses. The clients' son was training to be an Olympic swimmer, and stipulated that a 20-metre swimming pool be fully integrated into the design of the living spaces. They also wanted to retain their unlimited view on a very restrictive budget. Koenig studied the site and developed a rectangular plan parallel to the rear bank of the hill and far enough away from the front slope for the large pool to remain stable. A long private driveway leads onto the 100-foot by 175-foot property to a two-car carport and large private parking area.

The site is very windy and receives full sunlight during all seasons. Koenig was unable to plant trees to provide protection from the sunlight, as the wind from the ocean blows constantly, preventing tall vegetative growth there. The outdoor patios between the house and the carport are shielded from the wind by the mass of the house. To avoid uplift from high velocity winds, overhangs are totally omitted. To shade the interiors Koenig used a very fine sunscreen, Koolshade, a tiny horizontal louver, on the south and west elevations, (the same sunshades he used on Case Study House #21).

Outdoor service and storage areas adjacent to the carport are connected to the house with an entrance canopy. From the carport, the canopy slides between the two patios on the east side of the house, both with outdoor eating areas and a fire pit shielded from the wind. At the entry, the kitchen and the

1 Northwest elevation.
2 Sliding doors open to pool.
3 Outdoor patio between carport and house.

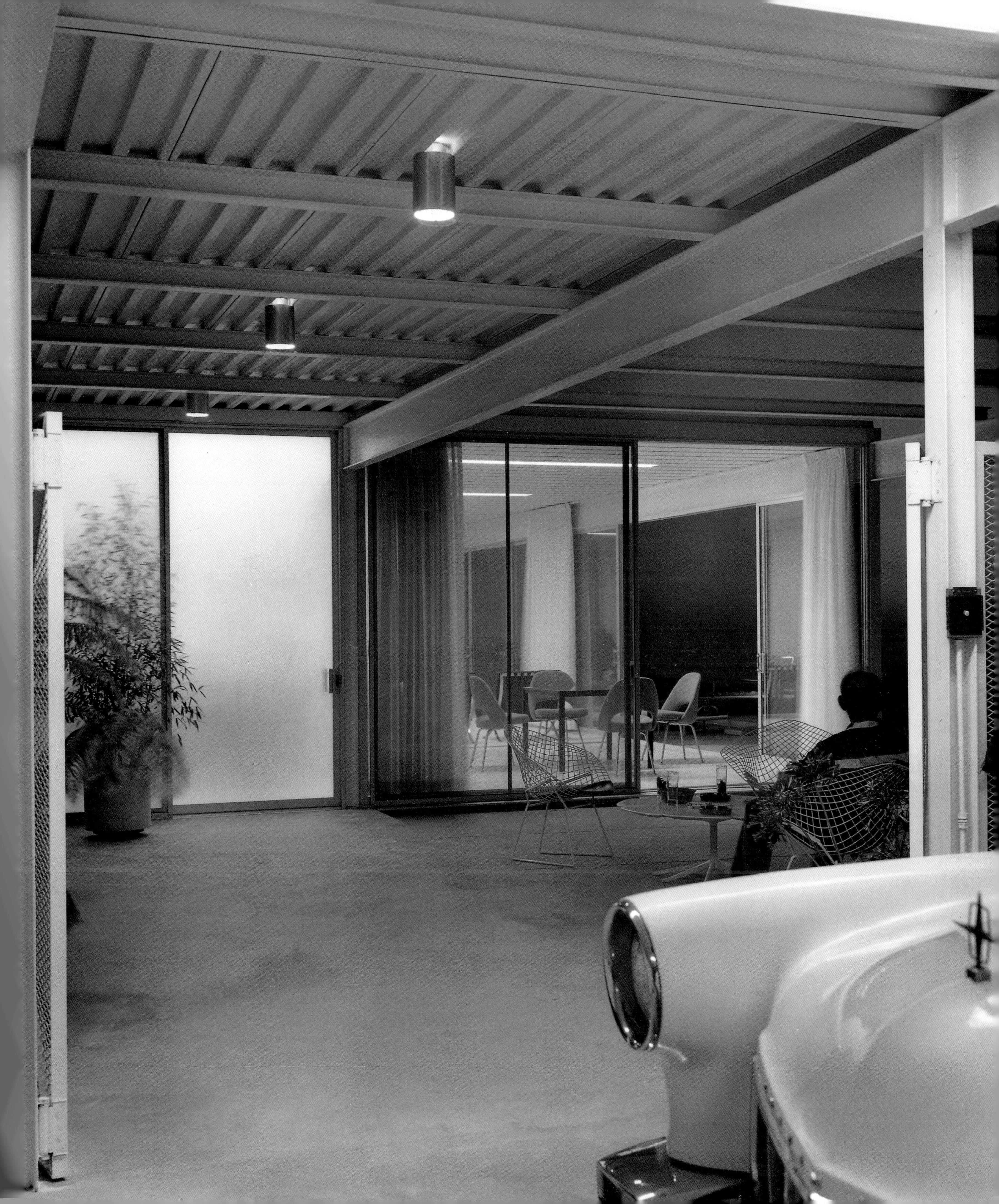

4 Infrared photograph with architect looking towards Santa Catalina Island, visible 26 miles away.

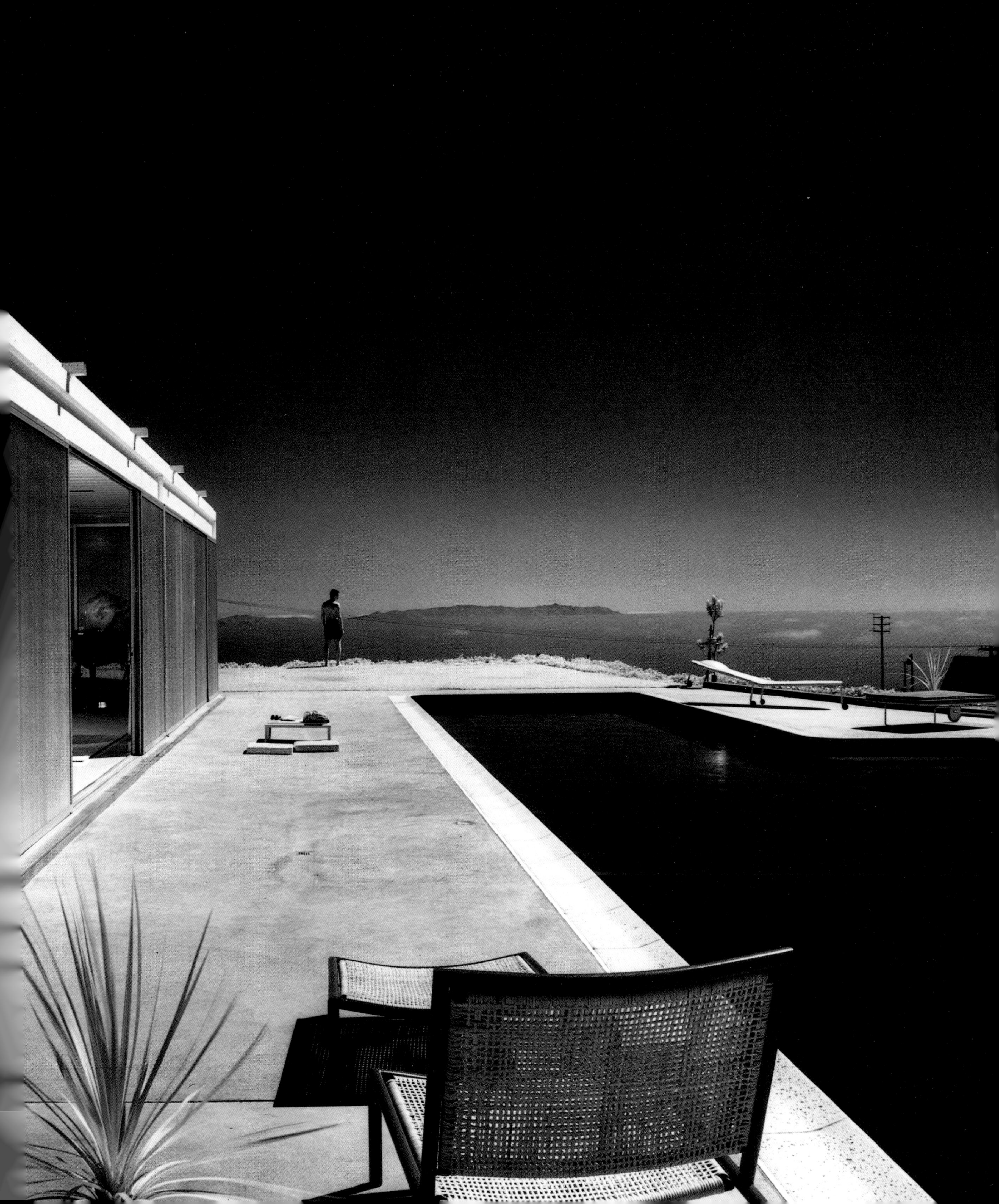

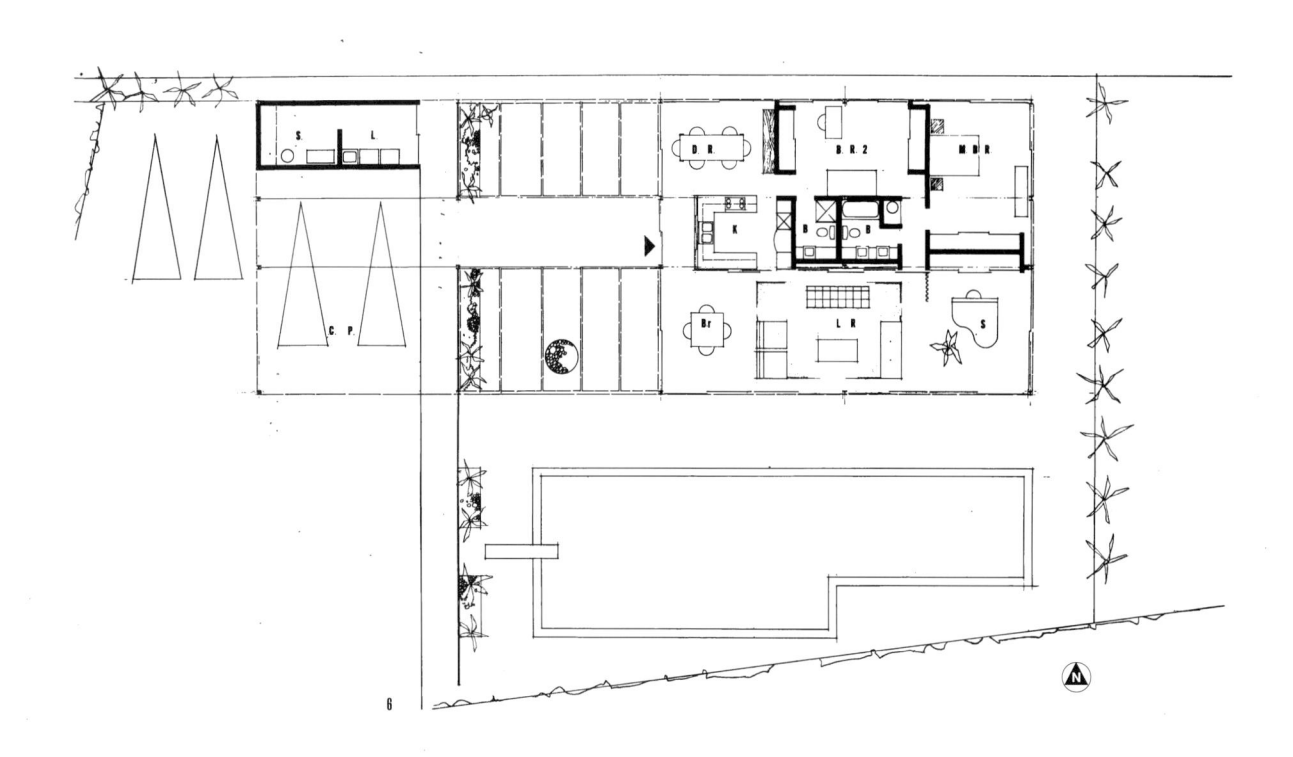

5

6

OBERMAN HOUSE

7

5 Pierre Koenig at the northwest corner of the house. Koolshade sunscreens protect the living area.

6 Site and floor plan.

7 The architect and the owner take a swim in the 20-metre pool.

two bathrooms form a central core that separates the general living area from the two bedrooms. The open kitchen is adjacent to four eating areas as well as the pool deck. The kitchen, with blue enamelled steel and walnut cabinets, may be closed off from the rest with interior sliding doors. The kitchen 'walls' do not reach the ceiling, emphasizing the fact that they are non-loadbearing. Steel roof monitors with operable overhead transom windows bring natural light and ventilation into the kitchen and bathrooms.

Koenig uses twenty 4-inch wide-flange columns to frame the house, the patios, and the carport. In plan, three horizontal bays run east–west to define the entire house. Five lines of columns placed 23 feet on centre and connected by 12-inch I-beams are used for north–south framing. East–west framing is achieved with 4-inch long span T-type galvanized steel decking between the beams. Acoustic board fastens to the underside of the steel deck except where obscure glass encloses fluorescent lighting troughs – employing the same system as in previous houses.

The informal dining area, living area, and study face the long side of the pool with 23 foot wide sliding glass doors that open to the pool deck. The master bedroom looks out across the lawn to the ocean and is separated from the study by a wardrobe wall. The east wall of the living area conceals a storage area behind sliding doors. The entrance canopy is differentiated by the use of $1\frac{1}{2}$-inch decking supported by 4-inch beams that serve as framing for the patios. Radiant heat pipes are imbedded between the layers of the double-poured terrazzo floor. The colour scheme both internally and externally is white, with white-on-white terrazzo floors throughout. However, colour is not entirely absent, and is achieved by capturing the changing light and mood of the sky.

8 View from carport to entrance showing outdoor patio transition area.
9 Interior view looking over pool with sliding door and sunscreen open.
10 Interior view of kitchen with living room and pool beyond.
11 Sliding glass doors open to reveal relationship of kitchen to two eating areas.

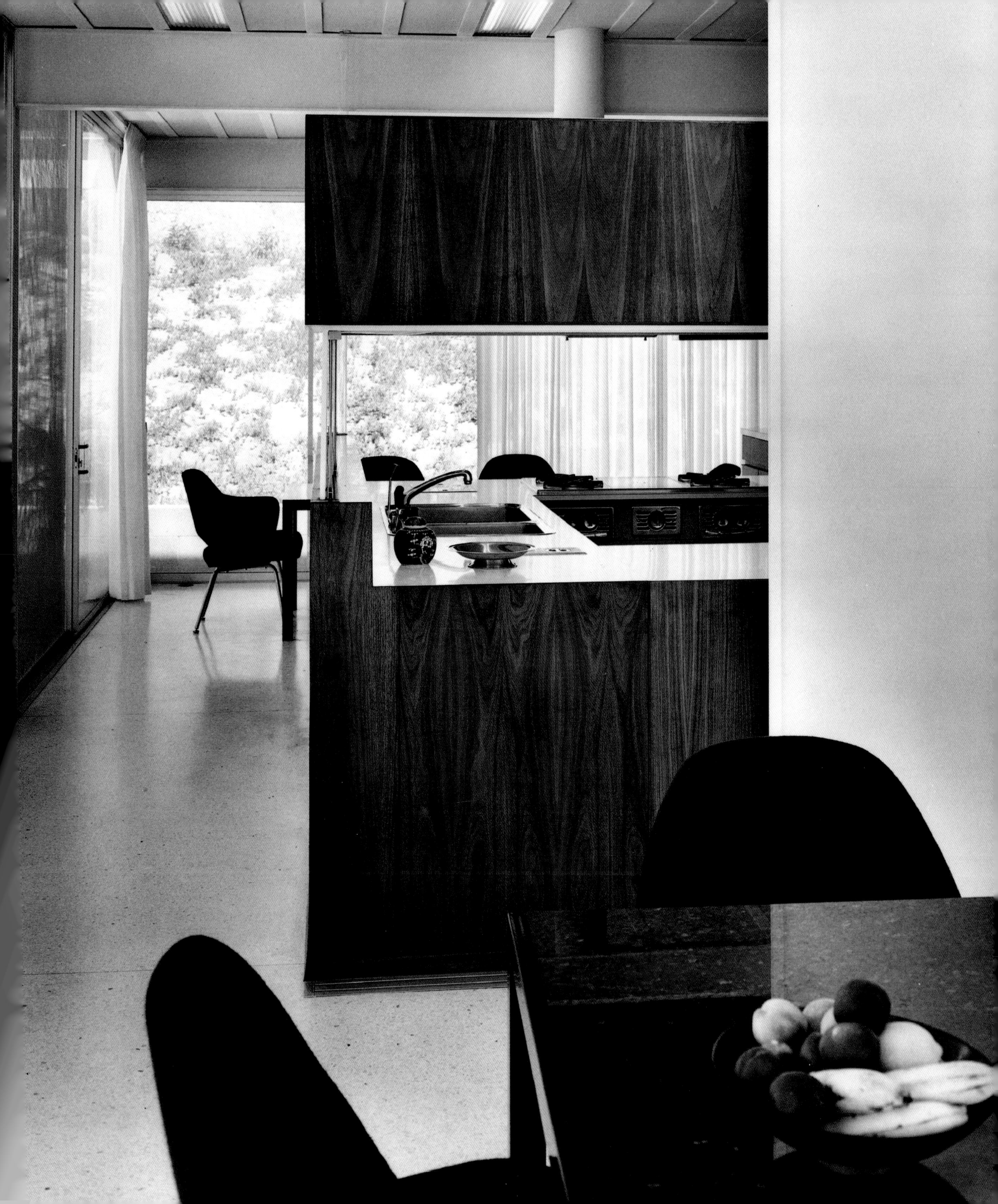

1

1 Street elevation with garage doors on left.   2 Rendering of front elevation.   3 View of southwest elevation as seen from below.   4 A privacy screen shelters the entry of the house on the right.

2

BEAGLES HOUSE

1963
Pacific Palisades, Los Angeles, California
3,000 sq ft
Structural Engineer: William Porush
General Contractor: Bruce Koch

The Beagles House is anchored to a steep hillside overlooking the Pacific Ocean with a sweeping southwest view of the sea. Typically, Koenig uses structure and planning to optimize the site, and in this case, the house has actually served to protect the landscape. In 1964 a severe landslide destroyed nearby buildings and evacuated large amounts of topsoil, and yet this steel frame house resisted the devastation and remains in its original condition. This particular location in the Pacific Palisades is known as an 'active slide area', and as a precautionary measure Koenig incorporated eight caissons in the design to anchor the building to rock deep below the soil. The resulting design is so efficient that it helps to stabilize the hillside.

The building is unusual as it is one of only two Koenig houses that are sided with stucco. Although Koenig preferred to side the house with his customary steel decking material, his clients insisted on a more traditional plaster exterior. The house has few openings on its side elevations. Instead, Koenig used full-height glass on the main elevations to provide spectacular ocean views.

In planning, Koenig employed what he calls 'an inverted plan', where the entrance from street-level leads straight on to the upper floor. The front door opens in the middle of the plan onto a two-storey central space with an open stairway. The flue of the fireplace rises through this circulation core of the house from the lower level. On the upper floor, the dining area, kitchen and play area are open both to this central volume and to the outdoors. Next to the play area are a bathroom and two bedrooms. An outdoor patio leading from the kitchen provides an informal dining area.

Downstairs, the positioning of the fireplace serves to extend the domain of the living room into the two-storey central space. The master bedroom, living room and additional bedroom face the ocean. The master bedroom has a master bathroom and dressing room, while the extra bedroom has a bathroom, laundry area and outdoor patio. Koenig used the lower front of the house, facing away from the ocean, to provide a large storage area. The garage is not detached, but enclosed within the main envelope of the house.

In lieu of a traditional 4-foot balcony, Koenig opted for an 18-inch window washing balcony. He provided a room-size outdoor eating area adjacent to the kitchen on the upper floor and an outside sitting room on the lower level adjacent to the living room.

3

4

5 Stairwell at lower level living area.
6 Central circulation core.
7 View of ocean from living room.
8 Upper (street level) floor plan.
9 Lower floor plan.
10 Service balcony and outdoor sitting area.

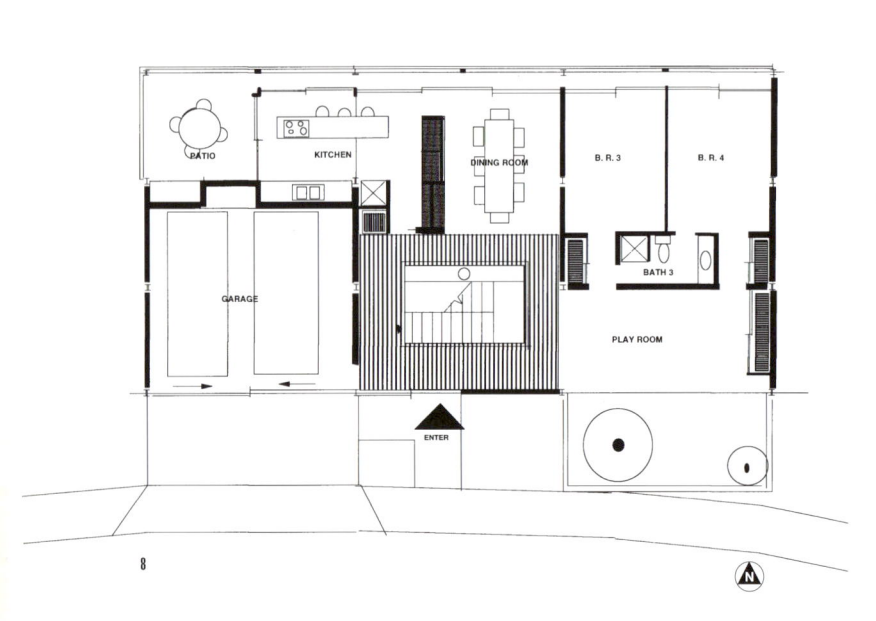

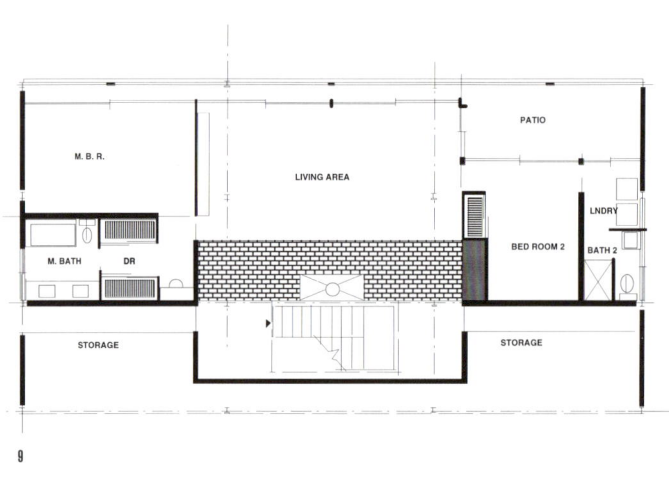

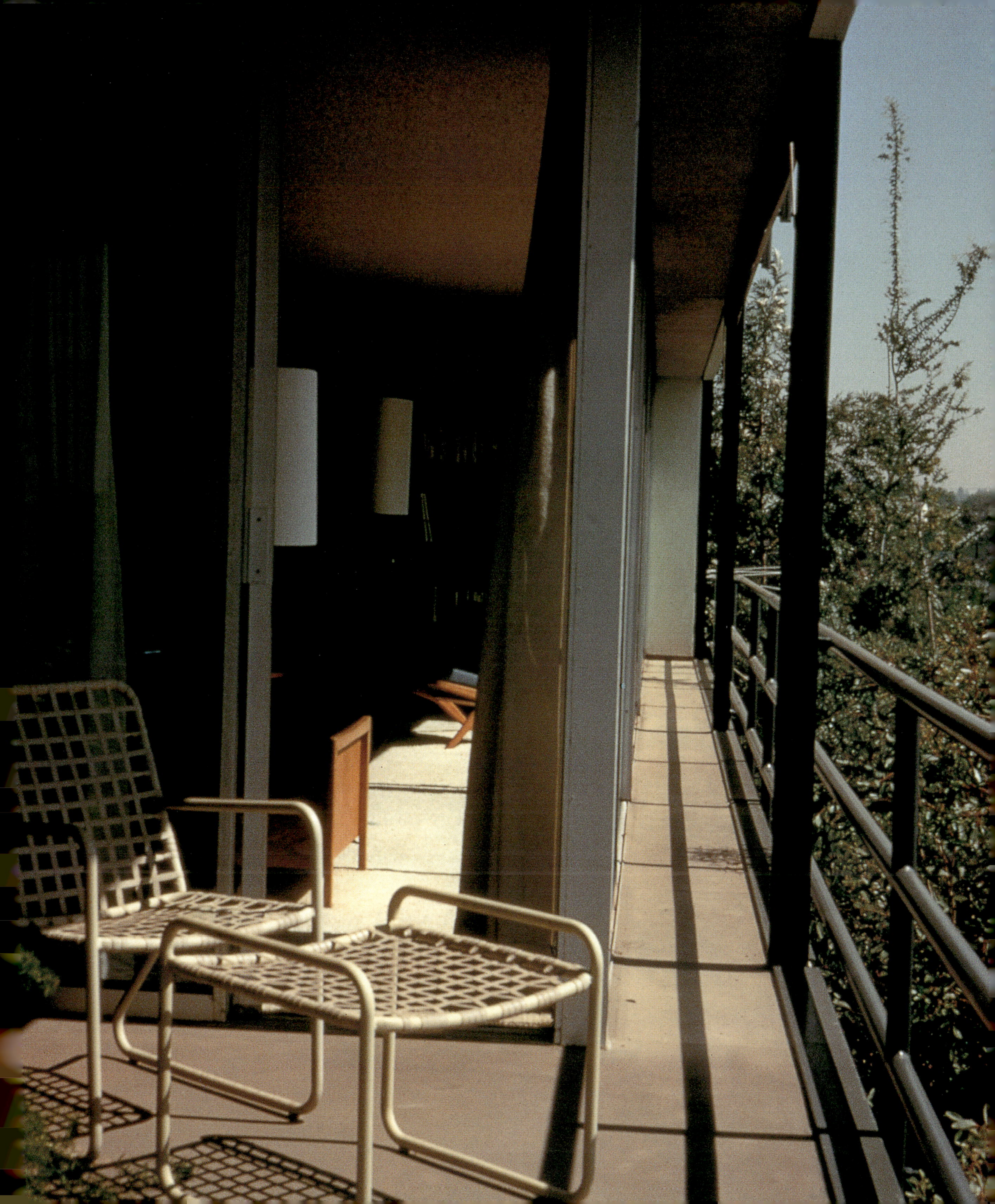

BETHLEHEM STEEL EXHIBIT PAVILION

1962
200 sq ft
Structural Engineer: Pierre Koenig
with William Porush
Display Design, Graphics: Pierre Koenig
Lighting: Pierre Koenig
Steel fabrication: Ferguson Door Co Inc
Construction: Jones-Bause

In 1962, the Bethlehem Steel Company commissioned architect Pierre Koenig to redesign their travelling trade show pavilion. The exhibit it housed was entitled 'The Steel Framed Home' and incorporated a display area for photographs, testimonial statements, product literature, data on steel-framed homes, and a house model. Koenig was to 'show maximum possibilities in the use of steel for residences and to develop a demountable display unit that could be easily assembled with a minimum amount of skilled labour.' Shown first at the 31st annual Garden and Home Show in Oakland, California, the exhibit travelled for two years to national home and industry shows throughout the United States.

The pavilion is a microcosm of Koenig's principles and demonstrates the value he places on the honesty of exposed structure. He created a sample of the experience of living inside an exposed steel-framed home whilst providing display areas to show built homes, including some of his own. The exhibit displays typical steel sections manufactured by the Bethlehem Steel Company for framing houses as well as details of wood–steel connections from the exhibit design itself. Koenig designed the pavilion without any covering or applied decoration to the steel structure, applying the same principles to this assignment as to his larger commissions. The mobility of this structure reinforces the idea of a flexible system, and Koenig liked the clarity of a system that does what it celebrates.

A perimeter channel defines the bottom and the top of the 10 by 20 by $9^{1}/_{2}$ foot pavilion. The steel members bolt together and the laminated wood floor is locked into place with tension rods. The photographs, display material, electrical wiring and lighting are permanently mounted and integrated into the building system for easy assembly. To solve the expected problem of uneven exhibition hall floors, Koenig elevated the floor line of the exhibit on half-inch diameter levelling bolts. The 'feet' are adjustable to accommodate the uneven exhibition floors while accentuating the pavilion effect by raising the entire exhibit one step off the floor.

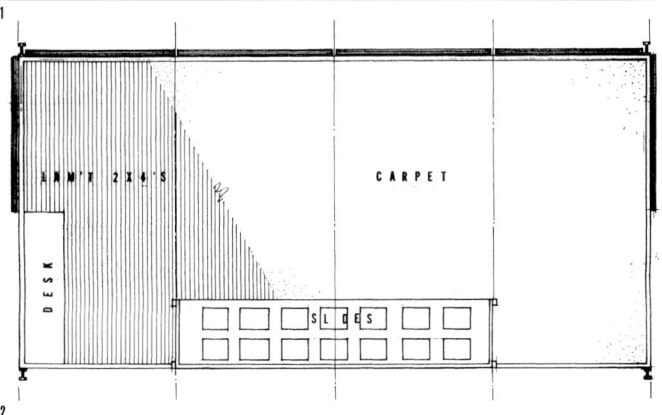

1 Front elevation of pavillion.
2 Floor plan.
3 Corner assembly for panels.
4 Roof assembly at centres.
5 Roof assembly at edges.
6 Floor assembly showing leveling bolt.
7 The assembled pavilion installed in an exhibition hall.

7

EEI FACTORY & SALES

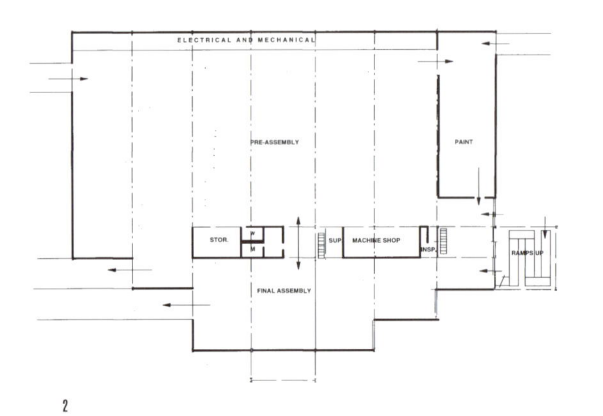

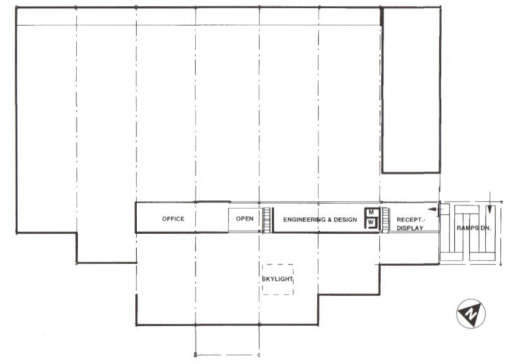

1

2 3

116

EEI FACTORY & SALES

1966
El Segundo, California
64,000 sq ft
Structural Engineer: William Porush
General Contractor: Smith Construction

Mike Jacobs, the president of Electronic Enclosures Incorporated (EEI), commissioned several architects to create design proposals for his new factory, showroom and office. He favoured Koenig's proposal because it simultaneously orchestrated assembly-line circulation, and resolved a difficult site configuration. The plot is an isosceles triangle and the building follows this shape. At 64,000 square feet, it is Koenig's largest project.

The building has steel perimeter columns, long span truss-joists, and pre-cast tilt-up exterior panels. A vast column-free production space occupies the majority of the lower floor. On the first level, toilets, storage areas, tool cribs and a machine shop form the core, while the reception, display and sales offices comprise the mezzanine. Sliding glass windows in the offices on the mezzanine allow views of the production loop on the floor below and communication with the workers. Customers enter the building from the car park via a processional ramp leading to the reception and showroom area.

An important planning consideration was to avoid fluctuations of temperature caused by the climate and by the heat generated by the machinery. Operable windows in the back of the trusses allowed ambient heat to escape, replacing it with cool air from outside. The individual workstations were also designed by Koenig, and have heaters and fans that a worker can operate. In the morning, when the factory floor is cold, individual workstation heaters and a radiant heat pad are activated. As the temperature rises during the day, individual fans are used at each workstation while windows vent and cool the overall workspace. The workstations also provide task lighting and a working surface.

In Koenig's design for the Franklyn Medical Building, he began to consider the idea of inhabiting the roof system. If the trusses are deep, they can be exploited both structurally and spatially: space between the cords is created, which can significantly increase the usable floor area. Koenig originally proposed this plan for EEI, and initially received his client's approval. However, once the working drawings were complete, the client reneged. As a compromise, Koenig changed the scheme to use long span truss-joists and abandoned his original experiment.

Koenig positioned the production loop at the south corner of the building. Circulation on the site was complicated because there was only one opening for the entry and exit of trucks. The front of the building is stepped to follow the oddly angled property line. The east and south elevation of each step is solid, whereas the north elevation of each step is all glass, allowing in natural light during the day, and a glimpse of factory work at night. The rear of the building is unpierced with large overhead doors leading into the factory, providing additional natural ventilation.

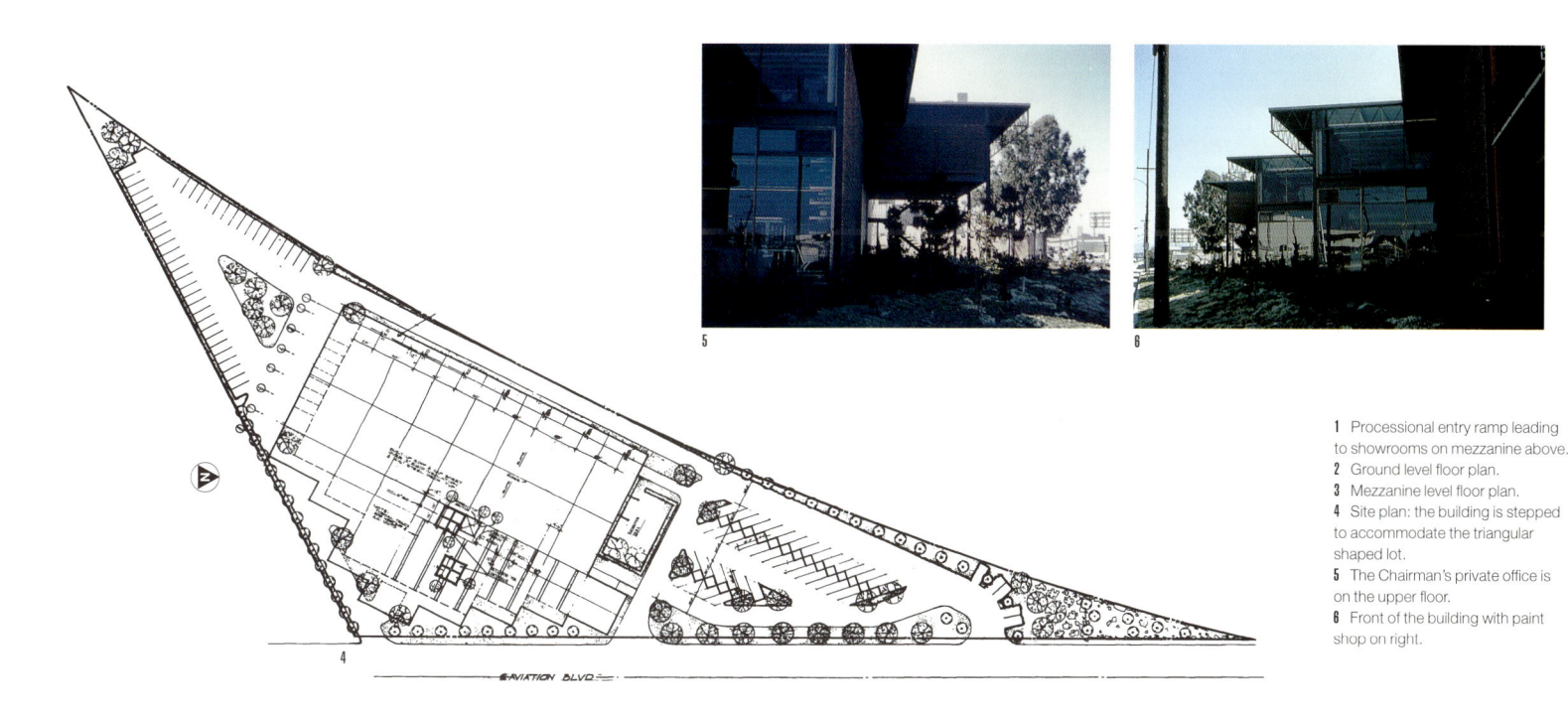

1 Processional entry ramp leading to showrooms on mezzanine above.
2 Ground level floor plan.
3 Mezzanine level floor plan.
4 Site plan: the building is stepped to accommodate the triangular shaped lot.
5 The Chairman's private office is on the upper floor.
6 Front of the building with paint shop on right.

1 West elevation of proposed house facing San Francisco Bay.
2 Top level floor plan.
3 Middle level floor plan.
4 Ground level floor plan.

WEST HOUSE

1970
Carquinez Heights, Vallejo, California
3,600 sq ft
Structural Engineer: William Porush
General Contractor: Carquinez Builders

Dr West was an oral surgeon in Oakland, California who had amassed a collection of modern art. He was familiar with modern architecture and with Koenig's work in particular. West had studied the work of many other well-known architects but he commissioned Koenig because he respected him as a 'true original'. West acquired land in Vallejo, on a ridge overlooking San Francisco Bay, and planned to build a series of modern houses for sale. His own house was to be the first one built.

The site of this 'bachelor's house' is 'high and beautiful' with a tremendous sightline west from the Golden Gate Bridge to the Bay Bridge and a view up the Sonoma River. The bare steel frame was made of Cor-Ten (rusting steel) which required no painting. The house occupied three levels. No living space was provided on the ground floor, only a carport and a furnace room with a sophisticated air-filtering system. As West was an asthmatic and prone to allergies, he insisted on a substantial mechanical system to condition the air. The middle level comprised the owner's suite, with a multi-purpose area, a bathroom and a bedroom. Koenig achieved privacy by limiting the amount of glass on the middle level. However, a single wall of glass was used to open the house to the main western view. The three remaining elevations were covered with solid panels. The top level was used for guests and entertaining. The living room, dining room and kitchen-dining areas were open to each other and surrounded by a glass perimeter wall, confusing the distinction between interior and exterior space.

West was constantly adding to his painting collection, and as he invited dealers and collectors to the house for viewings, he needed to be able to move the collection around as he wished. Koenig offered West an alternative method of displaying his painting collection. Instead of traditionally hanging artwork on the wall, paintings could be hung from the underside of the steel keystone decking material. Koenig employed a similar system at the Metcalf House. This way, paintings could hang anywhere in the room.

West passed away before he could move in. Eventually, the house was demolished and the remaining land was never developed as it was governed by a right-of-way clause claimed by a utility company.

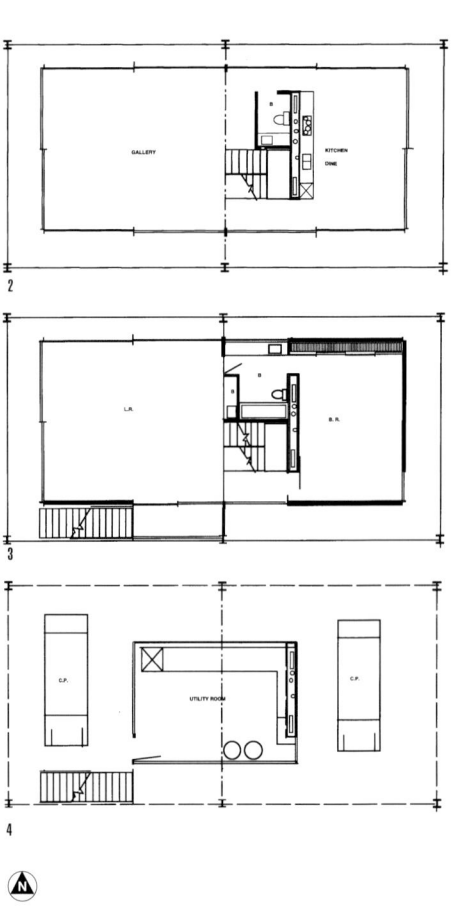

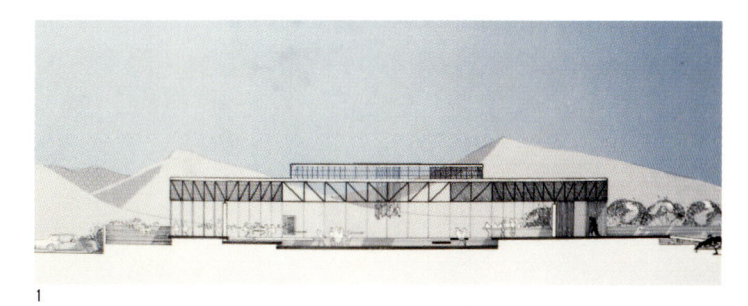

FRANKLYN DINNER CLUB

1981
Thousand Oaks, California
14,400 sq ft
Structural Engineer: William Porush

Dr Franklyn was a plastic surgeon and something of an architectural connoisseur. He was familiar with many of the architects in the world and enjoyed discussing potential projects with them. Franklyn first encountered Koenig when he was a draughtsman in the Candreva and Jarrett office. Later, when Koenig had his own office, they collaborated on several projects, largely unbuilt. Koenig designed a pool and gazebo for his residence, a steel stable, a medical building and the Franklyn Dinner Club.

Franklyn bought some land in Thousand Oaks at the summit of a dormant volcano that was levelled by the Navy for use as a landing strip to practice carrier landings during the Second World War. The site has a sweeping view of the valley and the surrounding mountains, and it is highly visible from the Ventura Freeway.

After receiving the commission, Koenig and Franklyn visited several large restaurants to examine successful design features and shortcomings. Koenig said 'I did the kitchen myself, because he (Franklyn) said a good way to go broke quickly is to hire a kitchen specialist. He showed me the ones that had a specialist, and at the time they were all overdone.' The Franklyn kitchen was small, but serves a large dining area, minimizing the need for cooking staff. Koenig arranged the equipment carefully, placing service and supply areas on the level below the kitchen and connecting them with a dumb-waiter. In this way the dining and serving area is not compromised by storage needs. Server stations are located throughout the restaurant, and a variety of dining, dancing and lounge areas surround the central space and bandstand providing flexible seating arrangements.

The club is octagonal in shape to maximize the surrounding view, to provide site circulation, to promote efficiency in the structural form for long spans, and to accommodate a multi-level open space. The roof is a 120 foot wide square spanned by deep truss-girders supported by four columns. The trusses cantilever an additional 40 feet over each side of the square, creating a roof width of 200 feet in total. Glass sliding doors wrap around the entire perimeter of the building allowing for ample air circulation and an efficient fire exit system (should the need arise). A large roof monitor over the central dining and dance floor opens to ventilate the large room and counteract overheating. By ventilating the room naturally 'we can open the doors and roof and within a few minutes take all the hot air out of the interior'. Koenig had ruled out the possibility of a mechanical ventilating system at an early stage. 'Not only are the energy costs high, but in large spaces it is rarely a comfortable climate indoors, either too hot or too cold. It takes too long to balance fluctuations.'

After Koenig had designed the Dinner Club, the local authorities said they would not approve any designs that did not conform to the Spanish style. Thousand Oaks City Hall is on the slope just below Franklyn's site and the authorities were concerned Koenig's building would divert attention from it. Koenig contested the decision and had almost received a permit, when the authorities unfavourably changed the zoning on the property. While disputing the zoning change, Franklyn died, and the project was never built.

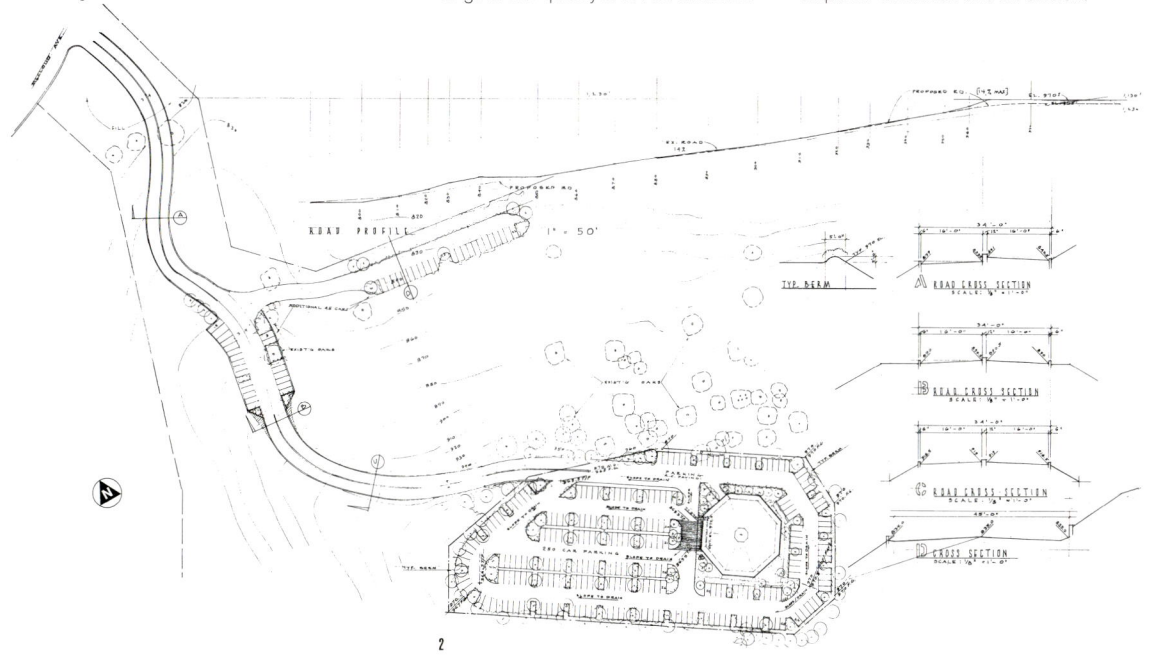

1 Section elevation shows depressed parking and sunken dance floor. The roof monitor rises above the roof level and vents hot air.
2 Site plan showing parking around and below level of main dining area.

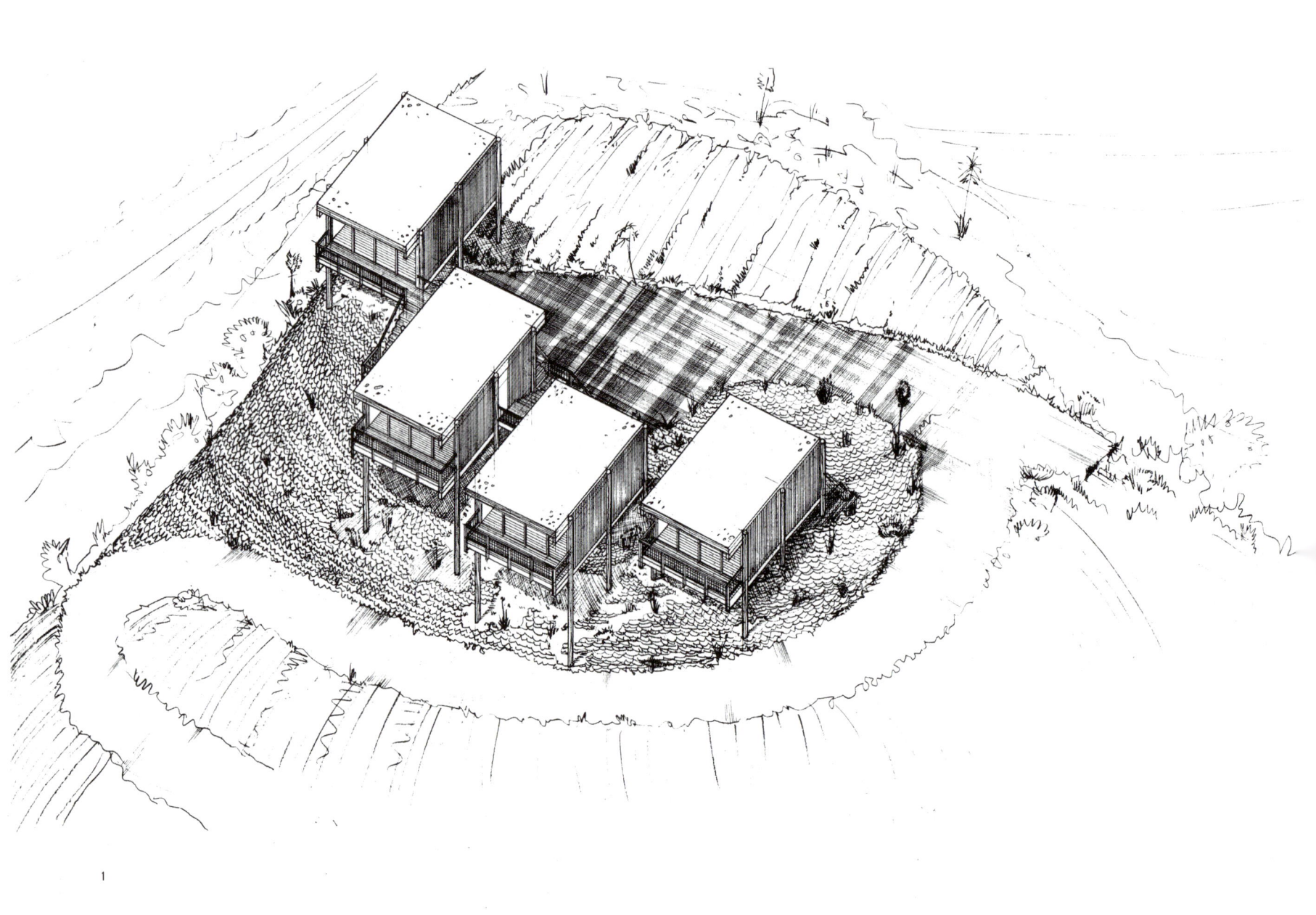

BURTON POLE HOUSE

1 Bird's-eye view of proposed modules.
2 Supporting structure is outside the building envelope.
3 X-bracing provides lateral stability.
4 View of ocean from one of the modules.
5 Floor plan: the four modules have transition zones between them.

1

2

3

4

BURTON POLE HOUSE

1979
Malibu, California
2,400 sq ft
Structural Engineer: Tom Harris

In 1978, the Burtons asked Koenig to design a 2,400 square foot house for their hillside Malibu site. They didn't want to build the whole house at once, and to solve the problem, Koenig divided the functions of the house into four modules so that the owner could build one module at a time.

The plot has strict tract restrictions which limited potential construction techniques and ruled out the possibility of building in steel. For the Burton Pole House, Koenig decided on a wooden pole system assembled similarly to the steel frame. 'In both cases, parts are prefabricated off-site, shipped to the site and the frame is assembled with a crane.' However, unlike steel, the wood structure cannot provide moment connections. Instead, X-bracing cables located below the floors support cantilevers, leaving the underside of the house free from the ground plane.

In Koenig's words: 'My philosophy is not to cut and fill the site, but to build on the side of the natural slope, leaving the landscape as untouched as possible. The pole house allows us to do that.'

Koenig wanted to plant the poles in the ground so that they would rise out to become the frame of the building. He abandoned this plan because it is impossible to align, straighten and plumb the poles at the same time. Opting for a mechanical system, he attached the poles to the caissons in a similar way to setting steel columns.

The walls are separated from the poles by a gap of about half an inch. The colours and textures of the materials differentiate the bearing structure from the non-bearing structure. There are very few openings on the side elevations, but extensive glass on the front opens the house to the ocean view.

From the outset, the house was designed to be constructed in segments so that part of the building can be inhabited while the rest is under construction or remains unbuilt. The plan is divided into four modules, with the two central modules now built. The owners inhabit Module 2, housing the recreation room and the office or guest room, and Module 3 comprising the kitchen, dining and living room. On construction, Module 4 will be the master bedroom suite, and the owners will move into this segment. Module 1 will have an office or studio and a spare bedroom. Although the distance between the modules is the same, their heights vary. Indoor and outdoor transition zones between them accommodate these level changes.

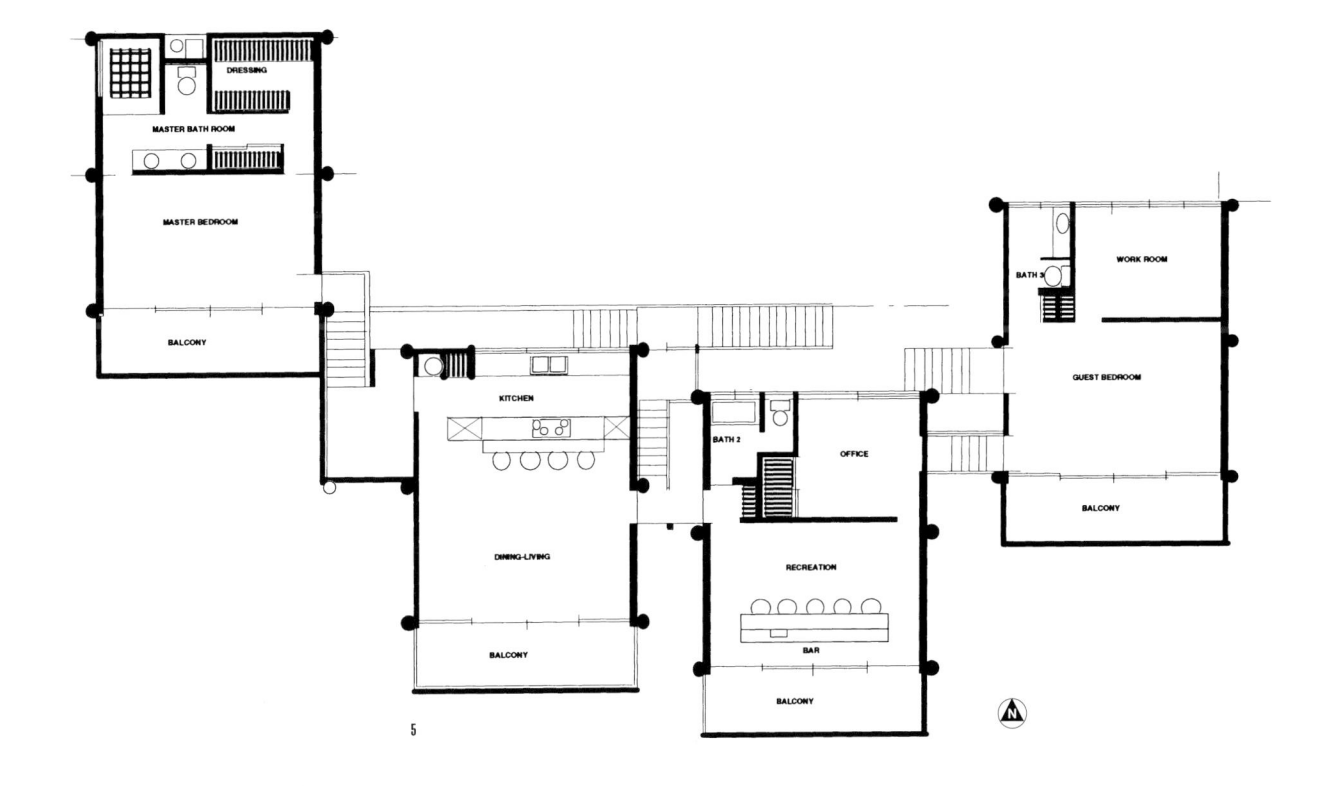

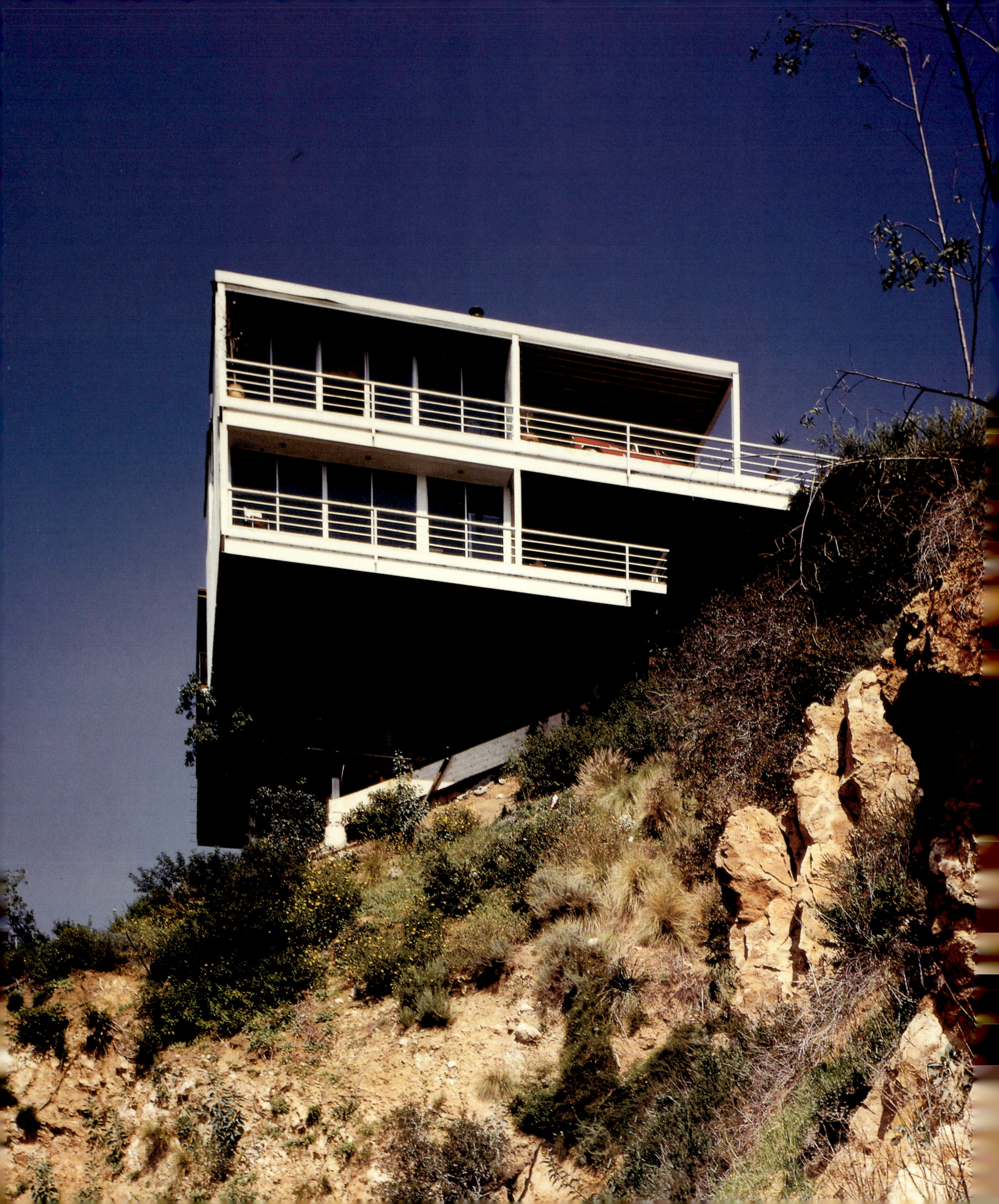

GANTERT HOUSE

1983
Hollywood Hills, Los Angeles, California
1,800 sq ft + 1,200 sq ft carport
and covered area
Structural Engineer: Dimitry Vergun
General Contractor: Michael Gantert

Koenig calls this house 'the most difficult project I've ever done.' The site has an incline of more than 45 degrees, and as such was previously deemed 'unbuildable' by the city. The Ganterts commissioned Koenig to design an inventive solution to the challenges of the site and to retain its spectacular view of Hollywood. With the use of modern building systems and materials, as well as some careful planning, the house stands triumphant. With glass from floor to ceiling, Koenig likens the spatial experience to 'being suspended in space, somewhat like being in a dirigible'.

Koenig designed a two-way cantilevered system using welded steel moment connections to achieve the required square footage. The two and a half levels are supported by only four columns. When the structural engineer first visited the site he was so stunned by the steep drop that he returned to his office to rethink his calculations.

Although the 'footprint' of the foundation is only 300 square feet, the top floor comprises 1,620 square feet, including the carport and approach. The lower floor is 1,260 square feet, including the covered deck, and the furnace room below is 120 square feet. To accomplish this, Koenig cantilevered the house twelve feet in two directions with 18-inch wide-flange beams supported by four 12-inch by 8-inch wide-flange columns, attached to concrete caissons sunk twenty feet into rock.

Because there is no horizontal space on the site, almost all the components were prefabricated, trucked in, and assembled with a crane. Scaffolding could not be used, so everything had to be installed from the inside of the steel frame, a method Koenig considers to be preferable to more traditional construction techniques. Tongue-and-groove plywood over lightweight steel joists make up the floor, while the roof consists of composition roofing over insulation over exposed long-span steel decking. The exterior walls are insulated, formed of short-span steel decking with gypsum board on the interior.

A large skylight over the central stairwell brings sunlight to the floor below and to the kitchen on the north side of the top floor. The entry space, living area, dining area, kitchen, service porch and guest bathroom surround the stairway. Downstairs, there is a master bedroom and a master bathroom, two guest bedrooms, and a guest bathroom. A covered deck with a jacuzzi heated by solar panels is located adjacent to the downstairs hall.

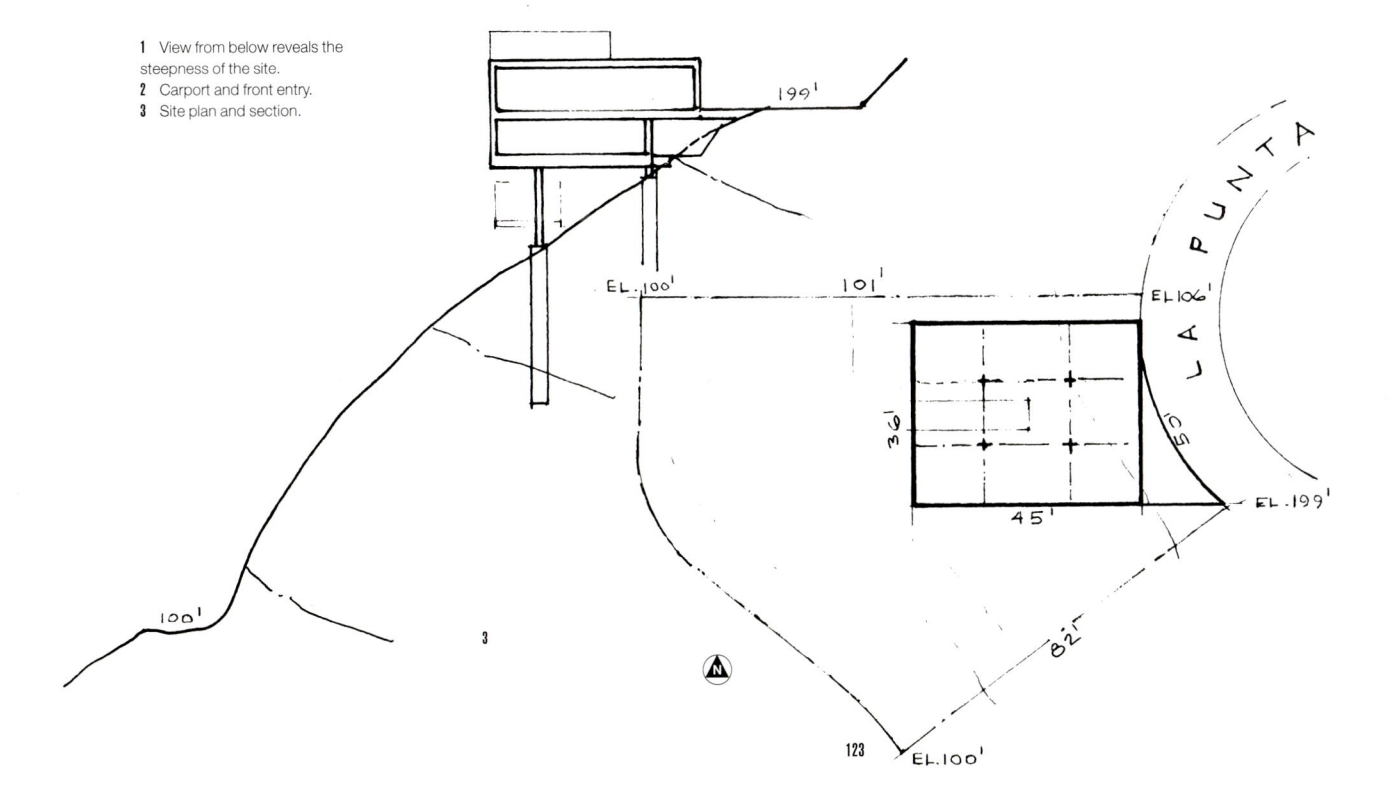

1 View from below reveals the steepness of the site.
2 Carport and front entry.
3 Site plan and section.

4 5 6

8

4 The hillside setting provides spectacular views.
5 Hammock on the play deck under the house.
6 Skylight brings sunshine into the stairway below.
7 Perspective rendering of proposed house with its mechanical room below.
8 The house cantilevers over the valley below.

6431

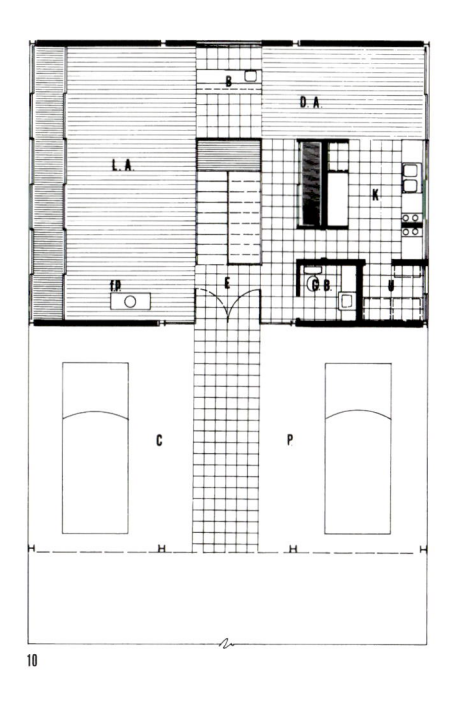

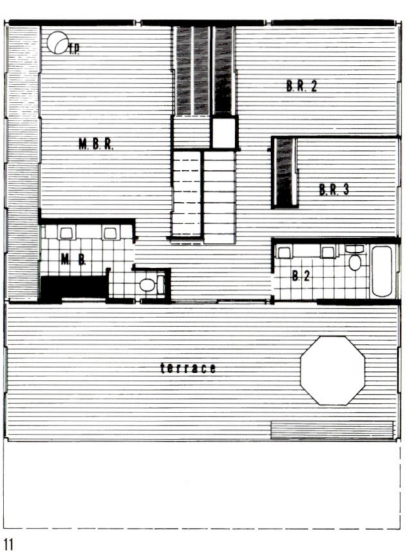

9 View through front door shows living room and skylit stairwell.
10 Upper floor plan.
11 Lower floor plan.

STUERMER HOUSE

1985
Oahu, Hawaii
1,600 sq ft including garage
Structural Engineer: Dimitry Vergun

In 1984, the Stuermers commissioned Pierre Koenig to design a house on the east side of the island of Oahu. The owner's property is on a steep perch on the side of an ancient volcano and has an exceptional view of the Kaneohe Bay. The site, because of its precipitous drop and mixed soil composition of lava and mud, is difficult to build on. Koenig proposed a 'vertical solution' in which the concrete pad and house footprint are very small. He reduced the foundations by supporting the structure with four 12-inch by 12-inch steel columns and concrete footings, thereby minimizing the amount of cutting required through the lava.

The house rises four levels and captures wide views of the bay. The plan is arranged so that only the first and second level are used for everyday living, with the third floor used as an entertainment area to reduce the amount of vertical travel during ordinary activities. A 20-foot by 20-foot concrete pad provides a two-car garage on ground level. From the ground level, a stair rises on the west side of the house. The first floor has an entry area, two bedrooms and two bathrooms. A glass-enclosed stair leads to the two floors above and provides access to the roof. The second floor has the kitchen and the living area and one bath.

Every floor has a five-foot balcony that wraps around it on three sides, accessible by sliding glass doors. The wide balconies and overhangs protect the interior of the house from direct sun. The roof is an excellent observation deck and allows access to solar panels and a satellite dish. No other artificial heat or cooling is required.

Koenig proposed fabricating the parts of the house in the mainland US, then shipping them to Hawaii for assembly on site, since material costs are very high in Hawaii. Koenig knows this method to be cost-efficient despite the shipping costs: in the early 1960s, he designed a small pavilion-like retreat house that was fabricated in Los Angeles and shipped to Maui in a cargo crate. Koenig's thinking then was typically ahead of its time. 'They sent the parts by boat, trucked the crate to the site, and put the pieces up like an Erector Set.'

The Stuermer House remains in the planning stages; construction will commence when the owner retires to Hawaii.

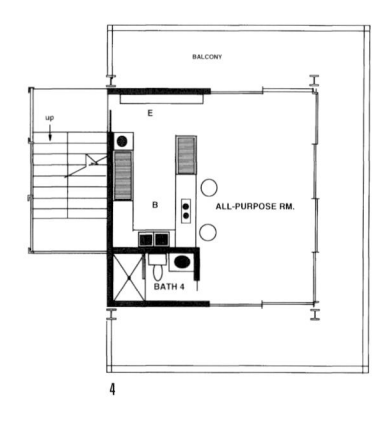

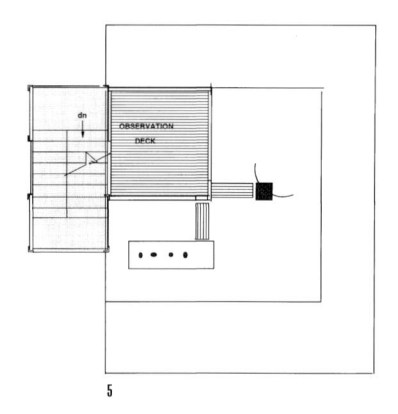

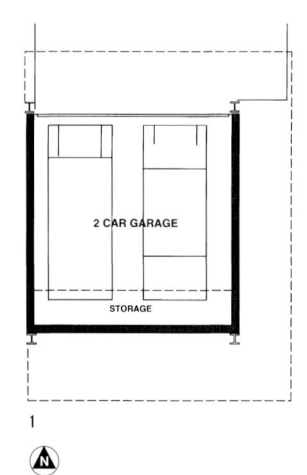

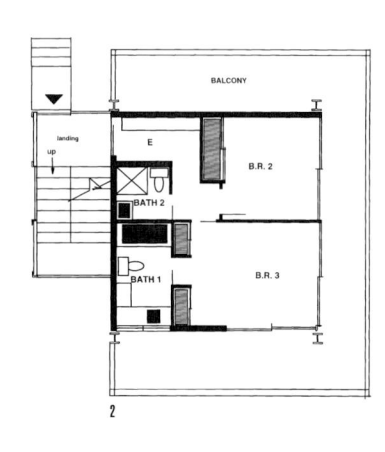

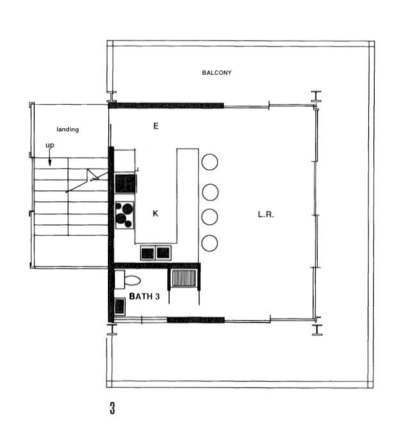

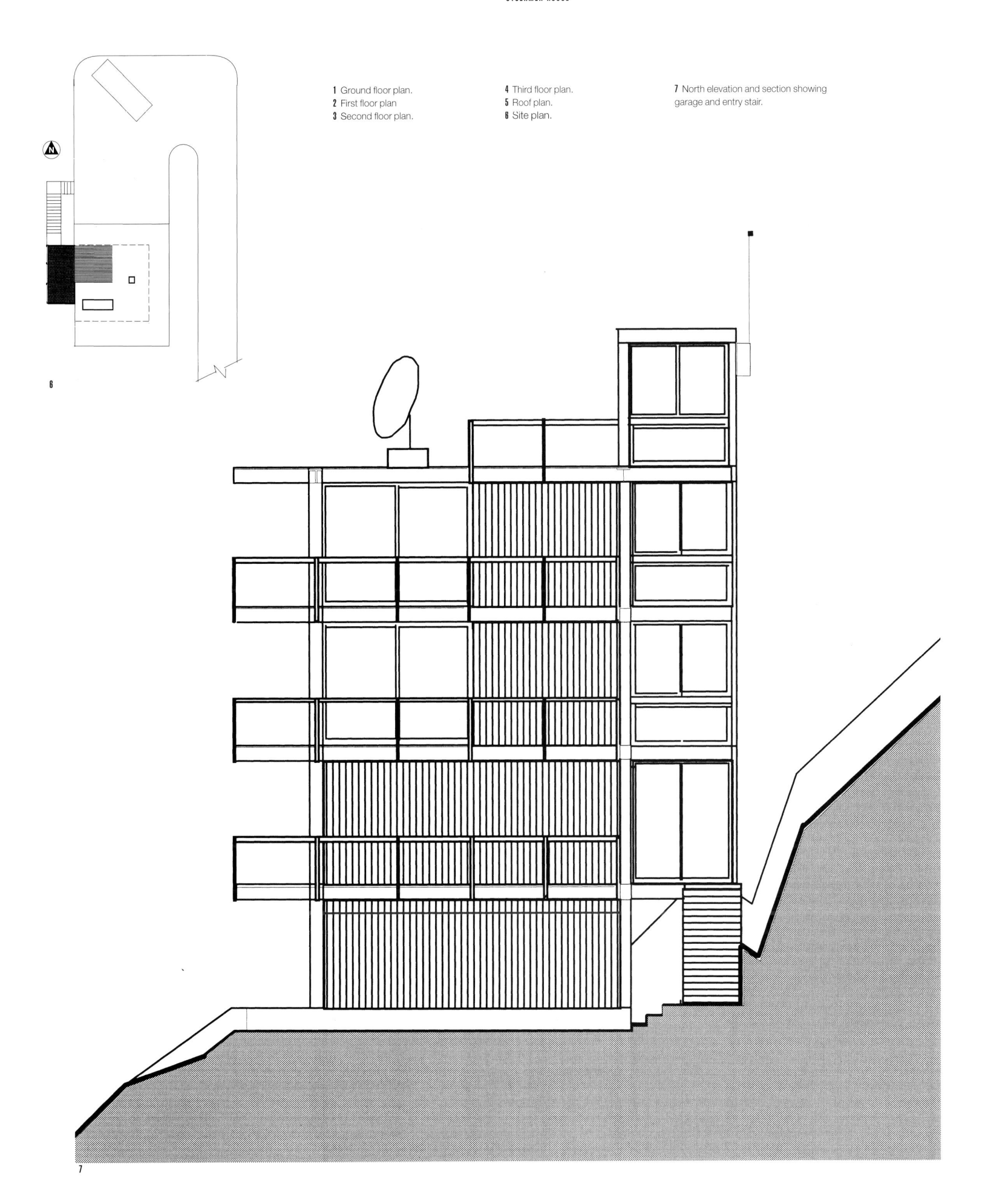

1 Ground floor plan.
2 First floor plan
3 Second floor plan.
4 Third floor plan.
5 Roof plan.
6 Site plan.
7 North elevation and section showing garage and entry stair.

KOENIG HOUSE #2

1985
Brentwood, Los Angeles, California
3,000 sq ft + 600 sq ft carport
Structural Engineer: Dimitry Vergun
Heating Engineer: George Rusher
General Contractor: Pierre Koenig
Interiors: Pierre Koenig
Landscaping: Pierre Koenig

Thirty-five years after Koenig designed his first house in Glendale, he designed and built a second house for himself in West Los Angeles. Koenig had lived in an existing house on the westside site for twenty-five years before demolishing it to build one of his own design. While living on the site he studied the movement of light and air, and his observations informed his approach to the volumetric arrangement of the living space.

Koenig believes sun, seismic forces, wind and sound must all be considered in his design. He orchestrates the movement of sunlight throughout the house so that sun penetrates the house in the morning and is kept out during the afternoon. Cool wind ventilates through a special 'wind' door on the ground floor with exhaust exiting at the top of the atrium. The carefully calibrated height of the atrium breaks the point of inflection for soundwaves and thereby avoids reverberation. All steel connections are moment connections, providing resistance to seismic forces while allowing clear spans and free use of the space. As with all Koenig's projects, the steel frame was erected in a single day.

The house steps back from the street in three graduated levels before reaching full height, mitigating its visual impact on the neighbouring one- and two-storey residences. The low volume at the front is Koenig's office, separated from the main house by an internal outdoor patio. In planning the circulation, Koenig conceived of two clear and open pathways, one for guests and one for residents. The guest enters the house from the street, without passing through any functional or ambient areas. The resident enters from the service alley and the carport at the rear of the house, through a back door at the eastern corner of the kitchen. Both pathways meet at the central atrium, and are referred to by Koenig as 'directional space'.

Although restricted on both east and west sides by neighbouring houses, the spacious interior belies the dimensions of the narrow site. The primary view is vertical and volumetric, opening towards the sky; and yet the house is essentially introspective in response to its urban setting. Though there are few openings on the sides of the house, glass doors open up the house on both north and south elevations, providing access to the patio and the back garden.

All living areas open on to the enclosed atrium, lined at the top with operable sliding glass doors. The steel stairway in the centre of the atrium rises up to a bridge between the bedroom wings on the first floor before rising again to a small roof deck. Opaque glass sliding doors close off storage areas and rooms from the central space.

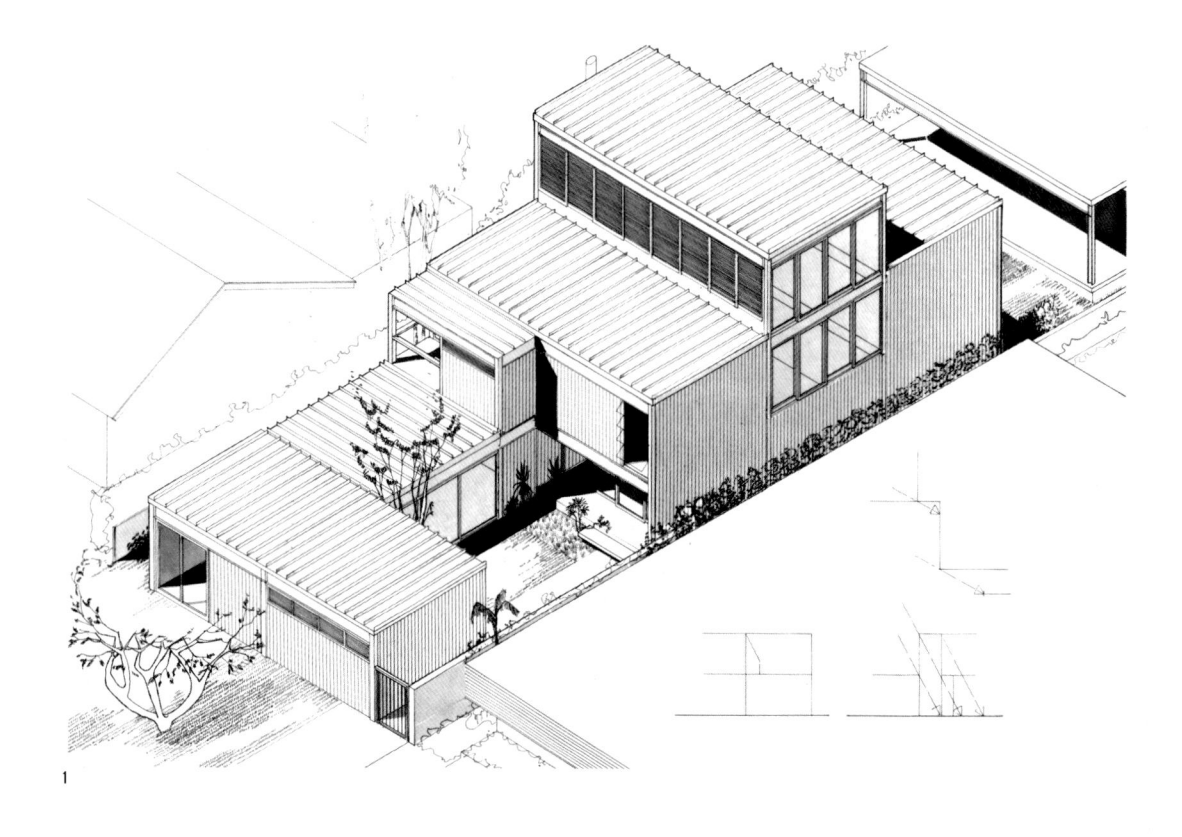

1

1 Bird's-eye view of proposed house. Diagrams, right, show angles and penetration of sunlight.

2 View of the living area from the top of the central atrium.

3 View of the house from the street.

4 View of the house from the carport.

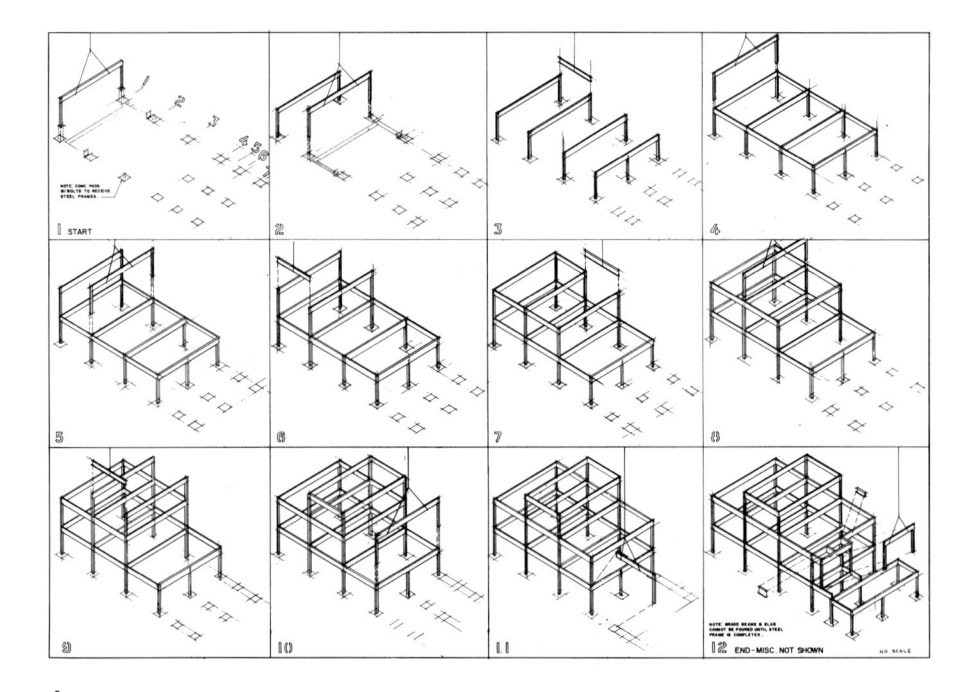

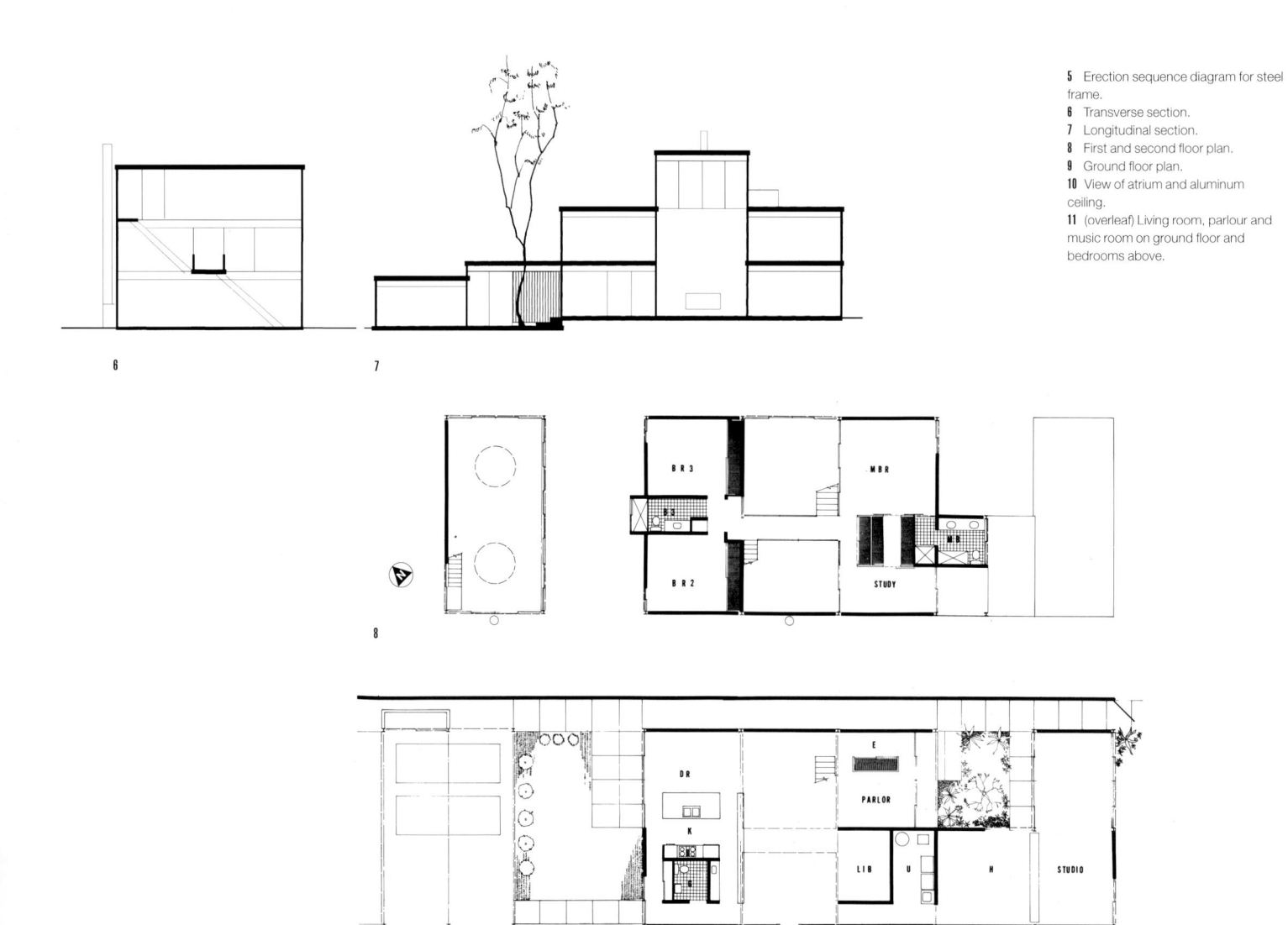

5 Erection sequence diagram for steel frame.
6 Transverse section.
7 Longitudinal section.
8 First and second floor plan.
9 Ground floor plan.
10 View of atrium and aluminum ceiling.
11 (overleaf) Living room, parlour and music room on ground floor and bedrooms above.

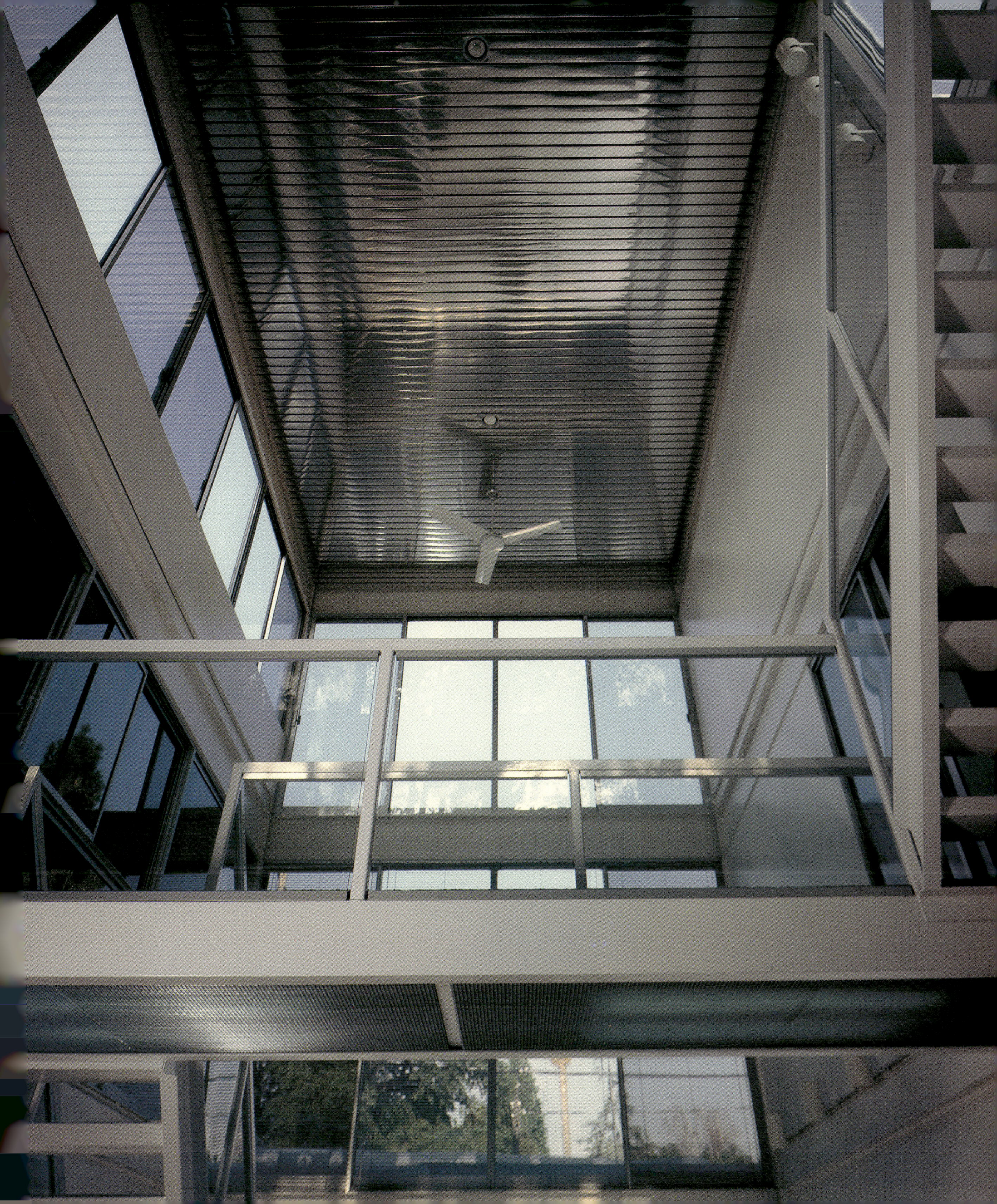

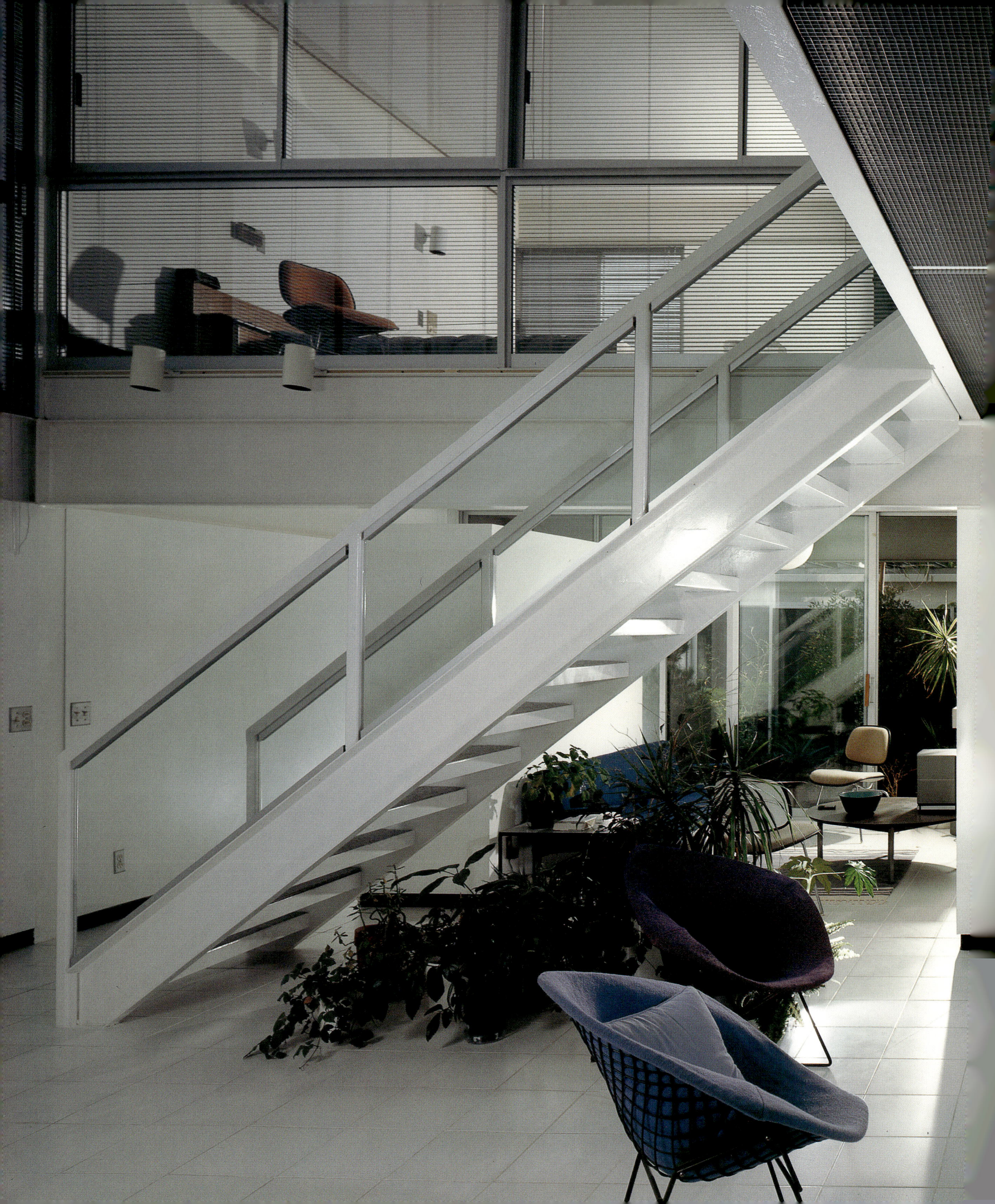

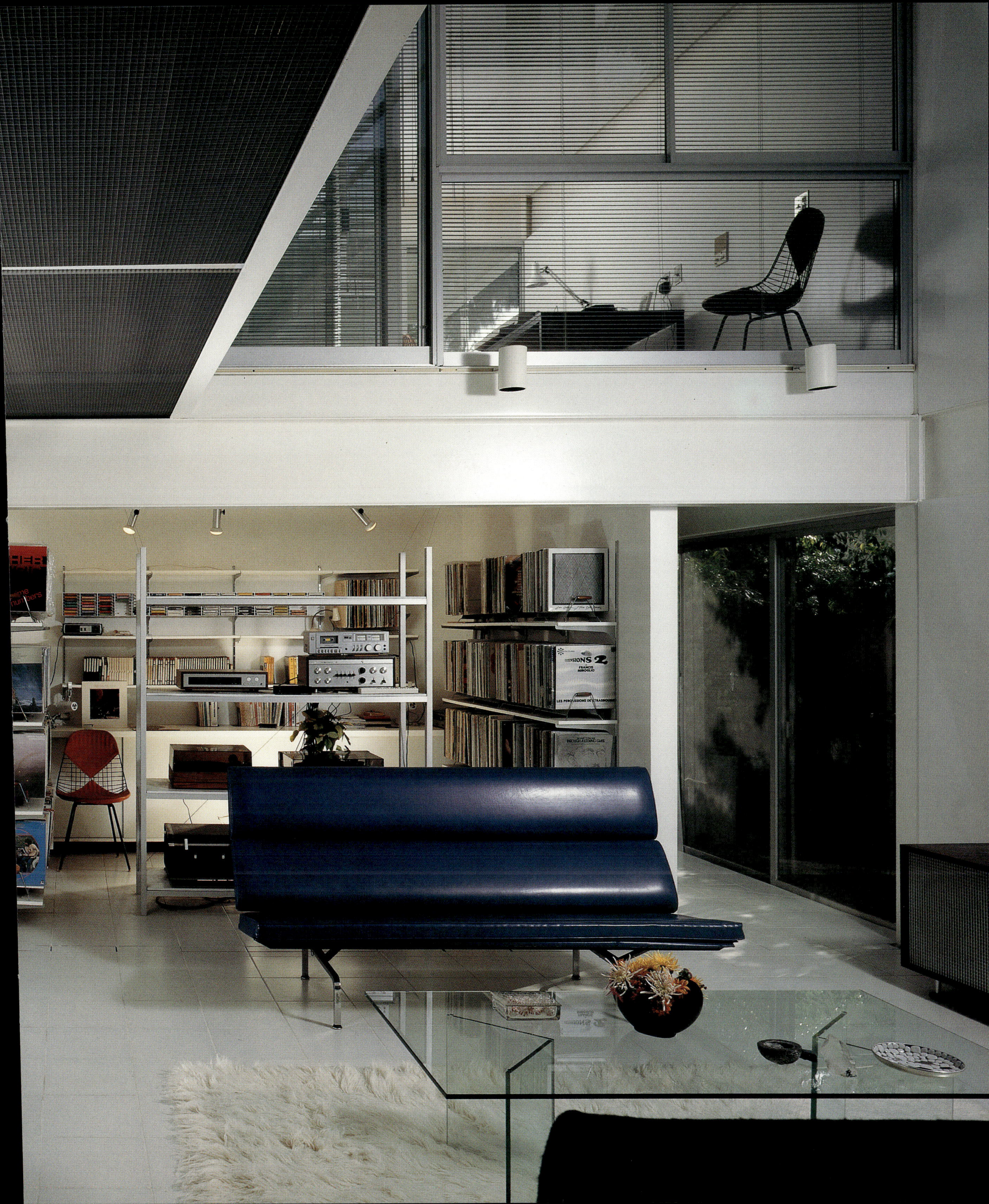

12

13

14

12 A bridge spans the space between the upstairs bedrooms. **13** The master bedroom looks on to the atrium. **14** Pierre Koenig's design studio c.1985. **15** Kitchen and eating area with adjacent living room on left.

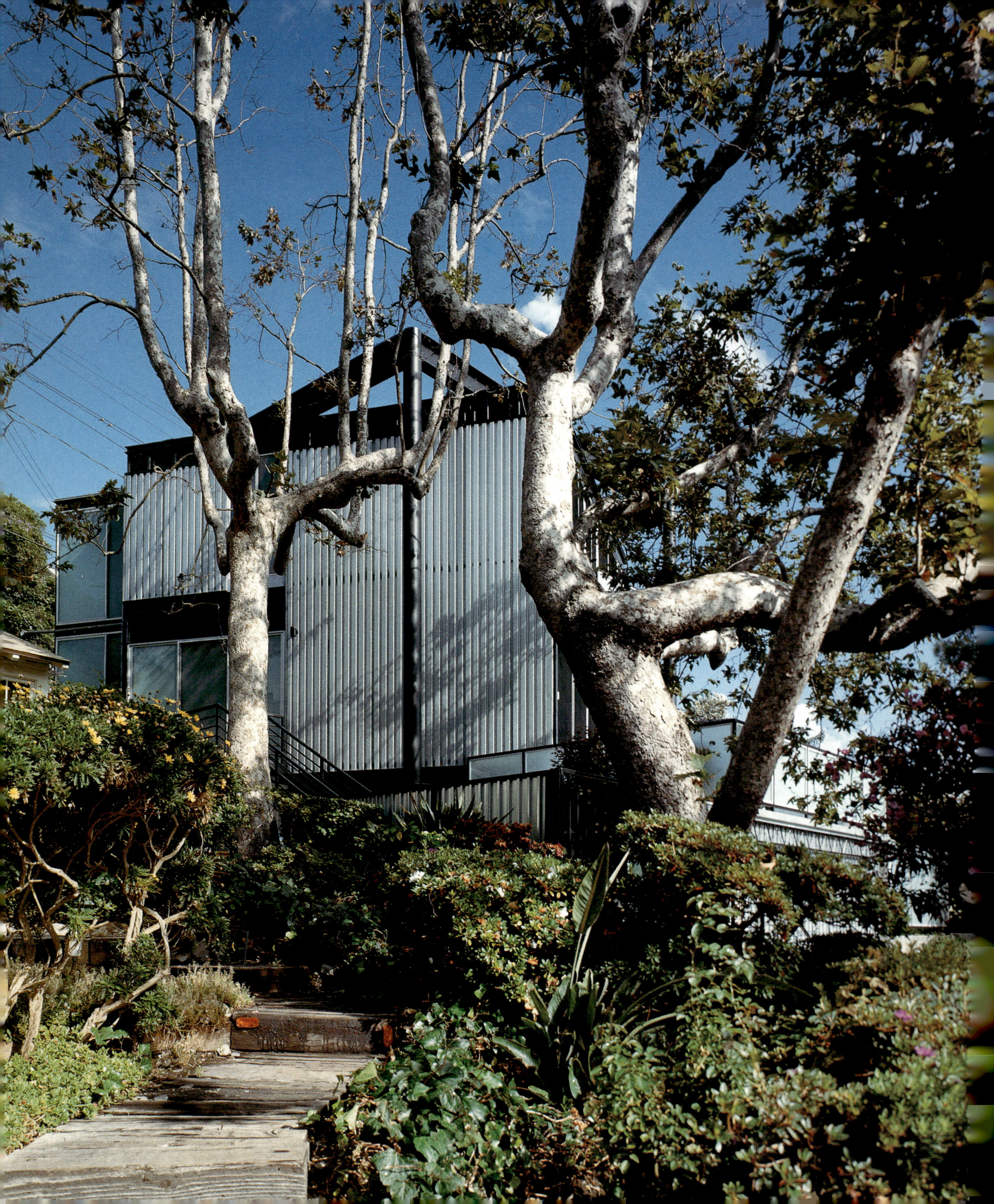

SCHWARTZ HOUSE

1994–6
Pacific Palisades, Los Angeles, California
3,100 sq ft + 400 sq ft garage
Interior Design: Joe Bavaro
Structural Engineer: Dimitry Vergun
General Contractor: R G West Corp
Landscape Consultant: Katherine Spitz Associates

The Schwartz House, built for a young professional couple, is perhaps Koenig's most 'expressive' house. Its shifted cube-within-a-cube form has a practical justification, allowing the main rooms to turn through 30 degrees to take advantage of the views towards the ocean along Santa Monica Canyon. The 'living cube' is rotated 30 degrees from the structural frame to orient the view 'down the street, rather than across the street' and to capture the breezes from the ocean. By rotating the living cube toward the south, the front elevation receives less of the low, hot, summer sun. The house is typically well-structured and rode out the powerful 1994 Northridge earthquake while still under construction without any signs of distress.

To create a level area on the sloping site, Koenig raised the two-storey steel frame one storey above street level, thereby generating space for the subterranean masonry garage. The house is disengaged from the garage by a space of two feet.

The primary steel structure rests on four concrete piles and is placed parallel to the site frontage. The secondary structure, which delineates the main building enclosure, is suspended within it. This shifting geometry results in what Koenig calls little 'bonuses' in plan, generating triangular balconies on the living and bedroom floors and allowing a virtually panoramic visual relationship with the site.

The service core forms a barrier between public and private areas and provides vertical access for all the mechanical and plumbing equipment. The bathrooms and laundry are attached to the central service core. The vocabulary of materials is familiar – galvanized profiled metal decking, unadorned steel framing, sliding glass doors and simple flat-fronted fitted furniture inside.

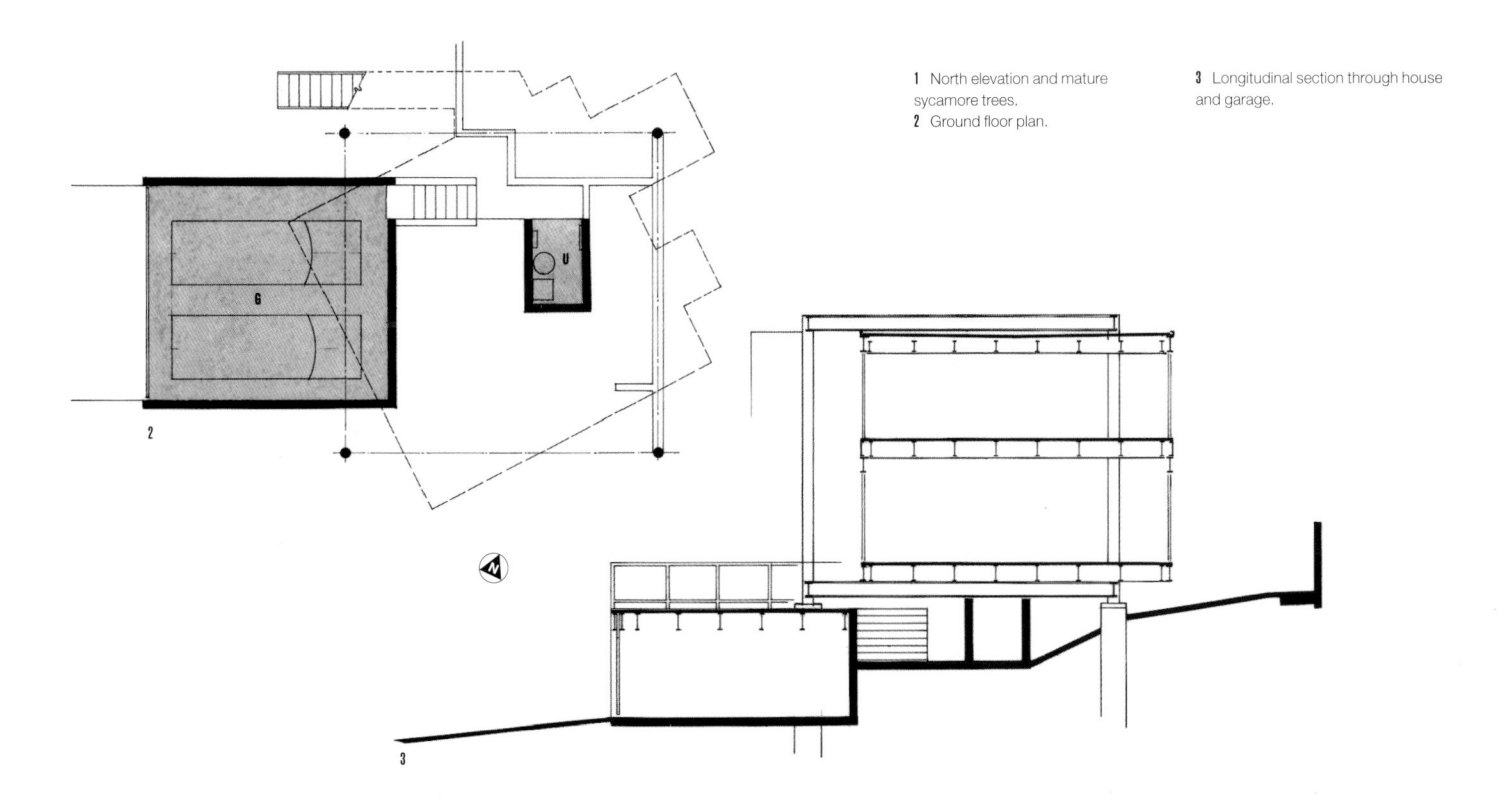

1 North elevation and mature sycamore trees.
2 Ground floor plan.
3 Longitudinal section through house and garage.

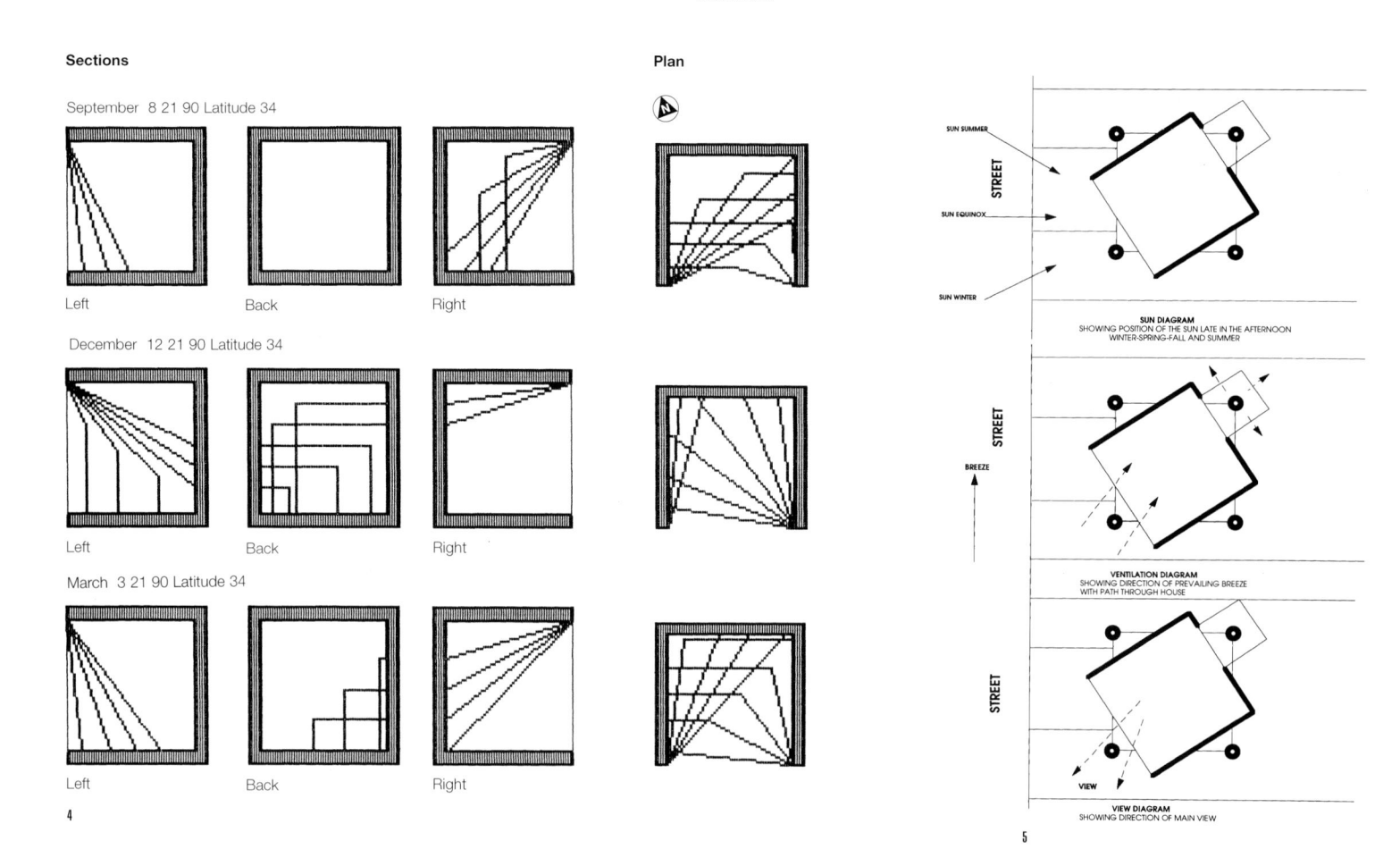

Sections

September 8 21 90 Latitude 34

Left   Back   Right

December 12 21 90 Latitude 34

Left   Back   Right

March 3 21 90 Latitude 34

Left   Back   Right

Plan

SUN DIAGRAM
SHOWING POSITION OF THE SUN LATE IN THE AFTERNOON
WINTER-SPRING-FALL AND SUMMER

VENTILATION DIAGRAM
SHOWING DIRECTION OF PREVAILING BREEZE
WITH PATH THROUGH HOUSE

VIEW DIAGRAM
SHOWING DIRECTION OF MAIN VIEW

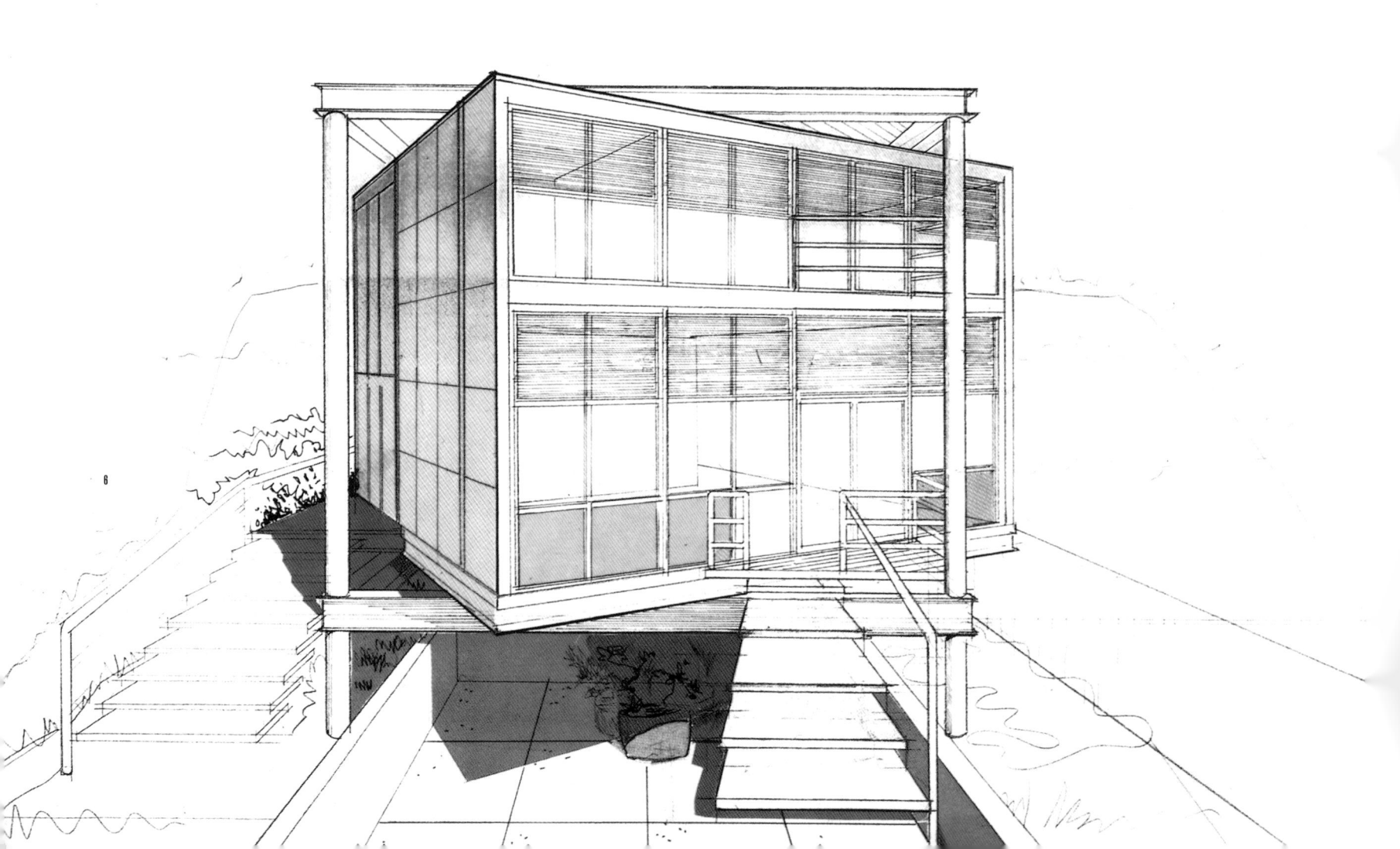

4 Computer-generated sun-angle study.

5 Three study diagrams show the sun, wind and view determinants.

6 Perspective rendering of proposed entry elevation.

7 Rear of the house with spiral stairwell.

8 Front elevation with stair to terrace above garage.
9 Entry stairway on north side of house.
10 Patio at ground level.
11 Night view of the house from the street.

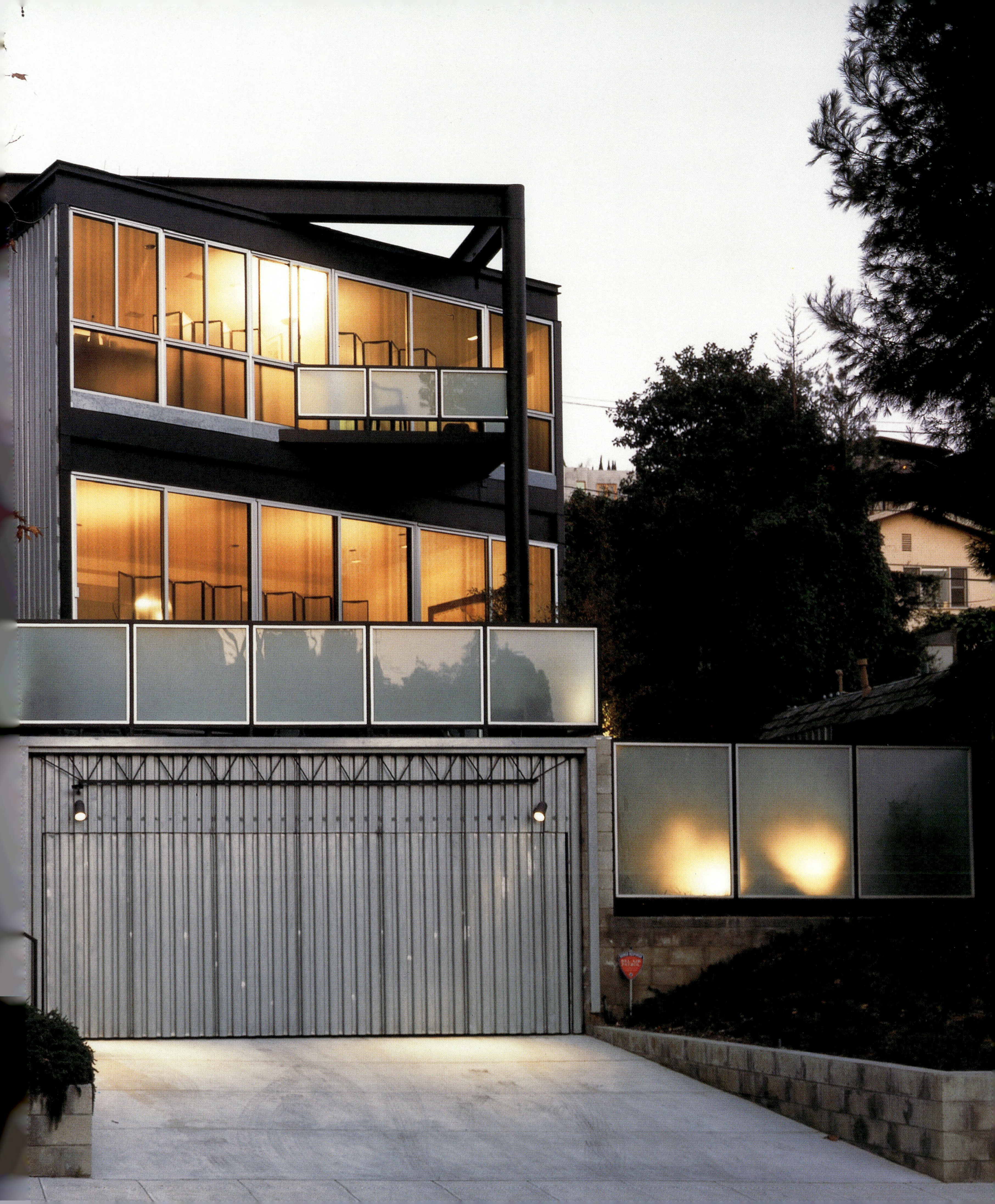

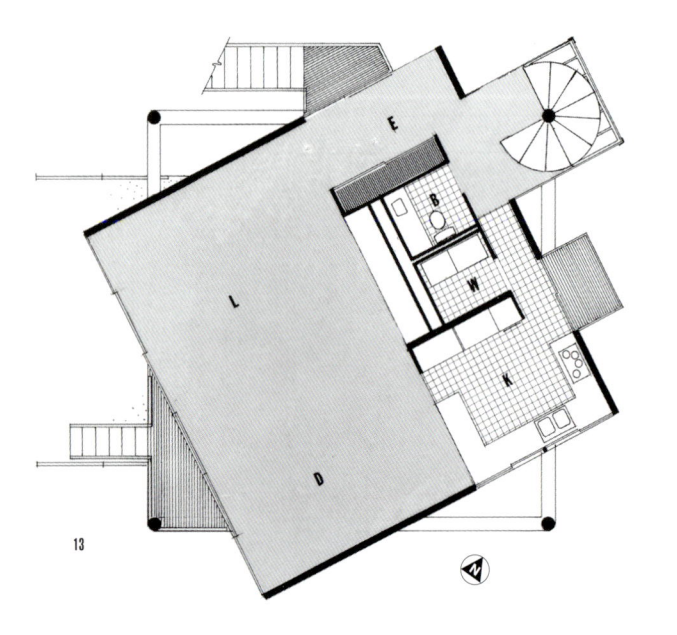

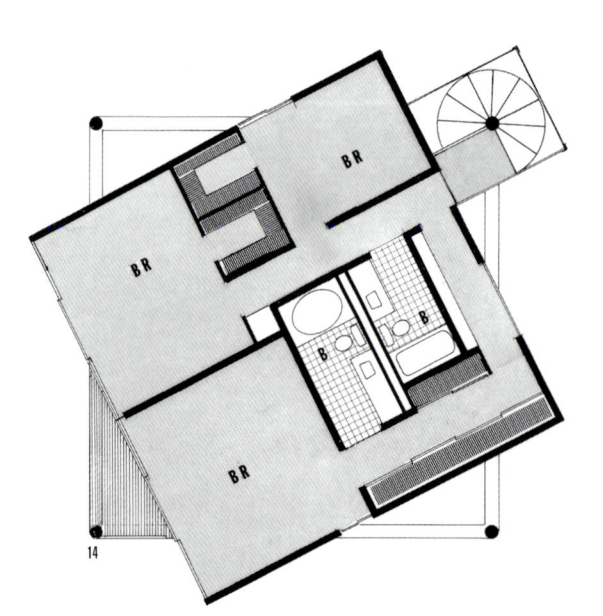

12

13

14

12 The living area includes the central core which serves on this side as a cabinet with blind doors.
13 First floor plan.
14 Second floor plan.
15 Kitchen and dining area.
16 The floor material changes around the spiral stair from wood to glass.
17 In 1996 an additional room was added under the house.
18 Additional bathroom.

LAGUNA HOUSE

1997
Laguna, California
3,000 sq ft + 600 sq ft carport
Contractor: R G West Corp

Designed for a client with an interest in the arts, this project represents a departure for Koenig: for the first time he has concerned himself with interior space that can be manipulated indeterminantly within the framework of a defined cube. In that sense it is an interesting departure for Koenig after decades of experimenting with low-cost prototypes. Within a steel-framed, cubic form, whose largest plan area is 40 feet by 35 feet, he has fitted three floors of accommodation in a free-form arrangement made possible by hanging the internal floors and partitions from the primary frame and bracing them horizontally with 'shock-absorbing' lateral restraints. The main frame is clearly expressed on the exterior of the living cube. Moment connections brace the cube in an east–west direction and diagonal bracing provides stiffness in a north–south direction.

This strategy was inspired in part by the extraordinary range of views offered by the site as Koenig describes it:

On this hillside lot, as you move up or down, the view changes: a few feet either way can produce an entirely different outlook. Here I have a three-dimensional indeterminate plan – every floor is shifted in space both vertically and horizontally relative to one another, and a different view and relationship to the sun is evoked from each situation.

The main living space, which cantilevers ten feet out from the primary enclosure, has the highest and widest view towards the ocean, and the greatest exposure to the sun. The other rooms are set back in varying degrees of shade, creating a different atmosphere in every space in the house. As Koenig says: 'Each level has its own environment. You have to go up and down short runs of stairs to achieve it, but it's worth it.' A large reflector on the roof redirects southern sunlight into the north side of the house through a large roof monitor. Solar collector panels are connected to the monitor. Fire exit doors are recessed into each side of the house, close to the property line.

The site on a bluff above the beach is a 'problem' hillside property, subject to soil erosion; this has led to a delay in obtaining permits. Previous housing in this area has proved physically unstable, but Koenig has demonstrated that the proposed structure and foundations will help to stabilize the hillside.

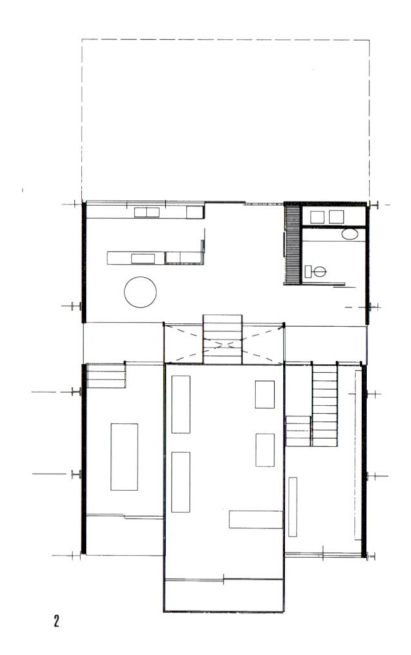

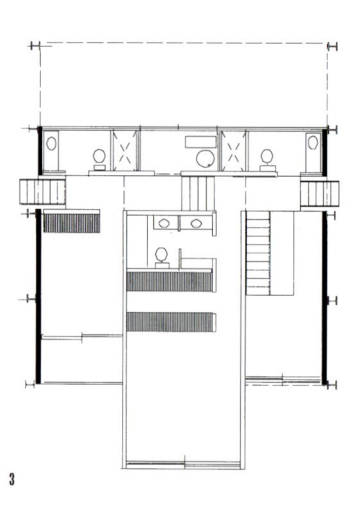

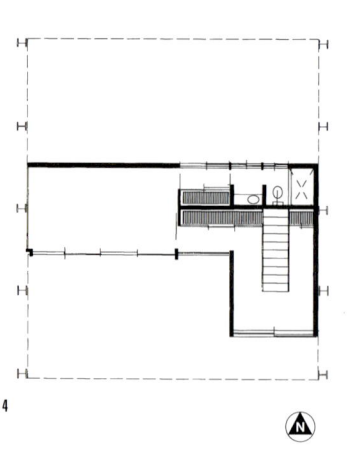

LAGUNA HOUSE

1 Living area dominates the plan by being higher and cantilevering further than any other area.   **2** Top level plan.   **3** Middle level plan.   **4** Lower level plan.   **5** Ghost drawing showing interrelationship of all planes, volumes and linear elements. The primary frame is grey, the secondary frame is red.

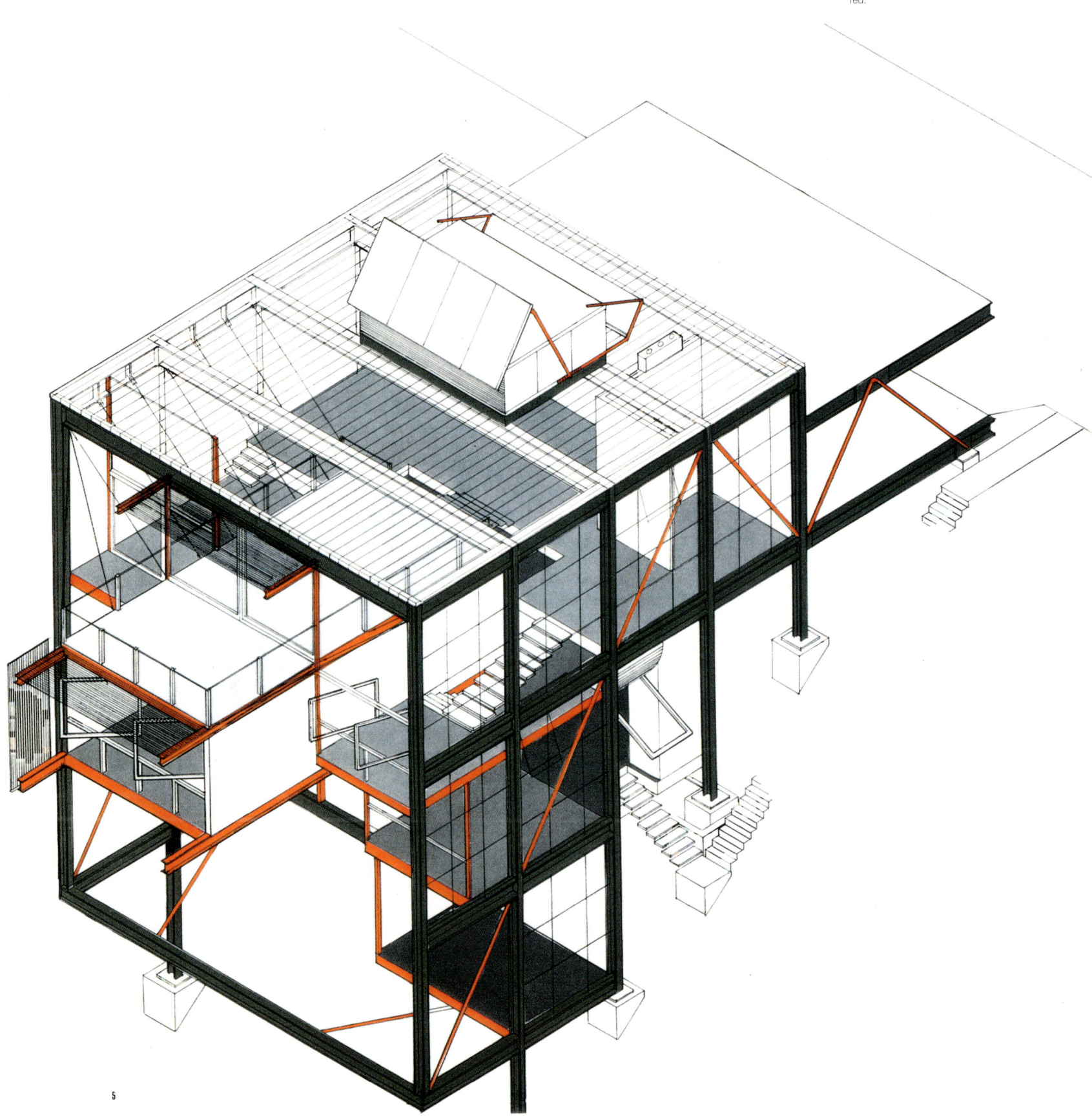

'BLUEPRINT FOR MODERN LIVING'
THE MOCA SHOW & THE MODERNIST REVIVAL

As the history of the Case Study Program shows us, even the most excellent designs for individual houses cannot, in themselves, lead to the sweeping changes required to house the majority of Americans in new ways. But as the legacy of the program suggests, innovation in housing across cultural, social, technological and economic boundaries is still urgent.
Dolores Hayden, 1989

The revolutionary ideas promoted by Arts and Architecture magazine throughout the two decades after the Second World War were again to cause tremors throughout the architectural community in the late 1980s, this time as the result of an exhibition entitled 'Blueprints for Modern Living: History and Legacy of the Case Study Houses', held in the Frank Gehry-designed Temporary Contemporary wing of the Los Angeles Museum of Contemporary Art (MOCA) from October 1989 to February 1990. The inaugural evening, coincidentally, was held on Pierre Koenig's birthday, 17 October 1989, a day that is better remembered in California for tremors of a different kind. The Loma Prieto earthquake in San Francisco, which caused devastation in the Bay Area, jolted Angelenos into a renewed awareness of the precarious toe-hold they maintain in a state, which for all its apparent virtues, spans a fault-line capable of generating momentous seismic upheavals.

Quite apart from that sharp reminder, the MOCA exhibition came during a reflective period in the city's history. The aerospace industry – which had flourished in Southern California in response to the same war that had created the materials and technology utilized by the Case Study architects – was now in serious decline. Los Angeles had grown increasingly racially diverse. Having become the western equivalent of the immigration gateway into the United States (which New York had provided on the East Coast in the previous century), Los Angeles by the end of the 1980s had developed into a baffling battleground of ethnic tensions that were soon to erupt in the riots of 1992.

The MOCA show was organized around the themes of 'day' and 'night' to contrast the 'centrality of the Case Study designers with the marginal role that design occupies today.'[1] The venue in which it was held was an ideal choice for such an ambitious undertaking, conceptualized by the curator Elizabeth Smith and the installation architects Craig Hodgetts and Ming Fung as a three-dimensional recreation of some of the best models in the Program, both realized and unbuilt. In order to engage the audience more directly, many of the exhibits were produced at full size, rather than as small-scale two-dimensional images. Judging from the reactions of the hundreds of thousands of people who visited the exhibition, and from the newspaper and international magazine reviews, the exhibition succeeded in its stated aim of providing an objective recapitulation of the successes and failures of the Case Study House Program in the light of the currents of social change then affecting the city.

The exhibition included walk-in reconstructions of Ralph Rapson's unrealized Greenbelt House – with its potential for finally allowing the Modern aesthetic to achieve a physical, rather than simply cerebral, *rapprochement* with nature – as well as Pierre Koenig's Case Study House #22. Visitors approached the dramatic replica of Case Study House #22 via a long ramp. At the top was a simulated swimming pool, made of gleaming black vinyl carefully crinkled to approximate moving water, and lit by rotating coloured lights that caused a sparkle on the house's white overhang. The house itself caused a jolt of recognition as people took advantage of the opportunity to inhabit an icon. The exhibition also displayed a range of typical furniture designs to be included in the houses such as Van Keppel-Green's indoor/outdoor lounge chairs, Charles and Ray Eames' moulded plywood furniture and a selection of kitchen appliances. The Eames House itself was included, cleverly shown sliced through in cross-section to indicate the method of its assembly from modular, industrial parts including steel framing, factory sashes, open-web steel joists and plywood sheeting.

A curving, corrugated aluminium wall – appropriately shaped in plan like the meteorological symbol for a hurricane – was employed by the exhibition

1

designers as a divider between the 'day' and 'night' themes. The daytime side of the wall had shelf-like niches cut into its thickness that presented a 'cyclorama' of objects intended to evoke the ambience of the period. Scripted with storyboards like a movie, this portion of the exhibition formed both an 'information wall' (presenting a graphic historical time-line of the period, also making use of video) and a circulation indicator, guiding visitors through a full-size replica of Ralph Rapson's unrealized Greenbelt House, with a courtyard packed with 1950s memorabilia, which captured the spirit of Rapson's original rendering. The storyboard described Ralph Rapson's prototype glowing in the sun, 'with Mom hanging up the laundry and Dad in the helicopter overhead.' On the other side of the wall, representing 'night' stood the replica of Koenig's Case Study House #22. Perched as it was at the top of a ramp, it simulated the relationship of the actual house to the city below, yet rather than the twinkling lights of Los Angeles, visitors looked out over a landscape of glowing TV monitors.

The monitors presented video-taped interviews with surviving architects involved in the Program, craftsmen associated with it, people who worked with *Arts and Architecture* magazine, and some of the clients who commissioned houses, all interspersed with other documentary material. Twenty-five wooden models of the Case Study houses, built especially for the exhibition, completed the display. Hodgetts and Fung took every opportunity to use the sizeable amount of space provided them to good advantage, and consciously set out to:

> ... capture the first-hand experiences of the architects, clients and builders alike as they struggled to define the goals of their houses, or to hurdle over long forgotten obstacles. As designers, we found meaningful parallels in their experience, which encouraged us to emulate many of the premises embodied in the Case Study projects. Installation design motifs recalled specific building elements drawn from the program, recomposed to suggest their significance to a contemporary audience.[2]

It is somewhat ironic that Hodgetts and Fung's rationale in the 'Blueprints' exhibition was to reassert principles of legibility and utility which they felt 'had become obscure or at least unfashionable in the indulgent designs of the 1980s', in a 'rebuke to the prevailing critical climate which equates architecture with overt displays of angst-ridden fastenings, iconoclastic textures and obsessive decor'.[3] The irony revolves around the fact that the very style they valorized as an antidote to this critical climate, and which the public 'consumed' as a result of the images presented at the exhibition, was itself promoted by image-master John Entenza to sell Modernism through the media. The Case Study House Program represents one of the most brilliantly conceived and consistently implemented public relations campaigns in American history that enmeshed *Arts and Architecture* magazine with the local broadcast media, national and international newspapers, manufacturers and advertisers. It is ironic also, that the comprehensiveness of the initiative made it all the more likely that it would succeed, although ultimately it was to fail.

One of the factors that was crucial in elevating the MOCA show above what might otherwise be considered as a trendy nostalgic retake of a period now wistfully believed to be the zenith of American power and prestige, was the concerted effort by the organizers to register the changes in cultural conditions that have occurred since the Case Study House Program concluded. The exhibition was significant because it did not merely present the Case Study House Program as a historical fact – and its design innovations as inanimate artefacts – but sought to regenerate the ideals it embodied in a wider social context. This was evident in an ambitious invitation given to an international group of architects to create new housing designs for the show.

The exhibition can be seen as a study of a Program which, in Elizabeth Smith's words, was 'a reflection of a certain set of assumptions and developments within culture and society at a pivotal moment in our recent history'.[4] In her introduction to the exhibition catalogue she posed the question of why the original Program had been thwarted, and why,

1 'Blueprints for Modern Living: History and Legacy of the Case Study House Program' exhibition at Los Angeles MOCA, 1989.

2 Case Study House #22 reconstructed at MOCA.

notwithstanding its final 'apartment' phase, it failed to attempt to explore multiple housing, as the competition sponsored by MOCA chose to do. She also hinted at a polemical agenda for the show by saying that, although Modernism has by now been widely slated for failing to meet its self-appointed goals of expressing the technology of the time:

> [A] belief in the potential of architecture and design to contribute positively to current social needs has resurfaced in contemporary thinking. This belief remains cautious, tempered by the awareness of the complex interdependence of economic, demographic, technological, social and cultural phenomena that shape architecture.[5]

The message ultimately was that while Modernism may have failed on several fronts, not least 'stylistically', its social aspirations must be re-evaluated in view of the continuing shortage of affordable housing. It also affirmed that the evolution of great architecture in Los Angeles, from houses for the elite by Greene and Greene, Wright, Gill, Neutra and Schindler, through the Case Study houses sponsored by John Entenza for the middle classes, must be taken forward to provide housing for all.

Pierre Koenig has offered his own perspective on the Program, its impetus and its failings:

> The major purpose was to promote Modernism. John Entenza's idea was that people would not really understand modern architecture unless they saw it, and they weren't going to see it unless it was built. The main importance of the Program was that hundreds of thousands of people went through these homes and experienced the principles they incorporated first-hand. There is a broader issue here, too, in the sense that, after the War, the housing shortage became acute, and many architects realized that it was necessary to design and build in a different way. Prefabrication and mass-production in wood, steel and aluminium of various components such as doors and windows, increased at this time; with a level of invention not evident today. There was a heightened interest in determining a process of construction, and yet the process of building houses, *en masse*, must be economical, by definition. The Case Study House Program only represented a part of what was going on, since hundreds of architects in Southern California and San Francisco were experimenting with similar ideas. John Entenza was astute enough to sense this and do something about it before anyone else did. He promoted this, but didn't start it. His talent was to promulgate ideas that many architects had at that time. My intention was to be a part of a mechanism that could produce billions of homes, like sausages or cars in a factory. In the end the programme failed because it addressed clients and architects, rather than contractors, who do 95% of all housing.[6]

While the Case Study House Program might not have revolutionized the building industry as Entenza had hoped, the wide media coverage given to it, as well as its broad public exposure through visits to individual houses, did ultimately influence public taste, easing the popular acceptance of Modernism. Builders, too, were influenced by these ideas, and houses based on open plans, relating equally to interior and exterior spaces, and reliant on the extensive use of plywood, glass and prefabricated fitted furniture and kitchens, came to symbolize a casual Californian lifestyle that the rest of America – and the world at large – could aspire to. Furthermore, the transfer from wood to steel in the Program in the early 1950s effectively short-circuited the 'Craftsman' bungalow tradition of the Bay Area, which thrived in Los Angeles prior to the First World War, and served to establish metal as an equally acceptable part of an updated regional tradition. It would be too easy to dismiss lightly the Case Study House Program as a good idea that managed to capture the buoyant optimism of the time, but which ultimately failed because industry remained unconvinced that the systems used could be economically mass-produced. Because its legacy is far too obvious, public resistance to change and a preference for cheaper alternatives must also have played a part in the failure of the Program to induce reform. What can be seen now, however, is that the interest in industrial materials and new technology begun there has gone on to generate an entirely new language, not necessarily confined to housing, which can be seen, for example, at the root of the contemporary 'High-tech' idiom that now enjoys such popular success; this is particularly true in the case of British architects such as Richard Rogers and Norman Foster who visited California as students in the early sixties and experienced Pierre Koenig's architecture at first hand. Both cite the lasting influence of the Case Study House Program on their work.

The Case Study House Program has also provided a touchstone for architects finding their way back to Modernism after what many now see as the wilderness years of Postmodernism, and other subsequent 'isms', in which style triumphed conclusively over content. Koenig identifies the MOCA show as the turning point in renewed public and critical interest in his work, but this renewal is really symptomatic of a more powerful groundswell, as he has observed:

> The show brought my projects back into consciousness. People came out of the woodwork from all over the world and told me how I had influenced them. There is a definite resurgence of interest in the Case Study period; but actually I have never considered myself to be out of the 'period'. I've been working consistently on trying to evolve, and improve things all the time. I was quite surprised when MOCA initially contacted me as if what I was doing was something out of a past age. Younger people want to know what happened with that Program. Like John Entenza, the museum curator Elizabeth Smith had a flash, perceived an idea, put two and two together, and it turned out to be the most successful show they ever had, and might ever have. Almost a million people saw it. It was the first time that MOCA had staged an architecture exhibition like that, and its ramifications have rippled all over the world. It was an incredible show: it was reviewed in periodicals in almost every language. I think Entenza would have been happy, had he lived to see it. It was the culmination of everything he had set out to achieve.

Koenig has become a beacon for the younger generation of new Modernists. They come in many guises, but all share a belief in the efficacy of space, its articulation and processional arrangement, as a crucial part of the architectural experience. In Koenig's recent projects he has been given the means for further spatial exploration, as more substantial clients continue to seek him out. Having already refined the ideal set of dimensions and the most efficient construction sequence, he has now been offered the opportunity to move to the next level of inquiry and is doing so with his customary zeal and thoroughness. Koenig's formal and structural language is an inspiration to those dedicated to a renewed investigation of Modernism. For him, the ineffable quality of what is contained takes equal precedence to the container.

The Schwartz and Laguna houses, Koenig's latest projects, are notable in this regard as attempts to explore spatial arrangement as well as the maximal limits of a designed system at this point on the historical helix. They are described by Koenig as attempts 'to do something different', to present himself with a new challenge because he has always sought to move forward.

The most important lesson that Pierre Koenig offers to young architects today, as the pendulum swings toward social and environmental consciousness in architecture once again, is the power of perseverance as an alternative to the ethos of instant gratification, which now prevails. The seemingly limitless range of invention that he has shown to be possible within a perpetuating constructional system has offered the prospect of another, more substantial and reflective way, which many may decide to explore because of him.

3 Pierre Koenig, Schwartz House, 1996.

PIERRE KOENIG

E-mail: pfkoenig@mizar.usc.edu
Website:http://www.-rcf.usc.edu/~pfkoenig/

Born in San Francisco, 17 October 1925.

Attended University of Utah, School of Engineering, 1943.

Flash Ranging Observer, US Army, 1943–6 (served in England, France and Germany). Awarded three battle stars.

Attended Pasadena City College, 1946–8.

Attended University of Southern California (USC), 1948–52.

Designed and built first exposed steel and glass house, Glendale, California, 1950.

Started own architectural practice prior to graduation, 1950.

Awarded Bachelor of Architecture from USC, 1952.

Appointed to Faculty, Department of Architecture, USC, 1964.

Assistant Research Technician, Southern California Counseling Center, 1964–6.

Granted tenure and appointed Associate Professor, Department of Architecture, USC, 1968.

Assistant Director, Undergraduate Studies, 1969–72, Institute of Building Research, USC; Konrad Wachsmann, Director.

Elected to College of Fellows, American Institute of Architects (AIA), 1971.

Director, Human and Land Resources Project (architecture and planning programme to assist minority group enterprises in the West), 1972–8.

Director, Comprehensive Planning Program for Chemehuevi Indian Reservation, 1972–8.

Director, undergraduate Building Science Program, School of Architecture, USC, 1983–present. Advisor to Building Science graduate programme.

'Blueprints for Modern Living, History and Legacy of the Case Study House Program, 1945 to 1966', major exhibition at Museum of Contemporary Art (MOCA), Los Angeles, 1989–90. Full-size, walk-through model of Case Study House #22 constructed in Temporary Contemporary Building.

'Wall to Wall', six-part BBC television special, 1994, about materials used in buildings throughout history. Episode six, 'Steel and Glass', featured three buildings by Koenig, with interviews and commentaries.

Appointed full Professor, Department of Architecture, USC, 1996.

Visiting lecturer at various institutions, including Yale University, University of California at Los Angeles, Pratt Institute, Harvard University, University of Texas at Austin, LA County Center Library, California State Polytechnic University at Pomona, California State Polytechnic at San Luis Obispo, Los Angeles County Museum of Art, Pacific Design Center, Art Center College, Southern California Institute of Architecture, Woodbury College, San Francisco Museum of Modern Art, Los Angeles Museum of Contemporary Art, Arizona State University at Tempe, and City College of New York.

Chronological List of Projects

1950
Koenig House #1
Glendale, CA

1953
Lamel House
Glendale, CA

Squire House
La Cañada, CA

Scott House
Tujunga, CA

1957
Burwash House
Tujunga, CA

1958
Radio Station KYOR
Blythe, CA

Metcalf House
Silverlake, Los Angeles, CA

1959
Bailey House (CSH #21)
Hollywood, Los Angeles, CA

1960
Stahl House (CSH #22)
Hollywood, Los Angeles, CA

Seidel House
Brentwood, Los Angeles, CA

1961
Beidelman House
Los Angeles, CA

Seidel Beach House
Malibu, CA

Willheim House
Brentwood, Los Angeles, CA

St Jean Prefab Tract
St Jean, Quebec, Canada

1962
Johnson House
Carmel Valley, CA

Oberman House
Palos Verdes, CA

Bethlehem Steel Co Pavilion

1963
Iwata House
Monterey Park, CA

Mosque
Hollywood, Los Angeles, CA

Beagles House
Pacific Palisades, CA

1966
EEI Factory & Showroom
El Segundo, CA

1970
West House
Vallejo (Carquinez Heights), CA

1973
Franklyln Medical Building
West Hollywood, CA

1976
Chemehuevi Prefab Tract
Havasu Lake, CA

1979
Burton Pole House
Malibu, CA

1981
Franklyn Dinner Club
Thousand Oaks, CA

1983
Gantert House
Hollywood, Los Angeles, CA

1984
Rollé Addition I
Brentwood, Los Angeles, CA

Stuermer House
Kaneohe Bay, Oahu, HI

1985
Koenig House #2
Brentwood, Los Angeles, CA

1989
Riebe Addition
(Johnson House)
Carmel Valley, CA

1994
Rollé Addition II
Brentwood, Los Angeles, CA

1996
Schwartz House
Santa Monica, CA

1997
Laguna House,
Laguna, CA

Professional Affiliations

Chairman
AIA Education Committee

Member
AIA Awards Committee

Member
AIA Education Committee

Member
California State Board of Architectural Examiners

Member
AIA 84/84 Committee

Research Assistant
Southern California Counseling Center

Member
ACLU Committee for the Investigation of the Century City Riots

Member
Committee to Save San Francisco Bay

Member
AIA Membership Committee

Member
AIA Library Committee

Honorary Member
LA Conservancy

Honorary Member
Society of Architectural Historians

AWARDS/EXHIBITIONS

Awards

1957
São Paulo Bienale Exhibition Award, São Paulo, Brazil

AIA–*House and Home* magazine Award

Architectural League of New York

1959
AIA–*Sunset* magazine Honor Award

Western Construction Honor Award

1960
AIA–*House and Home* magazine Award

1961–2
AIA–*Sunset* magazine Award

1962
AIA–*House and Home* magazine Award

1963
AIA–*House and Home* magazine Award

AISC Award, American Institute of Iron and Steel Award

1964
Best Exhibition Building, Portland, Oregon

Los Angeles Grand Prix

1967
AIA–Los Angeles Fiesta Award

36 Best Buildings in Los Angeles since 1945 Award

1983
AIA 200/2000 Award

1984
AIA Olympic Architect Award

1989
Los Angeles Department of Cultural Affairs Award

1996
AIA 100 Architects/100 Years

AIACC 25 Year Award for Excellence in Design

AIACC Maybeck Award for Outstanding Lifelong Achievement in Architectural Design

1998
Star of Design for Lifetime Achievement Award in Architecture, Pacific Design Center

Distinguished Alumni, USC School of Architecture

Distinguished Professor of Architecture, USC

Exhibitions

1957
São Paulo Bienale Exhibition, São Paulo, Brazil, (photo panels of Lamel House)

Architectural League, New York (Koenig House 1 and Lamel House)

1959
'Prize Winning Western Home Photos and Plans', Bullock's, Los Angeles, CA

1960
Architectural Gallery, The Los Angeles Building Center, Los Angeles, CA

1962
Building Exhibition, National Association of Home Builders Convention, Chicago, IL (Case Study Houses #21 and #22)

The Gallery, School of Architecture, Yale University, New Haven, CT (one-man exhibition: Koenig House #1, Lamel House, Case Study Houses #21 and #22)

1962–4
American Federation of Arts, New York, Traveling Exhibition (Case Study Houses #21 and #22); shown in sixteen cities across the USA

1963–4
The Bethlehem Steel Traveling Architectural Exhibition, USA nationwide

1964
'Environment USA', Museum of Modern Art, New York, NY (Case Study Houses #21 and #22)

1965
Museum of Modern Art, New York, NY (in the permanent collection of architecture)

Fisher Gallery, USC, Los Angeles, CA (Case Study Houses #21 and #22)

'Architecture in Southern California', Los Angeles Museum of Science and Industry, Los Angeles, CA

'Twentieth Century House', Museum of Modern Art, New York, NY

1967
California State College Architectural Exhibition, Los Angeles, CA

Santa Monica City College, Santa Monica, CA

1968
Agha Khan Architecture Collection, Harvard University, Cambridge, MA (Mosque drawing in permanent collection)

1972
Art Gallery, UCLA, Los Angeles, CA (Retrospective exhibition)

1983
'Architecture and Industry', Centre Georges Pompidou, Paris, France (Case Study Houses #21 and #22)

1984
'Olympic Architects', Museum of Science and Industry, Los Angeles, CA

1985
'Technology in Architecture', Museum of Science and Industry, Los Angeles, CA (permanent exhibition: two wind-derived forms from the wind tunnel, a heliodon used in the Natural Forces lab, and a full-size steel detail model from Koenig House #2)

'High Style, Twentieth Century American Design', Whitney Museum of American Art, New York, NY

1986
Arizona State University, Tempe, AZ (one-man exhibition, comprehensive retrospective)

Max Protetch Gallery, New York, NY (Koenig House #2)

1988
Fifth Alumni Exhibition, University of Southern California Architecture, Lindhurst Gallery, USC, Los Angeles, CA

1989
California State Polytechnic University at Pomona, CA

1989–90
'Blueprints for Modern Living, History and Legacy of the Case Study House Program', Temporary Contemporary Building, MOCA, Los Angeles, CA (full-size, walk-through model of Case Study House #22; $1/4$ in model of Case Study House #21; drawings, articles and videos)

1991
Pomona, CA (half-size model, smaller models and drawings of Case Study House #21, constructed by California State Polytechnic University students)

'Site Work, Architecture since Early Modernism', Photographers' Gallery, London, UK (selected works, 1950–85)

'American Design of the 50s', Harvard University, Cambridge, MA

'Master Architects and Designers', San Juan Capistrano Art Museum, CA (Case Study Houses #21 and #22)

1992
'Site Work, Architecture Since Early Modernism', Cambridge/Eastern Region Centre for Architecture, Cambridge, England (Case Study House #22)

Rendering of Case Study House #22, permanent display, Avery Museum, Columbia University, New York, NY; also exhibited in UK at Ikon Gallery, Birmingham; Orchard Gallery, Derry; Impressions Gallery, York

1992–3
'Koenig Houses #1 and #2 and Case Study House #22', Salon International de l'Architecture, Milan, Italy and Los Angeles, CA

Friends of the Los Angeles Public Library History Department, Bradbury Building Centennial, Bradbury Building, Los Angeles, CA (Case Study Houses #21 and #22)

1993
'On The Move', Santa Monica Art Center, Santa Monica, CA (Koenig House #2)

1994
'100 Architects, 100 years', AIA National Convention, Convention Center, Los Angeles, CA (Koenig House #2)

1995
'Case Study Houses #21 and #22', Bluher Gallerie, Cologne, Germany

'100 Architects, 100 years', AIA–Westweek, Pacific Design Center, West Hollywood, CA

'Steel Houses', RIBA Heinz Gallery, London, UK

1996
'To View from Here. Art Based on Architecture: Pierre Koenig', Art Gallery of Hamilton, Ontario, Canada

Craig Krull Gallery, Santa Monica, CA

25 Year Award and 1996 Maybeck Award, AIACC headquarters, Sacramento, CA

Sixth Venice Biennale, Venice, Italy

1997
Architecture Exhibit, Academy of Building Arts, Vienna, Austria

Hammer Gallery, Los Angeles, CA

'Architecture of Los Angeles', Galleria Sozzani, Milan, Italy

1998
'LA Obscura: The Architectural Photography of Julius Shulman', Fisher Gallery, USC, Los Angeles, CA

1998–2001
'End of the Century, One Hundred Years of Architecture', Tokyo, Japan; Mexico City, Mexico; São Paulo, Brazil; Los Angeles, CA; New York, NY

Select Bibliography

Cochrane, Peggy, *Koenig* (Andover/Detroit: St James Press, 1988)

Ford, Edward R, *Details of Modern Architecture* (Cambridge, MA: MIT Press, 1996)

Gebhard, David and Winter, Robert, *Los Angeles: An Architectural Guide* (Layton, UT: Gibbs-Smith, 1994)

Gebhard, David and Winter, Robert, *Architecture in Los Angeles: A Complete Guide* (Santa Monica, CA: Peregrine Smith Books, 1985)

Gebhard, David and Winter, Robert, *A Guide to Architecture in Southern California* (Los Angeles: The Los Angeles County Museum of Art, 1965)

Gleye, Paul and the Los Angeles Conservancy, *The Architecture of Los Angeles*, (Los Angeles: Rosebud Books, 1981)

Goldstein, Barbara, *Arts & Architecture, The Entenza Years* (Cambridge, MA: MIT Press, 1990)

Jackson, Lesley, *Contemporary* (London: Phaidon Press, 1994)

Jackson, Neil, *The Modern Steel House* (London: E & FN Spon, Van Nostrand Reinhold, 1996)

Jones, A Quincy and Emmons, Frederick, *Builders' Homes* (New York: Van Nostrand Reinhold, 1962)

Knowles, Ralph, *Energy and Form* (Cambridge, MA: MIT Press, 1974)

Mathews, Kevin, *The Great Buildings Collection. A Designers Library of Architecture on CD-ROM* (New York: Van Nostrand Reinhold, 1994)

McCoy, Esther, *The Case Study Houses, 1945–1962* (Santa Monica, CA: Hennessey & Ingalls Inc, 1978)

McCoy, Esther, *High Styles: Twentieth-Century American Design* (Park City, UT: Summit Books, 1985)

McCoy, Esther, *Modern California Houses, Case Study Houses 1945–1962* (New York: Van Nostrand Reinhold, 1962)

McCoy, Esther and Goldstein, Barbara, *Guide to US Architecture 1940–80* (Santa Monica, CA: Arts and Architecture Press, 1982–3)

Morgan, Ann Lee (ed.), *Contemporary Architects* (Andover/Detroit: St James Press, 1988)

Morrow Ford, Katherine and Creighton, Thomas H, *Designs for Living* (New York: Van Nostrand Reinhold, 1955)

National Design Center, *Design in Steel*, (AISC, 1963)

Odenhausen, Helmuth, *Einfamilienhause in Stahlbauweise* (Düsseldorf, 1961)

Priest, Margaret, *To View From Here* (Ontario: Hamilton, 1996)

Rosa, Joseph, *A Constructed View, the Architectural Photography of Julius Shulman* (New York: Rizzoli, 1994)

Rouillard, Dominique, *Building the Slope* (Santa Monica, CA: Arts & Architecture Press, 1987)

Site Work (London, UK: Photographers' Gallery, 1991)

Smith, Elizabeth, *Blueprints for Modern Living, History and Legacy of the Case Study Houses* (Cambridge, MA: MIT Press, 1989)

Steele, James, *Los Angeles Architecture: The Contemporary Condition* (London: Phaidon, 1993)

Weisskamp, Herbert, *Beautiful Homes and Gardens in California* (Stuttgart: Verlag Gerd Hatje, 1964)

Journals, Magazines & Newspapers

1953 February
Living for Young Homemakers, 'The Pioneering Urge in Action', by Edith Brazwell Evans, pp68–9

1953 October
Arts & Architecture, 'Steel Frame House by Pierre Koenig, Designer', pp24–5

1954 January
Arts & Architecture, 'Small House by Pierre Koenig, Designer', pp25

1954 September
Arts & Architecture, 'Patio House by Pierre Koenig, Designer', p24

1955 May/June
Aujourd'hui, Vol 3, 'Equipment de l'Habitation', pp60–61

1955 June
Arts & Architecture, 'Steel Frame House Designed by Pierre Koenig', by Pierre Koenig, pp22–3

1955 September
San Francisco Examiner, Modern Living, 'There May be a Steel House', by Barbara East

1955 December
Arts & Architecture, 'Hilltop House by Pierre Koenig', by Pierre Koenig, pp24, 34

House and Home, 'The New Language of Steel', pp144–5

1956 February
Arts & Architecture, 'Homes of the Future', pp6–7

Living for Young Homemakers, 'An Economical House Results From an Adventurous Spirit' pp102–3

1956 April
Arts & Architecture, 'Steel House by Pierre Koenig', by Pierre Koenig, pp18–19

Mobil + Decoration, Vol 4, 'Form in Gefahr', p189

Newsweek Magazine, 'I Built This House Because', pp50–1

Time Magazine, 'I Built This House Because', pp74–5

1956 May
Mobil + Decoration, Vol 5, Cover photograph

1956 June
House and Home, 'Will Metal Take Over?', p169

1956 October
House and Home, 'Glamorous Steel House of Stock Parts', pp208–9

1957 March
Arts & Architecture, 'Low-Cost Production House', by Pierre Koenig, pp24–5

1957 May
Architectural Review, 'Genetrix: Pierre Koenig 32', p386

1957 July
LA Times, 'What I believe, A Statement of Principle by Pierre Koenig', by Esther McCoy

1959 February
Arts & Architecture 'Announcement of Completion of CSH No. 21 by Pierre Koenig' by John Entenza and Pierre Koenig, pp18–25, 30

1960 July
LA Examiner, Pictorial Living 'Milestone on a Hilltop', pp1, 2, 18–20, 22

Zodiac, Vol 5: 'Pierre Koenig' by Esther McCoy, pp156–62

1960 December
Bauen – Wohnen 'Wasser, Stahl und Glas' by Wolfgang Wieser, pp428–35

1975
Perspecta 15, Yale Papers on Architecture 'Backgrounds For An American Architecture: Arts & Architecture Case Study Houses' by Esther McCoy, pp54–73

1987 May
Los Angeles Magazine 'Homes of the Fabulous '50s' by Sam Hall Kaplan, pp100–9

1989 September
L.A. Style 'Real Homes for Real People' by Michael Webb, pp176–81

1989 October
The Contemporary (MOCA) issue devoted to 'Blueprints for Modern Living'

1989 November
Metropolis 'Poetry in Steel' by Michael Webb, pp46–51

1990 March
Art in America 'Utopia in the Suburbs' by Douglas R Suisman, pp184–94

Domus 'CSH No. 21 by Pierre Koenig' and 'CSH No. 22 by Pierre Koenig' by Jurg Lang, pp80–4

1990 July
Los Angeles Magazine 'Back to Camelot' by Paddy Calistro, pp120–8

1993 May
Progressive Architecture 'An Architect for Better Living', interview with Pierre Koenig by Abby Bussel, pp113–4

Progressive Architecture 'The Case Study Houses, Then and Now' by Abby Bussel, pp110–2

1993 June
Architectural Review 'Metal Framed Houses in Los Angeles' by Neil Jackson, pp66–8, 71–6

1994 November
RIBA Journal 'Another Splash, New House by Pierre Koenig' by Neil Jackson, pp48–53

1994 December
Global Architecture Houses, 44, 'Pierre Koenig', pp84–97

1995 April/May
Elle Decor 'Study in Steel: Pierre Koenig's Student Experiment Becomes a Classic' by Joseph Giovannini, pp162–4

1997 August
A+U (Architecture and Urbanism) article by Ken Tadashi Oshima, pp3–9

1997 December
54 Houses (Global Architecture), pp8–9, 26–8, 30–5

1998 January
Archalendar, University of Arizona

New York Times 'A Modernist Jewel, Rescued from Disgrace', by Joseph Giovanni

Los Angeles Times Magazine 'Second Time Around' by Stacie Stukin, p23

MAMA, Magazine for modern arkitecktur

Miami Herald 'A New Setting Shows Different Faces of Modernist Jewel', by Joseph Giovannini

Knoxsville Herald 'Riebe Carmel Valley House' by Joseph Giovannini

1998 February
Monterey Herald, Home and Garden 'Saving a Modernist Jewel' by Joseph Giovinnini

USC Trojan Family Magazine 'The Shulman Eye' p43

Toronto Globe 'When It's time to Film, a House Can Be a Star' by Joseph Giovannini

1998 March
USC Chronicle 'Picturing the Good Life' by Ed Newton, p4

Los Angeles Times, Calendar Weekend 'The Architectural Photography of Julius Shulman' by Booth Moore

Los Angeles Times, Calendar Weekend 'Obscura Explores Myths of LA Lifestyle' by Nicolai Ouroussoff

Westweek 98 Catalogue 'Pierre Koenig FAIA, Lifetime Achievement in Architecture', p37

Los Angeles Times Homes, Mossier, Deasy and Doe, p19

Society of Architectural Historians News 'Dialogues with Design' by Pierre Koenig and Neil Jackson, p3

1998 April
Space and Society 'Architectural Photography', by Peter Gössel

1998 July
Harpers Bazaar 'The Houses to Have in Hollywood' by Allison Silver, pp122–141

Los Angeles Times 'Designing LA Steel Life' by Connie Koenenn

Other media

1952
High Sierra, environmental motion picture by George Foy and Pierre Koenig

1959
Appearance on Kona TV, Honolulu, to receive Honor Award for Case Study House #21

1960
Constructing CSH # 22 amateur 8mm motion picture by R Stahl

Interview with Marjorie Trumbull, KRON TV, San Francisco, CA

Appearance on 'The Dorothy Gardner Show', KTLA

Constructing CSH No. 22 motion picture by Bethlehem Steel

1962
'Current Work' audio cassette lecture, San Fernando Valley Chapter, CA

1972
'Current Work' audio cassette lecture, Southern California Chapter, AIA

1973
Gathering in the Desert, 16mm motion picture by Koenig for Chemehuevi Program (USC), Channel 28, KCET TV

1988
'Metal Frame Buildings' audio cassette presentation, California Polytechnic University at Pomona, CA

Pierre Koenig, Steel Houses, motion picture by University of Grenoble, France

1989
'California Preservation Conference', Los Angeles seminar

Domus interview with Jurg Lang, audio cassette

'CSH No. 21, CSH No. 22 and Current Work' 'Blueprints for Modern Living', video cassette presentation, Los Angeles Museum of Modern Art, CA

1990
Case Study Program and Current Work lecture at California Polytechnic Institute, Pomona, CA, with a video cassette of Koenig's work by Dariouche Showghi

'History and Lessons of the Case Study Program', seminar for MOCA, Japan American Theater

'Technology and Aesthetics', video cassette lecture, Herbst Hall, San Francisco Museum of Modern Art, CA

1991
'Current Work' video lecture and slide presentation, Harvard University, Cambridge, MA

1994
The Great Buildings Collection CD Rom, University of Oregon, OR (New York: Van Nostrand Reinhold)

1995
'An Examination of the Forces that Motivate Creative People' Computer generated video by Steve Disken, 4 Friends, Art Center

1996
Masters of Architecture Lecture Series, Los Angeles County Museum of Art

1997
'100 Photos Collection', Vol. 1 by Julius Shulman, USC, Los Angeles, CA

1998
Digital Archives, USC, Los Angeles, CA

Tours & Lectures

1991
Swiss Federal Institute of Technology Student Tour

Japanese Architects Tour

AIA Women in Architecture Tour

1992
Da Camera Society Music in Historic Places Concert

Berlin Polytechnic Institute Student Tour

Historic Society Official Survey

Architects for Shelter Annual Home Tour

1993
Los Angeles Conservancy Tour

BBC Survey Tour

1994
The Los Angeles Conservancy/Netherlands Architecture Institute Tour

1995
French Architectural Graduate Students Tour (various schools)

Technical University of Munich Tour

Princeton University/French Foreign Students Tour

Pacific Design Center Tour, Westweek

Belgian Architects Tour

1996
Brentwood/Kaufman Library Modern Home Tour

University of Houston Architecture Class Tour

USC Great Houses of Los Angeles Class Tour

Southern California Institute of Architecture Tour

Alpha Rho Chi Fraternity Tour

1997
USC Architecture 418 Student Tour

Venice Art Walk

LACMA Service Council Tour

1998
The Steel Alliance, Members and Press

UCLA Extension, Architects Houses Class tour

Delft University of Technology, The Netherlands

School of Architecture of Seville, Spain

USC Great Houses of Los Angeles class tour

Technical Institute at the New Bauhaus, Germany

Notes

'Towards a Steel Architecture'

1 Pierre Koenig, in interview with Gloria Koenig, Los Angeles, June 1998.

2 'Steel Frame House by Pierre Koenig', *Arts & Architecture*, October 1953, p 24-25.

3 Pierre Koenig, 'Prefabrication', *Form* magazine, USC summer 1989.

4 'Case Study House #21 by Pierre Koenig', *Arts & Architecture*, February 1959, p 19.

5 Reyner Banham, *Los Angeles: The Architecture of Four Ecologies* (Harmondsworth and New York: Penguin Books, 1971), p 227.

6 Ibid., p 227.

7 'Case Study House #21 by Pierre Koenig', *Arts & Architecture*, February 1959, p 19.

8 Letter from Pierre Koenig to Robert Brady, 19 April 1960, archives of Pierre Koenig.

9 'Low-Cost Production House by Pierre Koenig', *Arts & Architecture*, March 1957, p 25.

'The Style that Nearly'

1 Esther McCoy, '*Arts & Architecture* Case Study Houses', *Blueprints for Modern Living: History and Legacy of the Case Study Houses* (Cambridge, MA and London: MIT Press, 1989), p 16.

2 Reyner Banham, *Los Angeles: The Architecture of Four Ecologies*, p 223.

3 Peter Schrag, *Paradise Lost: California's Experience, America's Future* (New York: The New Press, 1988).

4 'California', *Look*, September 18, 1962, p 30.

5 Thomas Hine, 'The Search for the Postwar House', *Blueprints for Modern Living*, p 172.

6 Esther McCoy, *Case Study Houses 1945-1962* (Los Angeles: Hennessey and Ingalls, 1977), p 8.

7 'Announcement – Case Study House Program', *Arts & Architecture*, January 1945, p 37.

8 'Case Study House Program – CSH 1' *Arts & Architecture*, February 1945, p 92–95.

9 Fiona MacCarthy, *William Morris: A Life for Our Time* (London: Faber and Faber, 1994), p 605.

10 Kathryn Smith, *R M Schindler House 1921-22* (Hollywood: Friends of the Schindler House, 1987), p 24.

11 Neil Jackson, *The Modern Steel House* (London and New York: E & FN Spon, Van Nostrand Reinhold, 1996), pp 10–13.

12 Case Study House #4, *Arts & Architecture*, August 1945, p 32.

13 'Case Study House Program: House for 1949', *Arts & Architecture*, January 1949, p 33.

14 Esther McCoy, *Case Study Houses 1945–1962*, p 57.

15 Esther McCoy, 'Remembering John Entenza', *Arts & Architecture: The Entenza Years* (Cambridge MA and London: MIT Press, 1990), p 19.

16 'Case Study House #21 by Pierre Koenig', *Arts & Architecture*, February 1959, p 19.

17 Esther McCoy, *Case Study Houses 1945-1962*, p 53.

18 *Arts & Architecture*, February 1959, p 19.

19 Neil Jackson, *The Modern Steel House*, p 98.

20 *Arts & Architecture*, May 1959, p 15.

21 Amelia Jones and Elizabeth Smith, 'The Thirty-Six Case Study Projects', *Blueprints for Modern Living*, p 71.

22 Paul Goldberger, 'When Modernism Kissed the Land of Golden Dreams', *New York Times*, 10 December 1989, p 42.

23 Reyner Banham, *Los Angeles: The Architecture of Four Ecologies,* p 223.

24 Ibid., p 231.

25 Ibid., p 238.

'Blueprint for Modern Living'

1 *Hodgetts and Fung: Scenarios and Spaces* (New York: Rizzoli, 1997), p 82.

2 Ibid., p 83.

3 Ibid., p 83.

4 Elizabeth Smith, 'Introduction', *Blueprints for Modern Living: History and Legacy of the Case Study Houses* (Cambridge, MA and London: MIT Press, 1989), p 13.

5 Ibid., p 13.

6 Pierre Koenig, interview with Kimberly R Kirkpatrick, Los Angeles, 16 October 1992.

Phaidon Press Limited
Regent's Wharf
All Saints Street
London N1 9PA

First published in 1998
© 1998 Phaidon Press Limited

ISBN 0 7148 3753 9

A CIP catalogue record for this book is available from the British Library. Library of Congress Cataloging in Publication Data available.

All rights reserved. No part of this publication may be reproduced, stored in a retrieval system or transmitted, in any form or by any means, electronic, mechanical, photocopying, recording or otherwise, without the prior permission of Phaidon Press Limited.

Printed in Hong Kong

Front cover: Stahl House (Case Study House #22), 1960.
Page 2: Bailey House (Case Study House #21), 1959.
Page 4: Pierre Koenig at Stahl House (Case Study House #22), 1960.
Back cover: Gantert House, 1983.

All quotations from Pierre Koenig were recorded in conversation between November 1997 and February 1998 unless specifically noted otherwise.

All drawings are reproduced from original illustrations by the architect.

Authors' Acknowledgements

The authors would like to thank Carole Gustin, Lisa Cutmore and Emma Highams for their help in preparing the manuscript; Sophia Gibb and Laura Cleobury for picture research; Danielle Oum for production control; the editorial team of Vivian Constantinopoulos, Anita Moryadas, Iona Baird, Paul Harron, Hannah Barnes-Murphy and Nadia Silver for their thoughtful input; Karl Shanahan for designing the book; Kim Colin for conducting extensive interviews with Pierre Koenig, contributing descriptions of individual projects and generally providing input that far exceeded her role; and particularly, Pierre and Gloria Koenig for their patient and creative involvement in the project.

David Jenkins
James Steele

Architect's Acknowledgements

I want to thank the staff at Phaidon: Kim Colin, Vivian Constantinopoulos, Anita Moryadas and Karl Shanahan for their efforts on behalf of this book. Also, I want to acknowledge my clients; my colleagues and friends at the University of Southern California; and my family, Jean-Pierre, Randy, Carrie, Chelsey, Karley, Tom, Lynne, Barry, Carol, Brandon and Jonathan. Finally I dedicate this book to my wife Gloria, with thanks for her ideas and help on this project and in our life together.

Pierre Koenig

Photographic Acknowledgements

Every attempt has been made to contact the photographic sources. The publisher will endeavour to rectify any inadvertent omissions.

Arts and Architecture (pp 6 bottom, 10, 17, 46)
Richard Barnes (pp 90–1, 92, 93)
Robert Beagles (pp 111 left, 112 left and right)
Lauren Becker (p 131 top)
Richard Fish Photographer (pp 75, 76–7, 84, 85, 86–7)
Pierre Koenig (pp 23, 28, 72, 73, 81 bottom right, 95, 110, 111 right, 112 centre, 113, 116, 117, 119, 120)
Modern Age Photo Service, Inc. (pp 4, 30, 32, 33, 34, 64 left and centre, 78, 88, 89, 114, 115)
Marvin Rand (pp 7, 148, 149)
Julius Shulman (front and back cover, pp 2, 6 left, 12, 13, 16 top, 20, 21, 22, 24, 25, 26, 27, 38, 42 top, 49, 50 bottom, 51, 52–3, 54–5, 56, 57, 58, 59, 60, 62–3, 64 right, 65, 67, 68, 70, 71, 94, 96, 97, 99, 122, 123, 124, 125, 126–7, 131 bottom, 133, 134–5, 136, 138, 141, 142 left, 144, 145 top and bottom left, 151)
Leland Y Lee (pp 102, 103, 104–5, 106, 107, 108, 109)
Tim Street-Porter (pp 15, 16 bottom, 42 bottom, 44, 50 top, 66, 69, 80, 81 top and bottom left, 82, 83, 142–3, 145 bottom centre and bottom right)
Carlos Von Frankenberg (p 137)